THE COMPLETE GUIDE TO

Vintage Textiles

Elizabeth Kurella

Dedicated to

Angela Zubersky Kurella

With thanks for teaching me to appreciate the
thoughtful handwork of our aunts and grandmothers.

Published by

**krause
publications**

700 E. State Street • Iola, WI 54990-0001
Telephone: 715/445-2214

Please, call or write us for our free catalog of antiques and collectibles publications.
To place an order or receive our free catalog, call 800-258-0929.
For editorial comment and further information,
use our regular business telephone at (715) 445-2214.

Library of Congress Catalog Number: 99-61253

ISBN: 0-87341-676-7

Printed in the United States of America

Preface

This book is dedicated to the appreciation of vintage textiles — in every sense of every word.

All that is made from fibers, threads, and fabrics is far too big a universe to fit under the umbrella of a single word. The term "textiles" is the best the dictionary can offer.

"Vintage" has a variety of meanings, all of which apply to this book. It can be the product of a single year, an exceptional product of an exceptional year, or simply an item that is at least a few years old. Choose whichever meaning you want; they all pertain to textiles discussed in this book.

To appreciate something is to recognize, understand, and justly value it. This book discusses the essence of textiles, advises you where you should concentrate when you look at them, what each feature means, and to whom all these things matter. There are also directories that list dealers, collectors, and associations. These will tell you who has specific vintage textiles, who wants them, and who knows the most about them.

Knowing and understanding often leads to fondness. If you like something, it's probably safe to assume you want it. As more and more people demand something, it increases in value and prices rise. There is sensuality, passion, intrigue, money, satisfaction, and encouragement hidden in musty boxes of old rags, and this is the perfect guidebook to finding it. When did an old coin, stamp, pot or desk ever hug you? Quilts do, and so do security blankets, old woolen sweaters and flannel shirts.

Too often, wonderful old textiles are consigned to the rag bag, used to polish motorcycles, cut up to make pillows, or plasticized and decoupaged into oblivion. The more prices rise, the less likely it is that they will meet this fate.

Truly, that's real appreciation.

Contents

Introduction

This book was written for anyone with any old textiles—fabrics, ribbons, clothes, flags, lace, tablecloths, doilies—that they want to identify, evaluate, sell, or buy. It provides a method of looking at vintage textiles to figure out what they are, and what, if anything, makes them special and possibly valuable. It tells how to find the one person who might want to own your special old textiles.

To those moving out of big old homes and into small condos, use this book to figure out what you have, and what makes it special. The big old tablecloths you no longer need might be worth a great deal of money. The vintage clothes crowding the closets might have eager takers.

Some things, however, should not go out on the open market. The quilt made by your great-grandmother that was on the bed when your father was born, a wedding dress remodeled into a Christening gown, the gaudy potholders that were in aunt Sophie's kitchen for forty years. All these are family heirlooms, and should stay with the family. While you still have time, use this book to understand what makes them special, and start teaching your nieces, nephews, and grandchildren.

If it is too late for that, don't give up. The beautiful handiwork of your grandmother may bring pleasure and comfort to someone who never knew their own grandmother. Or, someone may use it as an example to teach some old techniques. This book can help find that person.

To curators, docents, and volunteers at historic homes, museums, and pioneer parks, use this book to learn to recognize and understand textile treasures. Learn which of the proffered donations truly fit into the historic period you desire, which are worth keeping, and which should be declined or sold off. Whatever your location, it will be more attractive and convincing if the windows, tables, dressers, volunteers and mannequins all are dressed authentically and attractively.

To antique dealers, bring the boxes of textiles out from under the table, learn what they are, and offer them properly cleaned and identified. More and more people are becoming knowledgeable, and it is fast becoming essential to recognize haute couture, and to know the difference between embroidery and machine tapestry, between crochet, tatting, needle lace and bobbin lace. You should be able to point out and explain bound buttonholes, properly tailored rolled collars, silk topstitching, picots, padded satin stitch, eighteenth century chintzes, Gros Point de Venise, and trapunto. If you're able to do this, you can command better prices.

The universe of old textiles is so vast and complex, that heirs and auctioneers alike often just box it all up in mixed lots, send it to the Christian Neighbors or Salvation Army, or consign it to the rag bag.

Whatever ribbons, lace, and notions come out of the sewing box usually are mixed in with some lacy or embroidered sleeves or cuffs from an old blouse that were just too pretty to throw away, and a few old Scout merit badges. Blankets, bedspreads, and bed linens often are boxed up at auctions with embroidered guest towels and place mats and maybe a few bits of old tapestry. As textiles wear out, few people look carefully and think about what made them special in the first place.

Sorting old textiles requires a broad view to make a guess as to what each item might be and what era it might have come from. It also requires you to take a very close look to find details of technique and workmanship that tell what makes it special, and possibly valuable.

Making the effort to really examine old textiles can be well worth the trouble. Prices are rising for them, and one or two "finds" can pay for the hour or two of trouble.

Teens and Generation X'ers are discovering the vintage clothing markets because they provide a funkier, more unique and elegant look than chain stores offer. They gradually are learning that there is substance as well as style to the older clothes: better stitching, comfortable, natural fibers, more value.

The nesters and cocooners, who love to entertain extravagantly in their own homes, are discovering that the right table linens, whether they are quirky prints from the thirties and forties, or silky damasks and textured laces from the Age of Innocence, add as much to a dinner party as the perfect olive oil or balsamic vinegar. Seeking them out and doing them up is as worthwhile and fun, and certainly as satisfying as making the perfect mango chutney — only they last longer.

As decorators rediscover looks of the past, from Arts & Crafts to Victorian to Empire, they need the right doilies, table runners, curtains and drapes to complete the look. Vintage fabrics, table linens, and bed linens are more and more in demand. Often, a broken-in, slightly used, or near-perfect original is cheaper and cozier than a decorator reproduction.

After decades of studious neglect, people finally are beginning to discover the myriad of rich possibilities offered by vintage textiles. The moral of the story is, regardless of what is in the rag bag, attic, or closet, stop and take a close look before giving it away or setting it on fire. Before using an old raggy tablecloth as a dropcloth, or before cutting it up to make sofa pillows, examine it carefully. Somebody out there wants it just the way it is.

How to Use This Book

Vintage textiles are a zany, centuries-long maelstrom of spinning, weaving, cutting, dying, stitching, embroidering, felting, crocheting, knitting, painting and printing that forms a plethora of capes, gowns, doilies, table covers, draperies, veils, shawls, hats, coats, mittens, and an infinite amount of other items.

For centuries, all this material has been recycled: re-cut, re-dyed, re-embroidered, re-stitched into more quilts, capes, dresses, coats, hats, pillows, bedspreads, etc.

Trying to provide a meaningful market guide to this tangle of threads seemed a daunting task until we applied the Keep-It-Simple motto, and reduced things to the basics.

All textiles are based on an assortment of fibers, threads, and yarns. Before they become garments, draperies, doilies, mittens, or sweaters, the fibers and yarns have been manipulated in a handful of basic ways: the fibers are either woven, (weaving variations include needleweaving, darning, and bobbin lace), or they are crocheted, knitted, felted, or needle lace stitched.

Possibilities become endless only because this handful of techniques is combined, and embellished with dyes, paints, prints, and embroideries. Then they're recycled over and over. It's important to understand the basic scheme of things: Fibers are spun into yarns, yarns are manipulated to form fabrics, fabrics are embellished, and used to make and decorate things. With this knowledge, it is not as hard to keep your bearings in overstuffed closets and teeming flea markets and auctions.

The best way to organize the book was a difficult choice. Some people collect techniques: Hardanger embroidery, Point de Gaze needle lace. Other people want things, like bridal veils and handkerchiefs. Still others want both: Stevengraph silk woven pictures or Arts & Crafts embroidered pillows and table linens.

All things textile are made from the same base materials and techniques. They might be woven, crocheted or embroidered, or sewn into garments then cut up into patchworks, then decorated again with more embroidery, painting and dyeing, but they all draw their techniques from the same well.

The first section, Materials, serves as a reference for the basic techniques used to make most of the textiles found in the marketplace. It organizes the possibilities, and provides a basic reference for identifying something, and what, if anything, makes it special. Using this section you will develop an eye for the detail that sets special textiles apart.

The second section covers Things. They are organized roughly as the marketplace is organized:

Vintage Fashions includes vintage clothing of all sorts, from haute couture that commands brow-raising prices, to aprons that everybody has saved from their grandmothers and aunts.

Household Furnishings covers the doilies, tablecloths, curtains, towels, and oddities used to decorate our homes. It also covers the superb textiles of royalty and high society of past centuries, and twentieth century potholders, handmade tokens of friendship that are the currency of fundraising bazaars.

Finally, Fabrics of Society covers the quirky, funky odds and ends like bookmarks, feedsacks, handkerchiefs, and unfinished projects. The current star of this category is samplers, which have risen to price levels strong enough to encourage the forgeries and fakes.

In the real world, the categories overlap.

Everybody that looks at things made of threads sees something different. Some see the stitching, some see the actual item. Some see raw materials to make doll clothes, others see an old pillowcase. One person sees a lace curtain, another sees a bridal veil. Still another sees a century-old paisley shawl, while another sees yard goods for a designer winter coat. And another might see the raw material for fabulous sofa pillows, or upholstery for a set of dining room chairs.

Old threads have been recycled for so many generations you never know what will show up where. Quilts, especially crazy quilts, are archeological digs for the connoisseur. Cigarette silks, old embroideries, nineteenth century chintzes and bits of old cowboy shirts can all be found in quilts. Once, a patch on a nineteenth century lace ruffle I saw proved to be a fragment of seventeenth century lace. A collector eagerly bought the patch, while the rest of the lace ruffle was not worth saving.

The entry for each item includes brief historical information, a checklist for how to recognize it, and pointers on what features make it special within its category.

Information on who has it and who wants it is listed right with each category, along with listings of any collector's clubs, publications, and newsletters. Because there still are relatively few dealers who specialize in particular things, they are listed right with the category entry. They are listed again in a geographical directory at the back of the book to help connect collectors and dealers as they travel.

Textiles are far more likely than most antiques to have been saved even after they were far beyond their prime, and many have been remodeled, repaired, and recycled. In spite of all this, people are still interested for many different reasons. Some plan to use an item for its original purpose, some simply want to study the technique, and others draw inspiration for contemporary crafts. For this reason, lots of photos are provided in this guide that show pieces in all conditions and quality levels.

The table of Milestones will help you get your bearings in time. Knowing when the sewing machine was invented will help date that old dress.

Finally, a comprehensive index and cross reference is included to help find things with multiple names, or things that could easily fit into several different categories.

Panorama of Textiles

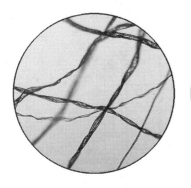
Cotton

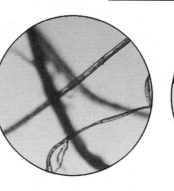
Linen

Wool

Silk

are spun to make.....

THREADS & YARNS

that are *Manipulated* by.....

Weaving

Felting

Knitting

Crochet

Knotting

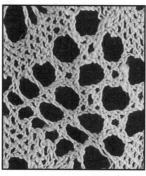
Bobbin Lace

Needle Lace

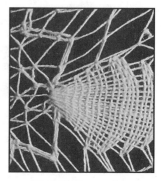
Needleweaving

to produce **FABRICS** which can be........

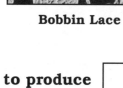

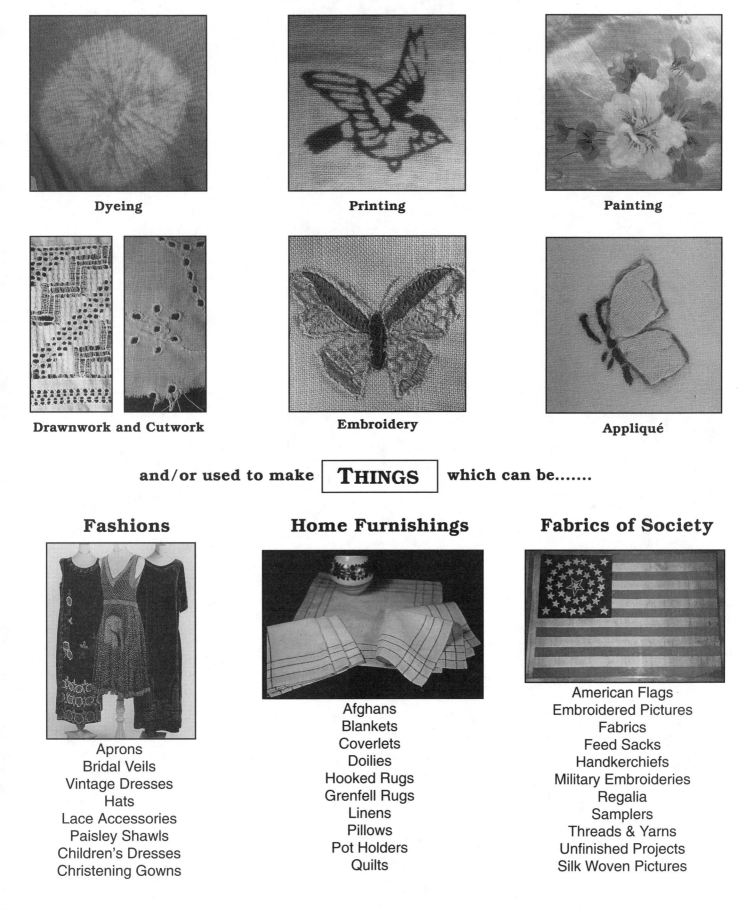

Embellished by...

Dyeing

Printing

Painting

Drawnwork and Cutwork

Embroidery

Appliqué

and/or used to make | THINGS | which can be.......

Fashions

Aprons
Bridal Veils
Vintage Dresses
Hats
Lace Accessories
Paisley Shawls
Children's Dresses
Christening Gowns

Home Furnishings

Afghans
Blankets
Coverlets
Doilies
Hooked Rugs
Grenfell Rugs
Linens
Pillows
Pot Holders
Quilts

Fabrics of Society

American Flags
Embroidered Pictures
Fabrics
Feed Sacks
Handkerchiefs
Military Embroideries
Regalia
Samplers
Threads & Yarns
Unfinished Projects
Silk Woven Pictures

Remodeled, Recycled and Reused and the CYCLE continues.

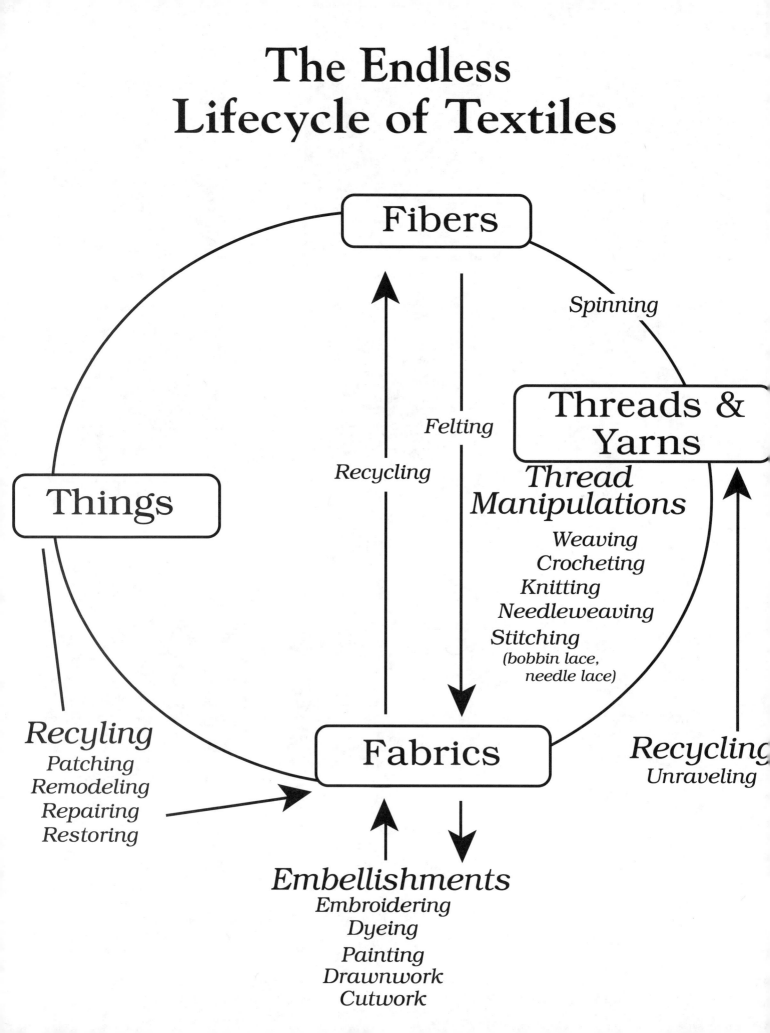

Pricing Vintage Textiles

Vintage textiles, more often than not, are one of a kind. Even through the Industrial Revolution of the nineteenth century, when the textile industry was the one to lead others toward mechanization, dresses, coverlets, blankets, sweaters, caps, and endless other textile products still were being made one by one, or were hand-decorated or finished by hand.

Also, vintage textiles have, since the beginning of time, been viewed as recyclable materials. Any incarnation — blanket, dress, tablecloth, doily — is viewed as temporary, waiting for fashion to dictate that they should be shortened, lengthened, patched, painted, embroidered, trimmed with lace, or turned into a rag rug or crazy quilt. Whatever form they take is assumed to be a mere suggestion. Until the middle of the twentieth century, most homemakers had the skills to sew, embroider, to crochet edging, add a line or two of rickrack, darn, patch, quilt, or braid a rug. Each time the frugal new owner was expected to make of it whatever their skills and imagination allowed.

Putting prices on anything made from thread and fabric is more complicated than matching something up with a hallmark or a picture in a price guide. Every vintage textile can appeal to any of several markets and hold different values in different forms to different people. Coverlet collectors lament every time a coverlet is cut up to make a coat, but for decades after the invention of central heating and L.L. Bean duvets, heavy double-weave wool and linen coverlets were just too warm to have any appeal as coverlets. Similarly, lace collectors cringe every time a pair of scissors is produced, because the simple truth is, sometimes lace collars have more value as raw material than as a collar.

In a perfect world, each hand-crafted textile would be discovered by the person that sees in it its most valuable features, and subsequently, it would be released from the endless cycle of reincarnations that render it unrecognizable. Not only is the world not perfect, but there are very few gurus out there to help point out the characteristics that make a vintage textile worthy of salvation. More quilt, coverlet, lace, embroidery, and vintage clothing clubs and study groups have started in the past few years, but most are still oriented to making new copies of old things rather than collecting the originals.

Thus, it is far more difficult to put meaningful prices on vintage textiles than on baseball cards or vases. Like any other antique, location plays a part in pricing. Prices in small towns in the Midwest typically are lower than at big city antique shows. Prices tend to be lower in antique malls than in specialist boutiques.

Mint condition means something far different in the world of vintage textiles than in other antiques. If the condition is otherwise sound, a filthy blanket, tablecloth, collar, dress, or coverlet can sometimes be washed or cleaned, and restored to pristine, if not mint condition. Also, different people get interested at different times in a textile's cycle of reincarnations. We cannot emphasize the fiber-thread-fabric-thing cycle enough. That's why we've presented it in two forms—the diagram and the panorama. One way or another, everybody should be able to understand it. Any point in the life cycle can be highly valuable. Scraps of pre-Columbian weavings, fragments of eighteenth century lace, bits and pieces of embroidered brocades from the seventeenth century — all can be very valuable, if the weaving, stitching, and fibers are of superb quality.

We did put prices along with photos and descriptions of pieces in the second half of this book. We also explain, whenever possible, where those prices came from — auction results, what a dealer is offering it for, or a price at a private sale.

In addition to putting prices alongside the pictures and descriptions, we are offering some tools to use to figure out for yourself what something is worth. In the long run, intangible factors — simple beauty, elegance, the comfort a quilt offers, the coziness a coverlet adds to a home, the glamour of owning a designer gown, the gratification of owning a sampler stitched over a hundred years ago by a mere schoolgirl — very strongly affect the price of vintage textiles. But the physical features of that object, including design, stitching, weaving and fiber, are what defines the age, origin, and true intrinsic value. These are things you can learn to see for yourself. Use those features to decide if a price you find on a flea market or antique shop item is reasonable, or to decide if the items in your own closet are intrinsically good, mediocre, or junk.

Refer to the Fibers, Threads, Fabric, Manipulations and Embellishments sections often when you are looking over vintage textiles. They offer a lot of basic information that will help you identify what you are looking at. Most importantly, they serve as a reminder to look at all vintage textiles with an open and alert mind.

Checklist for Evaluating Textiles

Two different sets of factors need to be considered in identifying and evaluating vintage textiles. Objective factors, or those that are an intrinsic part of the object, include materials, design, workmanship and technique. These are visible factors that merely require a sharp eye.

Another set of factors are subjective, and relate to the how the object fits into the universe. We will call them importance and congeniality. They change with society and the times. Who might have owned, used, or worn a thing, what events they attended while wearing or carrying it, and memories and feelings it conjures. These all add to its importance, or lack thereof. These are the wild cards, changing the value as the events and people are remembered or forgotten.

Congeniality is how much pleasure an antique brings, and how much fun is it to own. Things that are easy to show off to the neighbors are very congenial. Things that don't need to be washed and ironed, are unlikely to fade, wear out, crumble, or break are more fun to own than those that have to live in a cool, dark, quiet place and never go out to a party. Old sweaters, afghans, and quilts are congenial because they comfort and hug us on lonely, rainy, cold days.

Finally, condition and rarity complete the checklist. The importance of these final factors is determined largely by all the preceding factors.

Materials

Materials are the substances from which something is or can be made. In the universe of textiles, fibers are spun into threads, which are manipulated to form fabrics, which are embellished and made into things. Each of these aspects must be noticed and considered when identifying and evaluating vintage textiles. They provide the clues that tell how functional and beautiful the textile is, and also the clues that tell age and authenticity.

For the novice, it is enough that you learn to recognize natural fibers — cotton, silk, wool, and linen — and realize that the older textiles were made from these and their cousins. Synthetic fibers mean a textile dates from the late nineteenth century or the twentieth century.

Connoisseurs will notice even the direction of the twist in plied threads and yarns, and use this detail to determine what valley in Peru a certain pre-Columbian textile came from.

Many vintage textiles — garments, quilts, draperies — are made up of many fabrics and many layers. Sewing threads are the glue that holds them together. Check each one carefully. Are they original? Are they in good condition?

Experts who date vintage flags, garments, quilts, draperies, etc., will note every detail, from the twist of the thread, to whether it is mercerized or not, to the composition of each bit of fabric.

Design

Harmony, flow, complexity, simplicity, and balance all are universal elements of good design. Each style has its own hallmarks, which need to be acknowledged to determine whether or not we like that particular style.

Add points for special features. Pieces unique to a time period, such as the first Bizarre Silks, Art Nouveau, and Arts & Crafts designs deserve special note. Unlike dogs and cats, which must be perfect examples of their breed to win a title, textiles often are awarded more points when they are unusual, different, or just wacky. The most common, typical examples of each style get boring pretty quickly, and literally are a dime a dozen.

Consider the design of the object — the silhouette of the dress, the shape of the lace handkerchief, the necktie — then consider the design of the fabric used to make it. How they relate to each other plays a part in its total value.

Technique and Workmanship

These are two sides of the same coin, related but distinct and different. The difficulty of the technique is the trick. Is it a trick than anyone can do with little practice, or something that requires years of training? Workmanship is how well is it done. Are the stitches perfectly even? Is there a shading in colors and texture than could only be achieved by human care and thought?

Handwork alone does not guarantee value. This has been proven over and over again. When prices rose for handmade quilts in the early 1990s, China's huge labor force stepped in, and provided boat loads of charming, well-crafted handmade quilts for the mass markets. The same is true of simple crocheted, bobbin, and tape laces (Battenberg). Somewhere in the world, thousands of unemployed souls are ever-willing to produce doilies for pennies that will sell in the U.S. for a dollar or two.

It is important to look at each piece at least twice. Notice the technique and workmanship needed to produce the item, and the technique and workmanship needed too produce the materials used to make the item. A twentieth century dress, badly machine sewn in a boring, ordinary style may have been decorated with charming little embroidery. Extraordinary embroidery and lace are found surprisingly often in very common garments — handwork from the nineteenth century recycled in the twentieth.

Technique and workmanship also can be used to date pieces, and determine if the are original, repaired or remodeled. Most vintage dresses are a mixture of hand stitching and machine stitching, showing that they were remodeled and repaired.

In textiles, technique and workmanship very often are not recognized. It has been almost two whole generations since children were taught to sew a seam, darn a sock, and crochet an edge on a handkerchief by the time they were five. Most people today have no clue what handcrafts are difficult, and which are easy. We cannot even begin to appreciate the skill required to produce early textiles because so many steps were involved.

Technique and workmanship rarely are factored into the market price of vintage textiles. This makes the finest textiles the best bargains. Perhaps someday, when the world better understands the skill and effort required to make fine textiles, they will be appreciated and valued.

How the Features Relate

Evaluating vintage textile is a game of guessing, and judging the imagination, motives, aims, and skills of our ancestors who made them. How suitable are the fibers, threads and weaves for the design, and for the function of the textile? When the fibers, weaves, and embellishments in a single garment, tapestry, or tablecloth all are impeccably chosen and superbly crafted, the value rises exponentially.

Putting together a fabulous designer original gown, a superb quilt, an ethereal lace veil is more than the sum of the features. It is a portrait of the makers, and the thought put into selecting just the right fabric to complement the design, just the right shape, just the right suppleness. It is tangible evidence of brilliant problem solving, evidence of the heights that can be reached when human spirit, imagination, ingenuity, and skills are perfectly blended.

Importance

In addition to unique design, technique and workmanship, factors that give antique textiles importance are history, politics, economics, and just plain sentiment. Age alone does not.

The international press corps helped give importance to Diana's dresses. It is up to you to convey the importance of grandmother's wedding dress to the next generation. Your best audience is your own set of grandchildren. The likelihood that anyone else will be impressed in minimal.

Importance can be fleeting. While Diana's dresses still command tens of thousands of dollars at auction, Queen Victoria's lace-trimmed underwear sells for a few dollars; her Irish needle lace shawl for about two thousand.

Congeniality

To be congenial, textiles must make the owner feel good; be easy to wear, use, show off and display; impress the neighbors; require minimal maintenance and care. Any maintenance or care that is required should easily fit within the boundaries of known and available equipment, and techniques.

Congenial textiles should make the owner feel rich and famous and demand little in return.

Antique textiles are by nature less congenial than antique tables and chairs. Tablecloths wrinkle, soak up coffee and gravy, and demand to be washed and ironed each time they come out to a party. The table just sits there, waiting for the next fete.

Quilts and afghans may demand larger storage space and more care, but on the other hand, when did a stamp or coin ever hug you or comfort you on a cold day the way an afghan or quilt does?

Very often, the features that make textiles special cannot be seen without a magnifying glass, or even a microscope. The fact that such close scrutiny is needed to understand and appreciate the stitching clearly limits the market for lace and embroidery.

How a piece can be used also affects its value. A painting simply gets hung on the wall, a haute couture gown takes more imagination to display.

Technology in the future may help make textiles easier to display and show off, and broader knowledge will contribute more neighbors who will be impressed by the acquisition of a tapestry. We aren't there yet, but we're getting closer. Textiles that display well, like hooked rugs, samplers and tapestries, are the ones that are rising fastest in price.

Condition...

Remember the essence of textiles: fibers spun into threads, manipulated into fabrics, made into things. Keep that in mind, and consider each element when inspecting vintage textiles. Where the damage is, and what kind it is, determines how serious the problem is.

Lace, velvets, silks and linens that date back to Columbus, and some linens that date back to the pharaohs are still lively and healthy. Fibers that are sound, and protected from moisture, microbes, chemicals, and ultraviolet rays can last hundreds and hundreds of years.

...of Fibers & Threads

Deterioration in the fibers is most difficult to determine, but extremely crucial. Fibers that are rotted, or eaten away by microbes, bleaches, chemical dyes, or sunlight cannot be saved. They will continue to deteriorate and the textile will disintegrate.

...Of the Fabric

Learn to tell the difference between surface stains and stains that go clear through the fibers. Surface stains are easier to remove without damaging the fabric. Stains that go clear through the fibers usually are so entangled in the fabric they will never come out.

Sometimes it's possible to tell just by looking at a fabric whether or not dirt and stains can be coaxed out. Dirt gets embedded in knotted, tangled, tightly woven threads and refuses to come out. Dirt will be coaxed out of smooth, plain woven linens more easily than out of many tightly knotted laces.

...Of the Things

Complex old textiles — quilts, samplers, garments, bedspreads, draperies, tablecloths — are composed of an assortment of largely unknown ingredients. After a hundred years, or even a dozen, it is impossible to know exactly what fibers were spun into threads, what dyes were used, what materials were used for repairs, and how this mixture will react to cleaning agents and washing.

When buying or evaluating old textiles, look them over very carefully to see what stains, wear and tear, and damage they have. For any vintage textiles that represent a significant investment, consult a professional to help analyze them.

Look on both sides of vintage textiles — quilts, tablecloths, garments, curtains, and draperies. Look for bits of net that are supporting worn out areas.

Tears in otherwise sound fabrics often can be repaired; worn out fabrics will be too fragile to support mending.

Look at each part of each item. Garments, quilts, and tablecloths will consist of many different materials. Look carefully at each one. A velvet gown may be in good condition, but the silk lace sleeves may be disintegrating. Silk fabrics in a crazy quilt may be shattering while the velvets, linens, and cottons are still sound. Haute couture garments will consist of layers of facings, linings, and top fabrics. Check out the condition of each one.

May different techniques — stitched seams, embroidery, appliqué — will be used on vintage quilts and garments. Check each one for damage, repair, and disintegration.

Things closest to mint condition almost always are more valuable than those that are damaged, remodeled, or repaired. Recycling, however, has been such an integral part of textiles for so many centuries that a new incarnation of recycled pieces can still have great value.

What is it, and what is it made of is the key question with textiles. Crazy quilts assembled from luxury fabrics, if they are put together with imagination, a good sense of design, and great skill, can be every bit as valuable as the shirts, vestments, gowns, embroideries, and tapestries recycled to make them.

Rarity

Rarity is the sum of all of the above. Superb design, combined with the use of the finest materials and the most difficult techniques comprise the rarest items — especially those that have been used by notorious, famous, or well known people on a special occasion.

The rarest textiles, however, often are not the most valuable. So few people today recognize real quality in textiles that the rarest often goes unrecognized, and are especially unappreciated.

For that reason, fabulous textiles are still within the reach of ordinary folks who have the patience, and willingness to look closely and thoughtfully. Conversely, many of the most popular are ordinary in design, workmanship, and technique, and for their intrinsic worth, are overpriced.

Summary

This is by no means a fully comprehensive guide to evaluating vintage textiles. Additional features that apply to specific textiles are noted in each entry in the Things section, and ultimately becoming an expert in any area requires long, thoughtful experience and study.

This checklist is meant simply to provide a starting point to realizing that vintage textiles may be extremely complex. However, given a methodical approach to each aspect of them, even a thoughtful novice can be comfortable evaluating, buying, and using vintage textiles. An eager beginner with an open mind and a thorough checklist often does better than a complacent dealer.

Materials

Introduction

Drop back in time a couple of decades, just south of The Loop in Chicago. Enter the high-ceilinged shop of Helfand's Fine Fabrics near where the Circle Campus of the University of Illinois now stands. The first thing Mrs. Helfand would do is thrust a piece of fabric in your hands, and encourage you to feel it. "Fine fabric, ja?" she would ask. Then she would enumerate its features, one by one. The weave, the colors, the print, the drape.

"Why do you want it?" she would ask. "What are you planning to make?" The fabric had to fit the use. Unless, of course, the fabric was just totally irresistible. Then a use would be found on the spot. Sometimes fabrics were so beautiful they would just follow us home for no reason other than to feel and enjoy it. "A poem," said Archibald MacLeish, "must not mean, but be."

Mrs. Helfand wasn't alone in her approach. Smitty at Fischman's Fabrics in Chicago, and dozens of other sellers of fine fabrics — from Bambola in St. Gallen, Switzerland, to little shops off the Place de la Concorde in Paris and innumerable lofts on Seventh Avenue in New York — all made the same plea. Feel the fabric. Don't just look at it. See the weave, the print, the embossing, the embroidery, the pile. Notice and think about what you feel and see.

Years ago, a lace dealer in a shop in Camden Passage in London asked me to close my eyes and hold out my hands, palms down. She then draped a pair of eighteenth century Brussels lace lappets over my hands. "Feels like cream cooled in a village spring pouring over your hands, doesn't it, Luv?" she asked. Yes, it did, and I never forgot the sensation. I still have the lappets, and take them out now and then just to "feel the cream."

Vintage fabrics have no reliable labels with fiber content and washing instructions. There are precious few Smittys or Mrs. Helfands to guide us. Buyers are on their own, or left to blindly trust unknown dealers when shopping in antique malls, garage sales, or auctions.

Judging fabrics by feel is a great first step. Almost nobody carries a microscope or chemical test equipment to estate sales, flea markets, or antique shows. In the final analysis, the best way to judge quality, and to tell the difference between cotton and linen, silk and synthetic, camel's hair and polyester, is by feeling as much of it as you can, whenever you can. Drape the fabric over your hands, twist it, crush it, put it up to your cheek. Then, associate the feel with some memory, and store those memories carefully.

Each fiber, whether natural or synthetic, has basic intrinsic properties. These will determine, to a large extent, how the resulting fabric will behave: whether it wrinkles, absorbs water, feels warm or cool, silky or flat, whether it is stiff or supple. The quality, feel, and usefulness of the fabric are also determined by whether the fiber is tightly or loosely spun into thread, how many plys are combined into the yarn, how that yarn will be manipulated to form a fabric, and finally, how that fabric will be finished.

Fibers are spun into threads and yarns, those threads or yarns are manipulated to form fabrics or textiles. Dyes, paints, embroideries all are used to embellish textiles. Those textiles are used to make or decorate things.

Each manipulation is relatively simple: threads are interlaced in weaving, interlaced, twisted and braided in bobbin lace, looped and knotted in crochet, and stitched in needle lace.

Then the fun begins. Introduce color to the weave as stripes, checks, plaids, or intricate tapestry pictures. Embroider the woven cloth. Paint, tie-dye, or print the cloth. Cut holes and insert lace. Cut holes, and fill the holes with needleweaving or stitching.

Value and interest also are determined by how creatively, imaginatively and intricately the various manipulations and embellishments are combined, how brilliantly the fabric was embellished, and how carefully and appropriately the fabric was chosen for the particular use.

Each step along the way involved making choices. A particular fiber was spun in a particular way. The fiber plus the spin determined what the threads were suitable for.

Lacemaking requires fine threads with long fibers and reasonably tight spins. Smooth threads define the openwork better; tight spins don't fray and hold up better in the delicate structures. Threads shooting over the surface of damask make the shimmering patterns. Those floating threads must be strong enough to withstand countless plates and gravy bowls being shoved across the surface, and endless washing and ironing. Fine linen is strong in the wash, and gains luster with use. What is more pleasurable than angora for a sweater or baby bonnet, camel's hair for its lightness, softness, and warmth for a coat, felt for the poodle on a pink circle skirt.

Textiles are recycled, and the process repeats.

Notice each element in the cycle.

The fibers, threads, and fabrics all play a part, and are valued differently by different people.

All along the way, different people get excited over different aspects and stages of a textile. Some people collect fine old yarns, some people take old woolen sweaters and felt them, and recycle the fibers. Others rescue bits of fine embroidery or antique laces.

Each bit of fabric in a patchwork is unique. A single patchwork quilt may contain hundreds of different art forms: A dozen or more types of woven fabrics including damasks, calicos, dimities, herringbone wool. There might also be a dozen different lace techniques, hand dyed or printed fabrics, embroideries, machine-made tapestries of silk or cut bits of handpainted neckties.

A single fine tablecloth may include hand embroidery, drawnwork, needle and bobbin lace, filet and needleweaving.

Take a close look at each vintage textile that passes through your hands. Hundreds of years of imagination, skill, workmanship, and beauty are out there waiting to be discovered.

Fibers

The fibers determine how the fabric will perform. For instance, if it absorbs water it might make a good towel. If it's made of smooth lustrous fibers, it could be a table cloth or perhaps a shirt. The fibers also determine how the fabric reacts to staining, washing, and cleaning.

Many of the questions asked about the quality and care of vintage textiles relate directly to the fibers they are made from.

Dealers in vintage textiles and fashion who know their stuff shop with their hands as much as their eyes. They can tell the difference between linen and cotton, real silk and synthetics, and between good quality linen and good quality cotton by feel alone. They also can tell if the fibers are in good condition, or have been damaged by dry rot or overbleaching.

Color, texture, weight, and resilience all are part of the natural package with fibers. There is a wide range of quality levels in each fiber. Many factors influence the quality, from the genetic strain of the plant or animal and the weather while the plant is growing, up to the processing cycle. The finish of the fabric and whether it has been dyed, bleached, mercerized, or had flame retardants or other additives processed in, will have some affect on the performance of the fiber, but you can't entirely fool Mother Nature. The natural properties of the fibers change little.

The basic natural properties of the four most often used natural fibers — cotton, linen, silk, and wool — are presented together in the following table to allow comparison. Only the natural fibers are included. These are the fibers used in most vintage textiles. We present basic information rather than simple tips for a reason. If you know why something behaves as it does, you can figure out answers to many more questions on your own.

Natural doesn't necessarily mean better. No one fiber is inherently better than another. Each has its own place. Nothing beats synthetics for ski jackets and clothing to climb Mount Everest, just as nothing is better than the sheen and durability of fine linen for a formal tablecloth.

This table provides a few clues to help you tell the difference between linen and cotton. It also helps explain why linen fibers were so highly prized for tablecloths and why wool is fiber of choice for blankets. The table also explains the importance of knowing the fiber content before you wash, clean or repair old textiles What is good for cleaning one fiber may destroy another.

Use the information in the following charts wisely. They are provided partly to tell you how to identify and deal with certain fibers, and also to explain why certain fibers where chosen "in the olden days" for certain jobs. The chart also attempts to address what properties chemists were aiming for when synthetics were first developed. Plus, it tries to explain why it is best to call in experts in many situations when buying and caring for fine heirloom textiles.

Unless vintage fibers and yarns are carefully studied with a microscope or with chemical tests, they will, for the most part, remain a mystery. A single yarn may have been spun from several different fibers, and several different kinds of yarn or thread may have been combined to form a single sampler or hooked rug.

Embroideries often combine silk or wool embroidery flosses and threads on linen or cotton backing materials. Who knows what mixture of fabrics were stitched together to form crazy old quilts, or pulled together to form a hooked rug.

Regardless of whether the fibers are spun together in the same yarn, or two different yarns are combined, such as a linen warp and a cotton weft, the properties of the individual fibers will not be changed. In a blended thread, hot bleach will dissolve the wool fibers, leaving only the linen.

Experience is the best teacher. Handle as many textiles as you can, each time relating what you feel to things you have noticed in the past.

Features to note

Length of the staples or fibers

Each natural material has a normal range for the staples or individual fibers. In general, the longer the staple, the better the quality of the yarn or thread. Short fibers fray, and fabrics woven from short fiber threads "pill" more, shed more lint, and wear out faster.

Liveliness of the fibers

Resilience and elasticity generally mean the fibers are still in good shape. Fabrics that are dried out and chalky in textures often mean the fibers are either dry rotted, eaten away from too much harsh bleaching, stored too long in a hot muggy place or eaten away with mildew. Fibers in bad shape can't be revived.

Stains vs. dirt

Dirt usually is nestled between fibers. Many things that look terrible will wash or clean up well. Stains, however, almost always go deep into the fibers. Some stains, like rust, blood, and mildew actually are eating away the fibers. Treatments needed to remove the stains do even more damage to the fibers. Most stains leave a hole when they are removed.

	COTTON	LINEN
Type of Fiber	Seed hairs of plants	Stem fibers of plants
Length of Fiber	Up to an inch and a half Egyptian and American have longest fibers Chinese, Indian, African (other than Egyptian) have the shortest	Fibers 18 to 20 inches long
Shape of Fiber	Flattened tube with ribbon-like twists	Looks like microscopic, knobby-kneed bamboo stalk. Fibers are present as bundles in plant stems
The Better Kinds	Sea Island — extremely long staple, small diameter cotton grown in the U.S. along the coast of South Carolina. Almost extinct after boll weevil epidemic of 1930s. Pima — has extra long staples. Egyptian — very long staple cotton with small diameter. Can be spun into very fine thread for sheer and fine fabrics	Line are first quality, long, fibers. Tow are short, second quality, "leftover" fibers
A Few Key Properties	Twists make fibers cling to each other. Even short fibers will spin into thread easily. Longer fibers make finer, stronger thread. Fabric of long staples wears better, is softer, smoother, and more lustrous.	Bundles of long fibers give fabric a slightly more uneven texture than cotton. Linen also tends to be stiffer, less supple than cotton. Great length of fibers makes it possible to spin extraordinarily fine, strong threads.
Strength	Medium strength; less than linen. Loses strength when wet	Stronger than cotton; even stronger when wet
Natural color	Natural colors are white, cream, or buff	Natural colors are pale gray or yellowish
Luster	Naturally has no luster: • Has flat, chalky look unless treated • Mercerized cotton has luster	Fiber is naturally lustrous • Fiber becomes more lustrous with age and wear.
Affinity for Dyes	Fair affinity for dyes	Poor affinity for dyes
Heat Conductivity	Fairly good conductor of heat • Conducts heat away from body, makes it comfortable in hot weather	Very good heat conductor • Linen fabric feels cooler to the touch than cotton. This often is a way to tell the difference between cotton and linen.
Electrical Conductivity	Fairly good conductor • Does not build up static cling	Fairly good conductor • Does not build up static cling.
Elasticity	Not as elastic as silk or wool, more elastic than linen	Fibers are *not* elastic: • Repeated creasing and ironing in folds eventually cracks the threads. • Store rolled, flat, or with the folds padded to prevent cracking. • Wrinkles badly. • Difficult to iron unless damp.

SILK	WOOL
Animal (spun cocoons)	Animal hairs
Continuous filaments • Reeled silk threads are made by twisting together long filaments. • Spun silk is made by spinning together broken, chopped, and other short bits.	Depends on type of animal. Typically less than 2 inches. Some may be up to 8 inches.
	Scaly, and crinkled and crimped in all directions. Fibers naturally are very oily.
Raw silk is still coated with natural sericin gum. Tussah is raw silk from wild silkworms. Dupionni are irregular silk fibers resulting from two silkworms spinning cocoons together. Results in textured, slubby silk fabric.	Vicuna, Pashmina, Cashmere or Kashmir, are the finest, softest, and most delicate wool fibers. Camel's Hair, guanaco, llama, alpaca all are extremely fine Angora is hair of angora rabbit, mohair is hair of angora goat. Lamb's wool is first shearing of a lamb. One end of fiber should be rounded and uncut.
	Natural oils make wool resistant to dampness and dirt. • Brushing lifts fibers, removes lots of surface dirt. In the days before dry cleaning, a soft, firm brush was standard in any man's dressing kit. Scales and crimp make wool very resilient, but also make it turn to felt with heat and hot water.
Very strong when dry; loses strength when wet.	Naturally strong, but loses almost half of its strength when wet.
Ranges from yellow to gray, depending on what silkworms were fed.	Ranges from cream or yellow to dark brown and black.
Natural fiber (called fibroin) is coated with gum (called sericen) and is not lustrous. • Boiling fibers or threads in water removes sericen, gives silk shine. • *Natural, raw, or wild silks should not be washed.*	Coarse grades lustrous; good grades have low luster.
Good affinity for dyes.	Excellent affinity for dyes.
Not a good heat conductor: • Feels warmer to the touch than cotton or linen.	Poor conductor of heat • Warmest of natural fibers.
Poor conductor of electricity • Sometimes builds up static cling.	Poor conductor • Builds up static charge, especially when dry in the winter.
Very elastic • Has great resiliency. • Does not wrinkle badly.	Most elastic of natural fibers.

	COTTON	LINEN
Effect of heat	Withstands high heat: • Can be boiled to clean. • Does not scorch easily when ironed.	Withstands high heat: • Can be boiled to clean. • Does not scorch easily when ironed.
Effect of sunlight	Sunlight gradually oxidizes cotton fibers • Sunlight eventually will weaken and yellow vintage cottons.	Sunlight does not affect linen fibers as readily as cotton. • Linens survive whitening in the sun for more years than cottons.
Effect of alkalies (ammonia, borax, and many soaps are alkali).	• Most alkalis do not harm cotton.	Most alkalis do not harm linen.
Effect of acids	• Strong acids (sulfuric, hydrochloric, nitric) destroy. Weak acids will weaken fibers if not washed out and neutralized. • Weak acids (vinegar, lemon juice) do not injure. • Fruit juices are acid, and set as stains unless washed out quickly. Vintage stains usually are permanent.	Dilute acids are not harmful; ***concentrated will destroy wool.***
Bleaches	Cold dilute chlorine or hypochlorite bleaches ok; ***will destroy fiber if hot.***	Same as cotton.
Stain Removal Summary	Stain removal in vintage textiles is difficult because one can only guess what the stain really is. The following are additional reasons why stain removal is rarely successful, rather than a guide to actually removing the stains.	
Old food stains	Most old food stains, like fruits and meat juices, are acidic in nature. They will have permanently changed old cotton and linen fibers, and will not come out.	
Rust	Acids — hydrochloric, oxalic, tartaric, or citric — are needed to remove rust stains. Acids eventually destroy cotton and linen fibers. Rust removers sometimes do work, but don't be surprised if a hole forms where there was a rust stain.	
Blood stains	Iron in old blood stains turn to rust, and like rust stains, it is nearly impossible to get out.	
Perspiration, ring-around-the-collar	Perspiration stains that have been set for years almost always partially eat away the fiber. Linen and cotton often do withstand boiling, though, so for hopelessly stained items, it might be worth taking a chance if they're only going to be thrown out otherwise.	
Ancient starch	Years of starching cottons and linens builds up a barrier that water will not penetrate. Cottons and linens still in good shape typically do withstand boiling, which is sometimes necessary to break down the accumulation of old starch.	
Mildew	Mildew literally eats the fibers — it converts the cellulose into sugar.	

SILK	WOOL
Does not tolerate high heat • White silk turns yellow if boiled. • Scorches if ironed too hot.	Dry heat scorches wool, makes it brittle, harsh, and shiny. Moderate heat and steam make wool pliable and plastic: • Easily formed and shaped for hats, elegantly tailored garments. • Boiling reduces luster, strength. Boiling and agitation produces felting. • Gentle steaming can restore wool that has become flattened and shiny from ironing.
Sunlight gradually destroys fibers.	Sunlight gradually deteriorates wool
Alkalis attack silk. Many soaps are alkali, and should not be used, or used with great care.	Not especially harmful at cool temperatures; *very destructive at high temperatures.*
• More resistant to acids than cotton or linen. Vinegar (weak formic and acetic acids) does not harm silk • Some strong acids shrink silks, make them crepe-like	Dilute acids are not harmful; *concentrated will destroy wool*
Chlorine and hypochlorite bleaches weaken silk and turn it yellow • Hydrogen peroxide, potassium permanganate may be used carefully under the right conditions.	• Chlorine bleaches are harmful. • Potassium permanganate, sodium peroxide, and hydrogen peroxide sometimes can be used safely.
Vintage silks often were dyed, chemically treated to add weight, or otherwise are already "compromised." It is best to consult a professional before trying to treat stains in silk at home.	Most vintage woolens are in the form of hats, coats, dresses, or other things. This will have a bearing on how they are treated. It is best to seek professional help with vintage woolens.
Mildew rarely attacks silk • Bleaching agent may remove mildew, but will not restore damaged fibers.	Mildew rarely attacks wool — only after long periods of dampness.

Threads and Yarns

Grab a few bits of thread, yarn, and string, sit down with a glass of wine and a good magnifying glass, and start to unwind. While you are relaxing, untwist the threads and yarns. You will discover an entire invisible universe.

The exact time when threads and yarns (continuous strands of fibers) were invented is lost somewhere in prehistory. Typically, we think of threads as the fine strands used to sew up garments and make lace, yarns as the fluffy stuff used to make sweaters and mittens, and strings and cords are what we tie packages with. The textile industry typically uses the term "yarn" as an umbrella term that covers them all. We'll follow that policy here.

The idea of yarns is very simple. The irregularities in natural fibers cause them to stick together and form long strands when they are twisted together. No doubt the first yarns were very simple. As humans discovered different uses they required the many different properties of the yarns. The fillings in weaving didn't have to be very strong. The warp threads held them together and in place. The warp threads, however, would shred if they were not strong.

The idea of plying, which is twisting more than one yarn together to add strength, probably was one of the first innovations. Cording, or the twisting together of several strands of plyed threads, had to be invented before the sewing machines could run reliably at any useful speed.

Researchers intent on dating fabric artifacts like dresses or flags sometimes use the thread as a clue to the date. Using the threads and yarns as a way of dating, however, has its limits. Boxes of old yarns and threads constantly are emerging from old warehouses in quantities large enough to allow even an occasional industrial-sized production of old designs and patterns.

More casual vintage-shoppers should at least notice the spin, uniformity, and feel of threads used in weaving linens and fabrics. They should also seek out some truly fine old lace to understand how fine threads really were spun "in the olden days." This will serve as a benchmark to realizing how delicate antique laces truly are.

If we have lost quality in the fineness, suppleness, and uniformity of lacemakers' threads, then we have gained immeasurably in yarns for knitters, handweavers, and other yarn crafts.

If you notice the fibers, spin, and feel of knitting yarns you'll have an easier time recognizing the difference between art-to-wear handmade sweaters, mittens, and caps, and the run-of-the mill, store-bought variety. Composite yarns blending an assortment of fibers, colors, weights, and twists into the same length give new artistic possibilities to old crafts.

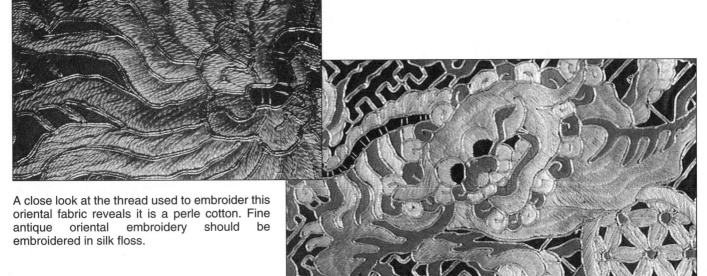

A close look at the thread used to embroider this oriental fabric reveals it is a perle cotton. Fine antique oriental embroidery should be embroidered in silk floss.

Features to note

Fiber

The properties of fibers were covered in the preceding chapter. Novelty yarns, however, deserve some note. The collectibles of the future will be those that take best advantage of the blends and variations in yarns available today.

For instance, adding synthetics to yarns used for handweaving and knitting allows amazing versatility. Small amounts of luxury fibers used in yarns can add value much the way herbs and spices add flavor to a favorite recipe.

Twist

A yarn's "twist" is determined by how tightly the fibers are spiraled around the center. It is measured in turns per inch. The twist has to be just right for each fiber and each purpose. Too loose, and the yarn shreds and falls apart. Too tight and it stresses the fibers, sometimes causing them to break.

- Loosely twisted yarns are used for soft fabrics with nap, like flannel and fleece.
- Warp threads usually have a higher twist than weft or filling threads. The higher twist makes them strong enough to withstand high loom speeds and abrasion of weaving.

Many professional weavers, lacemakers, and sewers also make note of the direction of the twist. If the spirals are in the direction of slope of the letter "S" when the yarn is held in a vertical position, it is called an "S" twist. If the spirals twist in the direction of the slope of the letter "Z," it is called a "Z" twist. Craftspeople try to minimize motions that will untwist and weaken the threads while they work.

Extremely high twist makes a yarn kinky. This is deliberately used in crepe fabrics with a crinkly surface.

Threads used for lacemaking usually must have a fairly high twist to make them smooth and strong enough to resist shredding.

Ply

Two or more single yarns are twisted together to form a heavier, stronger plyed yarn.

Two and three ply gives strength and uniformity to sewing thread.

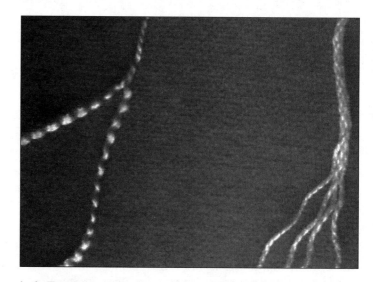

Left: Two yarns twisted together in the "S" direction to form one stronger yarn. This is called a two-ply yarn. Right: This cord is made up of four two-ply "S" yarns twisted in the "Z" direction. It might be described "2S4Z." The direction of the twist in a ply and cord sometimes can identify the origin of a textile.

Cording

Cord is two or more strands of plyed yarns twisted together. This is sometimes used to weave industrial fabrics. Some sewing thread is corded, especially threads intended for high-speed sewing machines, where it is important the thread not fray or break.

Size

"Size" of threads and yarns is expressed in terms of length per unit of weight.

Different systems are used for different fibers. Number 50 cotton, for example, is different than Number 50 linen.

In general, the higher the number (yards per ounce), the finer the yarn.

Fabrics: Manipulations

Fabric is material or cloth made from manipulated fibers or threads.

There are only a handful of distinctly different techniques that form unique kinds of fabrics: felting, weaving, crochet, needleweaving, needle lace, bobbin lace, crochet, knitting and knotting. Learn to recognize the essential characteristics of just this handful of generic techniques, and suddenly you will find you are quite literate in the language of textiles. You will understand them, be able to describe what you have, and know when a dealer does or does not know what they are talking about.

Beyond this handful of manipulations, things get complicated very quickly. Each of these techniques has dozens, if not hundreds of variations, and each can be decorated in another handful of different ways: dyeing, painting, drawnwork and embroidery. Each of these techniques for embellishing again has dozens of variations.

Regardless of how complicated a specific object becomes, recognize that the foundation of it all is one or a combination of the basic thread manipulations. Look for those manipulations, and you will be able to figure out the hardest textile puzzles.

Felting

Unwoven felt. Most common varieties of felt are formed from fibers that have been irreversibly welded together. It has no distinguishable structure or grain. The type most often found in craft stores is made of synthetic fibers. Better quality felt was made of wool.

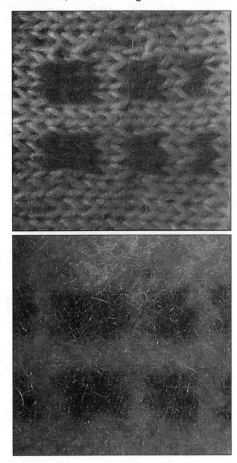

Felted knit. Knitted fabric before and after felting. Knitting a garment before felting makes it possible to work controlled, colorful designs into the fabric

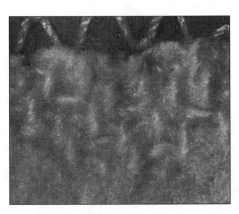

Felted plain weave. The moths have begun to nibble away the top layers of this felt, revealing the woven structure underneath.

Who hasn't accidentally made a piece of felt out of a favorite wool sweater, blanket, or cap by sending it through the hot wash cycle, or by tumbling it in a hot dryer? Very likely, the first felt also was made by accident, perhaps by a horseman who had placed a fleece under his saddle to protect the horse, then found it had turned to felt after a long, hard ride on a hot, sweaty horse.

The scales on the wool fibers lock together when the wool is wet, hot, and agitated or beaten. This makes felt. Wool makes the best, sometimes called the "true" felt. Today, it is nearly impossible to find real wool felt. Almost everything found in the craft stores is matted of synthetic fibers.

The process may start with loose fibers, like the horseman's wool fleece, or it may start with a woven or knitted fabric. Starting with a woven or knitted fabric is much more expensive, because there is the added expense of forming the fabric before it is felted. The fabric or garment is made two or three sizes too big, then shrunk and felted in a hot water wash with agitation. This is expensive and time consuming, requiring the time and effort of designing and weaving or knitting, plus the time and effort of the unpredictable shrinking process. Forming the fabric first, however, makes it possible to put colorful, controlled designs into the felt.

Decorative, colorful unwoven felts are made by mixing dyed or colored wool fibers. Felts may be decorated with paints, dyes, appliqués of other colored pieces of felt or fabric, or embroidery.

Felts were used wherever wool was available, and warm, relatively waterproof clothing was needed, or where attractive mats and rugs were wanted. This ranges across northern Europe and well into Asia.

Cut pieces of felt can be used as appliqués on other fabrics, or in crafts, to make ornaments, etc.

How to recognize felt

- Dense, somewhat stiff fabric with little or no discernible grain.
- It typically is stiffer and less pliable than a woven or knitted fabric of comparable thickness.
- Does not ravel.
- Typically is not very strong, and can be pulled apart with not a lot of force.

Features to note

- The best felt fibers are good quality wool with a matte finish.
- Wool should be clean and free of debris when it was felted.

For more information:

Vickery, Watson-Guptill, *The Art of Feltmaking*, 1997
Belt, S., *Folk Art Felt*, Krause, 1997
Sjoberg, Gunilla P.; *Felt, New Directions for An Ancient Craft* Interweave Press 1996

Weaving

Weaving, or interlacing threads or yarns at right angles to each other, is one of the oldest and most common ways of manipulating threads to form a fabric. At some point in their lives, nearly everyone has woven a basket, potholder, or placemat.

Threads running lengthwise in a woven fabric are called the warp. Threads running across are called the weft. (Other names for the weft threads are fillings, and picks.)

To weave the first woven fabrics, warp yarns probably were hung from a tree branch, and weighted with stones. The Navahos still tie the warp yarns between sticks, and interweave the pattern with other yarns.

To interlace threads, alternating warp threads on the loom must be raised and lowered. Eventually, someone figured out it would be faster and easier to weave if every other warp yarn could be raised at the same time, and a supply of yarn shuttled across the whole set of threads in one pass.

To do this, warp threads are run through wires with loops that are called headles. Many headles are held together in harnesses.

When a harness is raised, all the warp threads attached to headles in that harness are raised. The space formed between warp threads when some are raised is called a shed.

The steps in weaving are 1. shedding, or raising one or more of the harnesses; 2. picking, or passing the weft or filling thread through the shed; 3. beating up, or pushing the weft thread into place, and 4. taking up the cloth, or winding the finished cloth on the beam.

To form patterns in the weave, the way the threads interlace must be changed. Two harnesses are needed in a plain weave, where alternating threads pass over and under each other. To weave more complex patterns, warp threads must be raised and lowered in different sequences and in different combinations. To raise different warp threads at different intervals, more harnesses are needed. The loom becomes more expensive, the difficulty of weaving becomes greater, the time needed to weave the fabric usually is longer. Fabrics with complex patterns woven into them generally are more expensive or more valuable. These also were less likely to have been woven at home. The cost of the multi-harness looms, and the sophistication of the weaving process for patterned weaves suggests the most complex were left to professional handweavers, not homemakers.

Each one of the steps — shedding, filling, beating, and taking up the cloth — was mechanized in different ways at different times in history. Methods of passing the warp threads were mechanized first, and continually speeded up and improved over the decades. Methods of controlling shedding, or raising and lowering the warp threads, and beating, constantly were being changed and improved. Instead of being a revolution, mechanization of weaving was more of an evolution.

As the weaving process was powered by water, steam, and electricity and the looms began to weave faster and faster, the type of fibers and yarns that would be woven by machine changed. Fine pure cotton, wool, and other natural fibers were too easily shredded by the fast moving shuttles and warps, and had to be dropped. Stronger synthetics that were more able to withstand the harsh mechanized looms were developed.

Learning to look closely at how the threads pass over and under each other helps us understand what makes old, handmade fabrics interesting and valuable, and can reveal some interesting bargains in vintage fabrics.

Features to note

Count

The number of warp and weft threads per square inch is the fabric count. It sometimes is expressed as two numbers, 80 x 70 for instance, with the warp number first. The two numbers may be added together and expressed as one number, in this case 150.

- High count usually means more durable fabric with less unraveling and less shrinkage.
- Low count fabrics usually are softer, more pliable, and drape better.

Balance

The ratio of warp and weft threads per square inch is the balance.

- Warp and weft threads in unbalanced, low-count fabrics tend to slip or shift out of position more than balanced, high-count fabrics.

Off-Grain Fabrics

If the weave is skewed (one side of the fabric gets ahead of the other during weaving) or bowed (the center gets ahead of the sides) the fabric is said to be off-grain.

- Off-grain fabrics will not drape or hang right.

Plain Weaves

In plain weaves, yarns pass alternately over and under each other at right angles. Any fiber — cotton, linen, wool, or silk may be woven in a plain weave.

Balanced Plain Weaves

Balanced plain weaves have the same number of warp and weft threads, and the weaves are the same on the front and back. These are the easiest to weave, and require only a two-harness loom, which is the cheapest and easiest to operate, and the type most often found in home-crafted weaving.

Stripes, plaids, and checks can be woven into the plain-weave fabric by changing colors in the warp and weft. The plain flat surface is ideal to decorate with printing and embossing.

Plain weaves provide the ideal plain background for an infinite number of decorating processes. Then it is the finishing process — printing, painting, batik, tie-dye, cutwork, drawnwork, embroidery — plus the quality and appropriateness of the background that makes the finished product valuable and interesting.

Unbalanced Plain Weaves

Other decorative effects are achieved by using yarns of different weights in the warps and wefts, or by using different weights, textures, or fibers in different warp and weft positions.

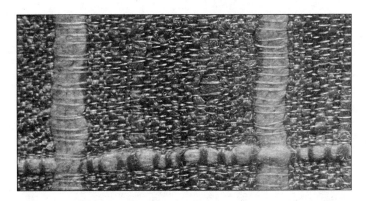

Unbalanced plain weave. Warp yarns are much lighter in weight than the filling or weft. In this novelty weave, occasionally heavy yarns are introduced for texture.

Balanced plain weave.

Unbalanced plain weave: Heavier filling yarns give grosgrain (grow-grane) ribbon a distinct, round crosswise rib.

A crosswise ridge or rib is created when the number of warp threads is much higher than the number of weft threads, when the weight or thickness of the warp thread is greater than the weft thread, or when the weight of the weft thread is greater than the warp. These all are known as unbalanced plain weaves.

Unbalanced plain weaves become very unusual and interesting when the blend of colors, textures, and fibers are imaginative.

Examples of Balanced Plain Weaves:
Lightweight, sheer or transparent fabrics:
Chiffon	*Organza*
Voile	*Organdy*

Lightweight opaque fabrics:
Batiste	*Crepe de Chine*
Handkerchief linen	*Challis*
China silk	

Lightweight, loosely-woven plain weaves:
Cheesecloth	*Buckram*
Crinoline	*Bunting*

Heavy, loosely-woven plain weaves:
Burlap

Medium-weight plain weaves:
Percale	*Muslin*
Chintz	*Gingham*
Calico	*Chambray*
Polished cotton	

Examples of Unbalanced Plain Weaves:
Broadcloth	*Grosgrain*
Taffeta	*Rag rugs*
Shantung	*Upholstrey fabrics*
Poplin	

Plain basket weave

Two or more yarns may be treated as a single thread, resulting in a texture called basket weave. When the two threads are worked in both the warp and weft, the fabric is a full basket. The fabric is called a half basket if two threads are worked only in one direction, either warp or weft.

Their neatly defined weave provides a good background for counted cross stitch, embroidered samplers, drawnwork, and other needlework.

Because there are fewer interlacings per square inch, the fabric is more flexible and wrinkle-resistant than a plain weave with a similar number of threads per square inch.

Examples of plain basket weaves:
Dimity	*Hopsacking*
Oxford cloth	*Monk's cloth*

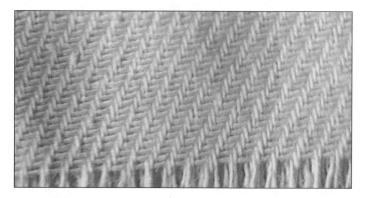

Warp-faced twill. Right or face of warp-faced twill. Threads floating across two or more weft threads create diagonal lines on the surface of the fabric.

Twill Weaves

Fabrics with a distinct diagonal line formed by floating each warp or filling yarn over two more filling or warp yarns are called twills.

Because warp threads have to be raised and lowered in a more complex way than for a plain weave, a more complex loom is needed. At least four harnesses are required for twills.

The diagonal will run from left to right on the front and right to left on the back. Twills most often are found in solid colors, or with color alternating in the warp and weft threads. The uneven surface does not work well for prints.

- Twill weaves often are found in vintage suits and dresses.
- Many wool tweeds (fabrics made of novelty, flecked wools) are woven as twills.
- With the great popularity and fascination with vintage jeans, there is more interest in the fabric used to make them.

Examples of warp-faced twills
(With predominant warps.)
Denim	*Chino*
Jean	*Gabardine*
Drill	

Examples of even-sided twills
(The same number of warp and weft yarns exposed on both sides of the weave.)
Surah	*Herringbone*
Serge	*Houndstooth*
Sharkskin	

Plain basket weave. A full basket weave, with two threads worked as one in both the warp and weft directions.

Satin Weaves

Threads carried in long floats over several warps or wefts create the characteristic shiny surface of satins. Most typically, warp or weft threads carry across four threads and interlace with the fifth. The interlacings progress diagonally across the fabric.

To keep an obvious diagonal ridge from forming, an irregular pattern of interlacings has to be established. This makes the weaving process more complex, and the fabric more expensive.

- Because sheen is the objective, bright filament threads, especially silk or synthetics, are the most common fibers used.
- Sateens usually are made with spun yarns of cotton or other fiber. The surface is finished or treated to enhance the shine.

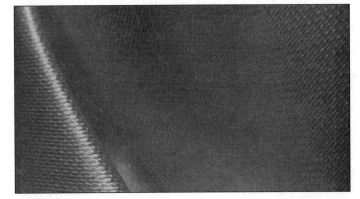
Satin weave.

Pile Weaves

A three-dimensional fabric is produced by weaving an extra set of warp or weft yarns along with a base fabric. By leaving this extra set of threads slack, or by weaving it over a wire, a looping pile is formed. This pile can be cut to form tufts, or left as loops.

The pile sometimes serves a useful purpose, such as increasing the absorbency of cotton or linen towels. Other times the pile is strictly decorative, as in elaborate silk luxury velvets.

Velveteen usually is made with spun yarns like cotton, and pile is quite dense. Velvet usually refers to luxury fabric of filament-spun fibers like silk, with a fine silky surface.

Novel pile surfaces produced with techniques other than weaving include: Chenille and Tufted rugs.

Interesting pile weaves include examples with:
- Complex designs that include piles of different heights in different areas of design.
- Designs created with cut and uncut areas of pile.
- Areas of pile in otherwise flat surfaces.
- Crushed, embossed, or sheared pile may create other dimensional effects.

Especially valuable examples include:
- Patterned pile effects combined with other elaborately patterned weaves, including brocades, or jacquard weaves.

Examples of pile fabrics:

Terrycloth	*Velour*
Velvet	*Corduroy*

Pile fabric. Velvet, velour, and velveteen all refer to fabrics with an overall soft pile surface.

Pile fabric. Corduroy is an everyday, wear-to-school-or-work pile fabric. Tufted pile is arranged in rows called wales.

Patterned or Structured Weaves

Patterns other than stripes, checks, or plaids require very complex interlacings of the warp and weft threads. This means some method has to be established to raise and lower specific warp threads at precise intervals. The dobby and jacquard attachments were two ways of doing this.

Both are relatively expensive, require a lot of space, and were quite complex to operate. For the most part, patterned weaves are the products of professional rather than home weavers.

Dobby Weaves

The dobby is an attachment for looms that makes it possible to produce novelty effects in very small repeats, such as dots or small stripes.

In a fabric like Dotted Swiss, which has tiny dots woven into the surface, threads are allowed to float across the surface between the woven dots. These floats later are clipped or shaved off.

In fabrics like huckaback or huck toweling, the floats are very short, and are left in. In huck toweling, they are left to increase the absorption of the towel. Because they pop up at short, regular intervals, they make a handy gauge for embroidery. Huck towels very often are decorated with colorful geometric designs done in running stitch embroidery.

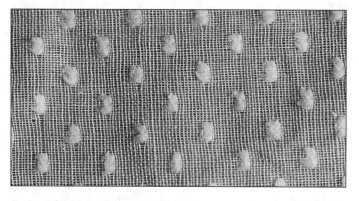

Dotted Swiss, a popular fabric for summer dresses in the first half of the 20th century.

Huck toweling. A popular homecraft of the early 20th century is created by running colored embroidery threads under the short threads floating at regular intervals across the surface. The effect is colorful geometric patterns.

Examples of patterned or structured weaves:

Huck or Huckaback	Dotted Swiss
Waffle cloth	Pique
Madras	

Leno Weave

Adjacent warp yarns are crossed over one another before each filling is inserted in the leno weave. This twisting holds the filling or weft in place in very low-count fabrics such as curtain materials, some mosquito netting, and some bags for laundry and produce.

Handwoven leno weave with extremely large spaces between the warp and weft is used as the basis for burato lace. The plain background net is formed, then a design is hand-darned over the grid.

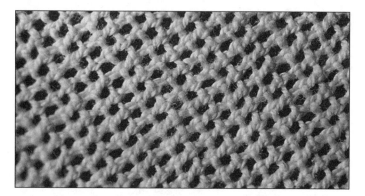

Leno weave.

Jacquard Weaves

We are so accustomed to seeing elaborate pictorial weavings today that it is hard to imagine what an exciting discovery the Jacquard process was.

Working elaborate patterns right into the weave was a labor-intensive process that required elaborate instructions that often took weeks or months to encode for the weavers. From this complex coded set of instructions, a weaver's assistant, called a draw-boy, selectively raised and lowered warp threads by drawing on different warps one by one.

Jacquard's invention of a punch-card system that would automatically raise and lower the appropriate warp threads to produce the design eliminated the draw-boy's job, but still proved incredibly labor-intensive.

Jacquard weave. 20th century upholstery fabric.

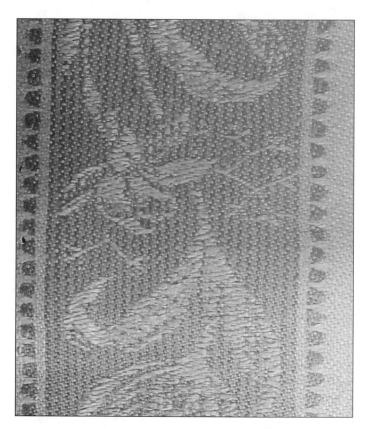

Damask napkin, detail.

The position of each individual warp and weft thread as they crossed had to be precisely drafted out on a pattern, and a separate punch-card prepared for each separate pass of the weft or filling thread. This was called a pick.

For even a comparatively short pattern repeat, say a foot long, there might be a thousand weft threads passing across the loom. This would mean a thousand different cards had to be punched and strung together in an accordion-folded train to be fed through the loom.

Each of this thousand or more warp threads had to be individually strung through a ring attached to a wire, then connected to the punch card system. The position of the holes in the punch card would determine which warp thread was raised or lowered for each pass of the filling thread.

Drafting the pattern, punching the cards, and stringing the loom might require days or weeks. The longer the pattern repeat, or the more variations in a pattern, the more expensive the fabric.

Professional weavers, such as those who made coverlets in the nineteenth century, would have a preset group of sectioned patterns, which might be combined in different ways. Different borders and corner blocks could be designed and combined to add individuality for coverlet customers.

Many kinds of Jacquard weavings are very collectible:
- Coverlets, especially those with many colors, unusual designs, and good provenance.
- Woven pictures, especially Stevengraphs, with many colors and the most intricate designs.

Vintage damask table linens with high thread count, long staple fibers, and excellent designs often are priced low, and represent an extremely good bargain.

Examples of Jacquard woven fabrics:
Damask
Brocade
Jacquard tapestry for upholstery, purses, etc.
Woven silk pictures, including Stevengraphs
Coverlets

Tapestry

Handwoven Tapestry

The dictionary definition of a tapestry — a textile with a design or picture that is formed as part of the weaving process — hardly does justice to the awe-inspiring Navajo rugs, the eighteenth century Indian cashmere shawls and the fantastic woven creations that kept the chill off castle walls with fanciful stories in thread.

Like lacemaking, and most other forms of fabric making, many new techniques and an assortment of new machines have been developed to weave pictures in threads. None of these have the texture of true handwoven tapestry.

Hand tapestry weaving goes back centuries to before the development of the multi-harnessed loom that we know today.

To understand what makes handwoven tapestries so special, a quick review of weaving terminology is needed. The warp threads are those that travel the lengthwise direction of the fabric. The weft, pick, or filling is the thread or yarn that travels across. Handmade tapestries have a discontinuous weft; each time the color changes, a new weft is introduced.

This raises an obvious question: How, exactly, does one drop the color of yarn as it crosses the weft and change to a new thread? What happens to all those ends and beginnings? The answer to that question reveals the essence, and the unique opportunities for design, in tapestry weaving.

To recognize handmade tapestry, first look to see whether there is a discontinuous weft, which is the most distinctive feature of handmade tapestry. Details that show exactly how colors are changed not only confirm that a tapestry is handmade, but they help evaluate the quality and the origins.

Basic slit technique

Each color ends with a turn, like a selvage. This leaves a hole or slit in the tapestry. These may be sewn shut at the end or left for decorative effect. There is a basic disadvantage to this technique, a weakness in the structure.

Dovetail

Alternating one or two warps with each color on alternating rows interlocks the weft threads as the color changes. This leaves a zigzag effect along the edge of the color change.

Single weft interlock

Different color yarns can be twisted around each other before turning to complete the weaving. This leaves a line, depending on what color is put forward each time the threads twist.

Some non-weaving techniques are used in tapestries:

Twining

With this technique, two threads are intertwined around the warps. This technique may be used separately, as in Chilkat Indian blankets and robes, or as an additional technique along with traditional tapestry weaves.

Chaining

A form of crochet-like looping can be worked across the warp threads. This usually is used as a decorative effect along with other techniques. It rarely is used alone.

Soumak

A single thread around the warps. It can be open — with the loops facing front and the carryover across the back — or closed, which is vice versa.

Features to note

Design
- Complex scenes that tell stories make extremely interesting tapestries.
- Backgrounds with lots of color, shading, and variety adds interest.
- The technique should reinforce and support the design. The technique the weaver chooses for color changes in diagonals, vertical and horizontal lines, and curving lines all demonstrate the skill, imagination, and technique of the designers and weavers.

Quality of the materials
- Yarn or threads must be strong, durable, and colorfast. Cheap tapestries will fade or run.
- High-tensile strength threads are important in the warp.
- Weft turns and relays are important to get an even, interesting texture.

Technique and workmanship
- Warps must be perfectly evenly spaced and tensioned so the finished tapestry will not pucker. The warp should not show from behind the weft.
- Ridges formed by the warp, concealed under the weft threads, will tell whether the tapestry was woven horizontally or vertically. This provides clues as to exactly how it was made, when, and in what workshops.

What makes tapestry valuable
- History, provenance, and workshop add to the value.
- Design, workmanship and technique must be of the highest quality for the tapestry to be valuable.

Condition is important
- Exposed warps, separations at the slits or color changes are signs of wear and deterioration. But, expect some deterioration in extremely old tapestries.
- Look for evidence of replaced wefts, such as fibers, textures, and yarns that don't quite match the originals.
- Fragments of handwoven tapestry are interesting and collectible when the technique, design in the fragment, and colors all are exceptional.

Slits or holes naturally result when colors change in tapestry. Photos courtesy of Anne Schumacher.

Alternately twisting the differently colored weft yarns around one or two extra warp threads is a way of changing colors without leaving a slit. This produces a zigzagging effect called dovetailing.

Raveling edge of old tapestry rug shows discontinuous weft threads wrapped around, and completely hiding, the warp threads.

Decorative textural effects can be worked into tapestries.

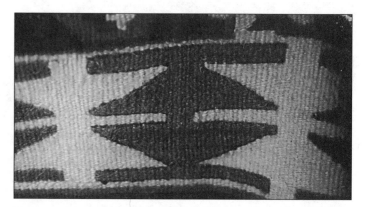

An outline yarn in a contrasting color masks the natural step effect in a diagonal color change.

Machine Imitations of Tapestry

The defining difference between handmade tapestry and machine-made tapestry is the weft, or cross-wise filling yarns. In handmade tapestry, the weft is non-continuous. Each time the color changes, the weft stops and a new color is put in.

In machine-made tapestry, the weft is continuous. When a certain color is not being used to form part of the design on the front, it floats across the back of the tapestry. The more colors used in the weaving, the thicker the tapestry because of the numerous threads floating across the back of the work. Sometimes, especially in paisley and other huge, highly decorative woven shawls, the threads carried across the back were clipped off by hand to reduce the weight of the fabric.

The threads are left on most tapestries intended for upholstery or for wall hangings and they add stability and weight to the fabric.

Features to note

Detail and lots of colors are hallmarks of the best machine tapestries.

- Figures in the best woven pictures will have noticeable personality, with flirting, roving eyes, and elegant, gesturing hands and fingers.
- Floral and garden pictures should have gracefully shaped petals, veining on the leaves and the petals should be delineated.
- Look for good quality materials, especially silks, wools, and other natural fibers.
- In general, the finer the yarns, the more detail is possible in the picture.

Wefts are continuous in machine woven tapestry. Colors not showing on the face float across the back.

Bobbin Lacemaking

Bobbin lace is a generic term for one of the basic techniques of thread manipulation to form lacy fabrics. It is relatively easy to learn to identify a lacy fabric like bobbin lace, and to judge whether it is a poor or excellent example. Learning to identify when and where it was made, however, involves much more study.

Bobbin lace evolved out of weaving and other thread manipulations, and emerged as a specific form of lacemaking in about the 1500s. By the late 1600s, it was raised to high art in Europe. In the nineteenth century, it was carried to Asia, Africa and the Far East by missionaries, and businessmen who sought cheap sources of labor. It is not native to the Far East, and designs often are stilted or stiff in design. Because it was an imported craft, and lacemakers were expected to produce quickly with minimal schooling, workmanship often is excellent, but techniques are often limited.

Because bobbin lace has a history of several hundred years, it appears in an amazing variety of styles, an astonishing combination of techniques, and in thread weights from gossamer-fine to nearly rope-like.

Regardless of the pattern, weight, or style, however, it always is based on the same handful of thread manipulations. Once these basic manipulations are recognized, it becomes easy to recognize a piece of lace as bobbin lace.

How to recognize generic bobbin lace

Bobbin lace is a type of free-form weaving, worked with many threads at the same time. It consists of areas that appear to be woven, threads that twist around each other, and braids made from either three pairs of threads, or plaited of four separate threads.

- Clothlike areas may be either linen stitch, which looks like woven cloth, or half stitch, an open diagonal weave.
- Threads running lengthwise in the woven clothwork will follow the shape of curves.
- By introducing twisted threads and holes, patterns can be woven into the clothwork.

The background may be either mesh or bars.

- Meshes with be intricate combinations of twisted and braided threads (see examples on following pages). Recognizing the precise paths the threads take are clues that distinguish handmade from machine. The mesh often is one clue that defines a specific style of bobbin lace.
- Bars will be braided threads.

Dense, clothlike areas will appear woven, with threads interlaced over and under each other.
Distinctive features of bobbin lace include:
  1. Linen or cloth stitch
  2. Half stitch
  3. Wheatears or tallies

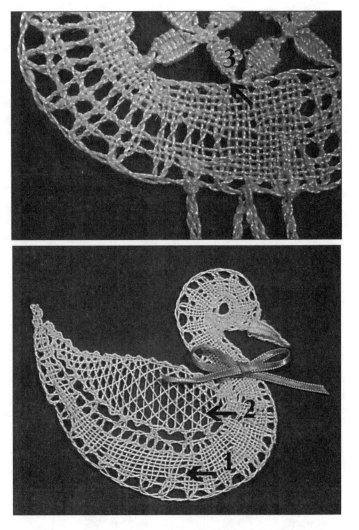

The four basic categories of bobbin lace

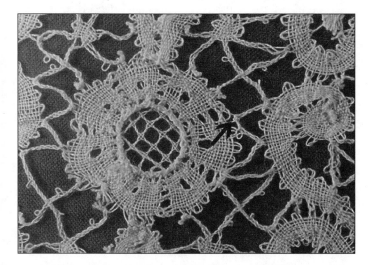

Non-continuous guipure (bar background). Motifs were made separately, brought together and assembled with connecting bars. Connecting bars start and end at the edge of the clothwork.

Continuous guipure (bar background). Background and design were made continuously. Threads continue from bars through clothwork.

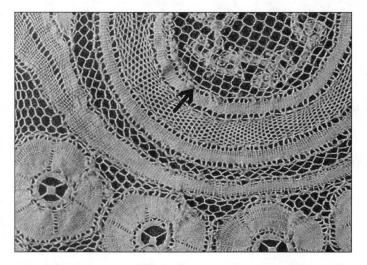

Non-continuous mesh background. Mesh was added after design was made. Nearly microscopic knots where mesh was ended show it was added in and isn't continuous.

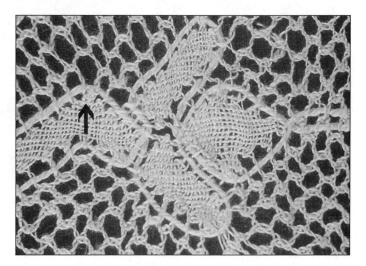

Continuous mesh background. Mesh was made at the same time as the clothwork design.
Threads continue directly from mesh into clothwork, and vice-versa.

Features to note

- Thread used for bobbin lace should be spun tightly enough to make a stable thread that will not easily shred.
- Thread should be lightweight enough that it clearly defines the design. Too heavy and thick, and the design is obscured. Too thin, and the design is stringy.
- Look for shading effects created by spacing stitches and a variety of types of stitches.
- Look for elaborate patterns and great variety in filling stitches.
- A few of the most sought after types of bobbin lace include seventeenth and eighteenth century bobbin laces with snow grounds and elaborate designs. Types of lace include Binche, Valenciennes, and Mechlin.

What makes bobbin lace valuable

- Fragments of bobbin lace are collectible when the technique and stitches are extremely complex and difficult, when the thread used to make it is extremely fine, and the design is very good and unusual for its age and type.
- Look for handmade mesh background. Snowflake, six-point star (Point de Paris), droschel, Mechlin, Valenciennes, and honeycomb, were especially difficult to work, and required great skill.
- If the technique is not unusual, the design must be exceptional, and the bobbin lace must be in the form of a useful thing that would be highly valued. Bridal veils, fans and handkerchiefs are a few examples.

Pieces with known provenance, especially those with crests, names, or royal insignia, may have added value.

How to recognize specific styles of bobbin lace

It is not difficult to identify a piece of lace as bobbin lace. To identify where and when it was made and possibly assign a name to the style, it is necessary to look very closely at precise details of the technique.

- Whether the lace was made all at the same time, in which case the background is continuous with the design, or whether the lace was made in little bits and pieces and assembled later is a first key clue. This divides the lace into one of two categories: continuous, also known as straight lace, or non-continuous, also known as part or free bobbin lace.

- Specific classic styles of bobbin lace made in well-known lacemaking centers typically have distinctive combinations of clothwork, specific edge or outline treatments, and unique methods of working the mesh and arranging and decorating the bars. For positive identification of the name and place of origin, the complete package — clothwork outline, mesh and bridges — must be identified. Dozens of such combinations are listed in the reference book *A Guide To Lace and Linens*, by Elizabeth Kurella, Antique Trader books, 1998.

Even when a lace does not match up with a complete combination of features, the presence of two or three of five can offer enough clues to suggest the origin.

Handmade Bobbin Lace Meshes

Valenciennes. This is one of the most commonly found meshes, but one most often overlooked. The presence of this mesh defines handmade Valenciennes bobbin lace.

Four-strand braids line all four sides, made continuously with the clothwork. Depending on the length of the braids, mesh may be round or square. Even with extremely high-power magnification the braids may be difficult to recognize.

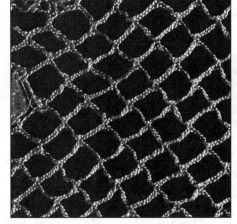

Valenciennes diamond mesh.

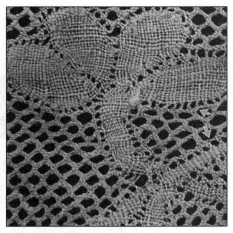

Valenciennes round mesh.

Droschel and Mechlin. Both droschel and Mechlin meshes have four-strand braids on two sides of a roughly hexagonal mesh and the remaining four sides are twisted threads. Mechlin is continuous with the clothwork. Droschel was always added in later, and the braids are slightly longer. Requires extremely high-power magnification to see.

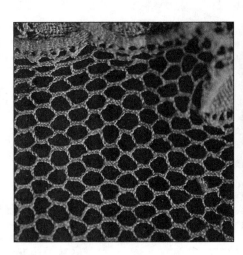

Droschel mesh.

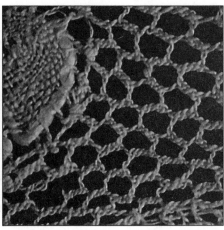

Mechlin mesh.

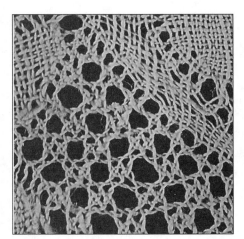

Five-hole mesh. Also known as cinc trous, fond de mariage and fond de la vierge. This checkerboard-like mesh is commonly named for the five holes in each of the little blocks. It often is found in early 18th century Valenciennes, Mechlin, and Binche bobbin laces, and forms the background in 20th century Flanders lace.

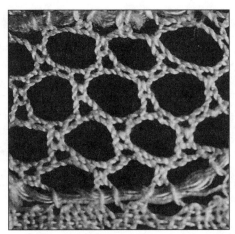

Honeycomb mesh. Named so for its distinctive resemblance to a honeycomb. The shape of the mesh usually can be recognized with the naked eye. A magnifying glass is necessary see the precise path the threads take, and to tell handmade from machine. The mesh usually appears as an accent in handmade Chantilly.

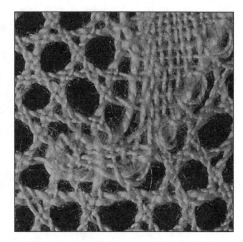

Six-point star mesh. Also known as Point de Paris or Jewish mesh for the six-point star. It was used as a decorative background mesh or an accent in many bobbin laces from the 17th century through today. The shape of the mesh usually can be recognized with the naked eye. A magnifying glass is necessary see the precise path the threads take, and to tell handmade from machine.

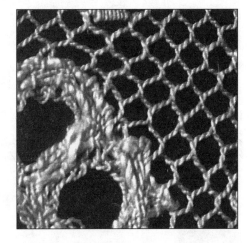

Point ground. Also known as Lille mesh. This mesh consists of pairs of threads twisted on all sides. It is the simplest of the bobbin lace meshes, and was copied faithfully by machine by 1800. Point ground is the basic background mesh in Bucks Point, Lille, Beveren, and Tonder bobbin laces from the mid 19th century to today.

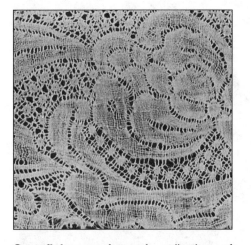

Snowflake meshes. A collection of meshes, including armure, partridge eye, partridge eye with halo, and several other highly decorative background meshes are named for their resemblance to snowflakes. They were extensively used as backgrounds in 17th and 18th century Valenciennes, Binche, and Mechlin bobbin laces, and were used widely as accents in Brussels lace. They reappeared as the background in circa-1900 Binche, also known as Point de Fee.

Machine Imitations of Bobbin Lace

Machines were eventually developed that could mimic the designs popular in some bobbin lace. Except for a very few very simple bobbin laces, machines never were able to duplicate the technique or stitching. That is the way to tell the difference.

Two basic categories of machines were used to imitate bobbin laces. The first were machines that ran with a continuous lengthwise warp and could manipulate the warp and weft to produce lacy fabrics. The two best known of these machines were the Pusher and the Leavers machines. These were especially good at imitating continuous mesh-based bobbin laces, or laces where the design and background were produced at the same time.

The second category of machine are the embroidery machines. The "aetz" or chemical lace process was the best known of these. A design was embroidered in a lock stitch on some form of substrate that later was chemically dissolved, freeing the embroidery as lace.

The Schiffli embroidery machine usually was the machine used to do the embroidery. These were especially good at producing the guipure bobbin laces — those where the motifs were connected with bars.

To tell machine imitations from handmade bobbin lace, it is necessary to closely compare each of the basic features including the clothwork, outline, mesh and/or bars, and the ornamental stitching.

Both categories of machine-produced bobbin lace often could mimic one, two or even three of the features of handmade bobbin lace, but there always was at least one feature that gave away the imitation.

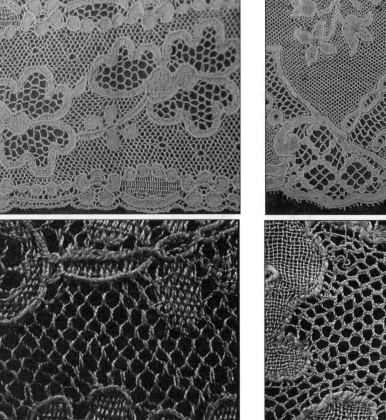

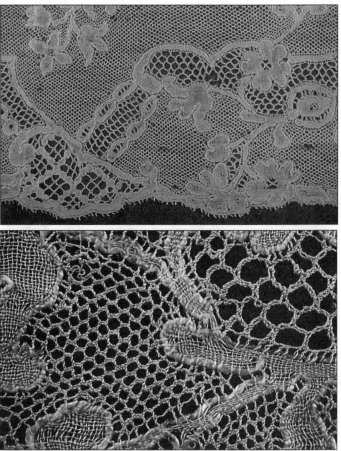

A machine imitation of handmade Mechlin bobbin lace. Note the slight grain in the texture of the clothwork of the machine imitation. The outline thread, known as a gimp, appears slightly raised on the face of the machine lace. It also does not completely trace the edge of all the motifs. In the handmade version, below, the gimp is woven right into the lace, and appears along the edge of all motifs.

Handmade Mechlin bobbin lace. The key difference between handmade and machine is in the mesh. An extremely strong magnifying glass is needed to see that two sides of the slightly hexagonal handmade mesh are braided (see detail of Mechlin mesh on page 36). In the machine version, there are no neat braids — machines were never able to duplicate the handmade Mechlin mesh.

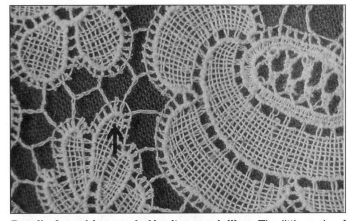

Detail of machine-made Honiton medallion. The little sprig of leaflets is typical of both English Honiton and Belgian Duchesse bobbin lace. A sprig like this with little segmented leaflets is sometimes called a leaf with taps. In the handmade version the entire sprig is woven continuously. Threads are carried as a bundle or as a little woven rib to the tip of the leaflet, then spread out and woven back as a broad area of clothwork. This is faked in the machine version with a heavy row of stitching.

Oval medallion pictured here is a extremely fine and delicate machine imitation of a design typically worked in handmade English Honiton bobbin lace. The machine imitated the design beautifully, but did not duplicate the thread manipulations as they would be worked in bobbin lace. The machine does a passable job of imitating the woven clothwork of bobbin lace. It is the details of the outline and edges of the motifs, and how the motifs are formed, that show the key differences.

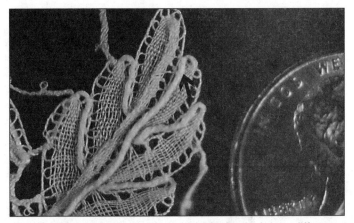

Detail of handmade Honiton bobbin lace. A key difference between handmade and machine appears in the edge of the woven clothwork. In the handmade bobbin lace, pairs of threads exit the woven clothwork, form the edge, and return into the clothwork. In the machine version, a single thread runs along the edge of each motif.

Needle Lacemaking

Needle lace is a generic term for laces built up stitch by stitch with a needle and thread. It evolved centuries ago from cutwork and drawnwork. As more and more threads were drawn out of a woven fabric, and areas of the original fabric were cut away to form a design, more and more areas were embellished with "stitches in the air" built up on the few threads remaining of the original fabric.

Eventually, lacemakers recognized it was not necessary to start with a woven fabric. A skeleton of threads could be laid down, and the lace built up over them.

Because it is such an old lacemaking form, needle lace was made into many different styles and designs, always changing to reflect the taste of the times. Over the centuries, hundreds of different forms were marketed under a variety of names. Some names reflected the style or combi-nation of stitches chosen, other names reflected the place where it was made.

What never changed over the centuries was the basic technique and some basic stitches used to make it. Looking at the technique and stitches rather than at the design makes it easy to recognize a piece of needle lace.

How to recognize generic needle lace

All needle lace is built up of threads, and the manipulations are done with a needle and thread, including stitches based on the buttonhole or blanket stitches, and variations of needleweaving and darning.

Needle lace often is combined with other techniques. In large items like tablecloths, shawls, or veils, needle lace is combined with bobbin lace, embroidery, and drawnwork.

The edge of each motif is defined with a thread. This is a skeleton that was established when the lace was made.
- It can be left plain.
- It can be covered with extra threads and buttonhole stitches to create a raised outline.
- It can be highly decorated with crowns of stitches.

Clothlike areas of the design are built up stitch by stitch with blanket or buttonhole stitches placed very close together.
- These sometimes are worked over an extra thread to make the clothwork even more dense.
- They can be highly decorative patterns, but still are based on variations of the buttonhole stitch.

The background can be either mesh or bars.
- The mesh can be simple long loops of thread.
- The long loops can be wrapped with additional threads, or covered with buttonhole stitches.
- The precise method of making the mesh often is one clue that defines the style and origin of a piece of needle lace.
- The bars will be covered with buttonhole stitches.
- The bars may be plain, or decorated with picots. The picots may be little spikes, little loops, or loops covered with spikes.

Features to note
- The more elaborate and unusual the design, the more attractive it is to collectors.
- Very often, the finer the thread, the better the lace.
- Laces with animals, figures, and birds are always the most interesting.
- In the best quality needle lace, each stitch will add to the overall effect. Look for rows of stitches to follow curves and shapes of leaves, flower petals, stems and scrollwork.
- Look for shading effects created by spacing stitches and a variety of types of stitches.
- Look for elaborately decorated outlines with raised edges and thorn-like picots.
- Look for elaborate patterns and great variety in filling stitches.
- A few of the most sought after types of needle lace include Gros Point de Venise, Reseau Venise, Alencon, Point de France, and Point de Neige.

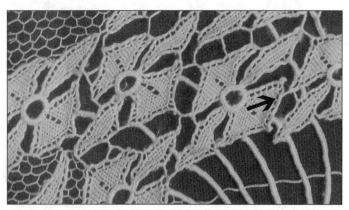

Detail of early 20th century Art Nouveau needle lace. Edge is flat. There is no raised outline.

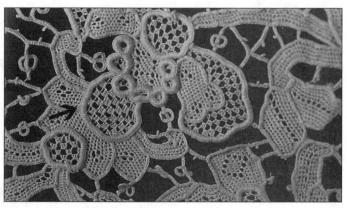

Detail of 20th century lace tablecloth. Note heavy raised outline, covered with buttonhole stitches.

Note distinctive texture of the buttonhole-stitched clothwork in both examples.

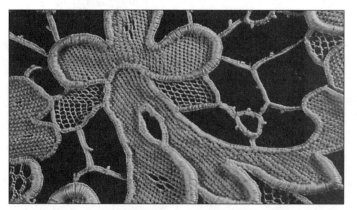

Detail of clothwork in needle lace. Each row is built up of little buttonhole stitches. To make the clothwork more dense, an additional thread can be run along the bottom of each row and the following row stitched over that thread and into the preceding row.

Point de Gaze. Also is known as Brussels mesh. It consists of long, looping buttonhole stitches with an extra twist in each stitch to lock it and keep it from slipping. It typically is worked in threads so fine it cannot be recognized with the naked eye.

Alencon mesh. It consists of long, looping buttonhole stitches that have been wrapped with another thread along the bottom of each row. The much-magnified, coarse version of the Alencon mesh shown here is used in a tape lace. The mesh, as used in handmade Alencon, is much finer, and can be recognized only with about ten to twenty power magnification. The mesh was introduced in the late 18th or early 19th century. Worked in extremely fine thread, and loosely enough to form a vaguely hexagonal mesh, it is found as a background in Alencon needle lace. In Burano needle lace, it is worked more tightly, and forms a more rectangular mesh. It appears in a heavy, coarse version in some tape laces, in mixed needle and bobbin laces of the 19th century and in other assorted large-scale 19th century laces.

Argentan mesh. This consists of long looping buttonhole stitches that have been covered on all sides with buttonhole stitches. It is shown here in extreme magnification. It typically cannot be recognized with the naked eye. Introduced in the late 17th century, it was used in spectacular laces through the 18th century. It nearly disappeared in the 19th century. Very large scale versions of this background can be found in early 20th

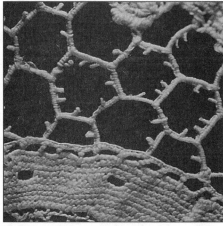

Point de France mesh. This consists of long looping buttonhole stitches that have been covered on all sides with minute buttonhole stitches and decorated with thorn-like picots. It is shown here in extreme magnification. It typically cannot be recognized with the naked eye. It was introduced in the 17th century, and appeared mainly in extremely fine and elaborate French needle laces through the early 18th century.

A heavy, coarse version appears in some generic tablecloths and other large scale items. This was introduced in the second quarter of the 19th century. It is found as a background in Point de Gaze (Rose Point) needle lace, and as a background in a combination lace sometimes called Point d'Angleterre with Brussels bobbin lace motifs, and occasionally in other 19th century mixed laces.

Machine Imitations of Needle Lace

Machines were eventually developed that could mimic the designs popular in needle lace. They never were able to duplicate the technique of stitching, however. That is how to tell the difference.

Schiffli machines were capable of embroidering in a lock stitch that would not unravel were developed in the third quarter of the nineteenth century. In the late 1880s, a method was perfected to of dissolve the substrate or background, leaving the embroidery free as lace. This was called chemical lace, or aetz for the Swiss-German word for burnt.

The machine-embroidered lace was capable of imitating the crisp-edged designs typical of needle lace, and many of the early designs imitated Point de Gaze, Alencon, Point de Venise, and other well-respected needle laces.

It is very easy to tell them apart. It just takes a close look with a good magnifying glass. Eventually, it becomes very easy to recognize most of the aetz lace even without a magnifying glass.

The key difference is all needle lace is based on variations of the buttonhole stitch. The machine never duplicated that stitch. Instead, it produced an irregular zigzag stitch.

Extremely magnified detail of handmade needle lace. Buttonhole stitches, partially obscured by the thorn-like picots, form the rings and cover the bars surrounding the rings. The dense clothwork areas in handmade needle lace are built up of row after row of buttonhole stitches. This gives the clothwork a very distinctive texture.

Actual size example of machine-made lace known as aetz, or chemical lace. Magnified detail of chemical lace. There is not a buttonhole stitch in sight. The bars are a form of zigzag stitch, and the clothwork has a fuzzy woven appearance.

Crocheting

Crochet is perhaps the most homespun of textile techniques, a creative outlet for any child, woman or man. It requires only a hook and a length of thread. With only a few lessons, nearly anyone anywhere anytime can start making a tablecloth. Even after arthritis has caused knobs on our knuckles, we can still grip an oversize warm wooden hook, find some soft, fluffy yarn, and go on making colorful afghans for our grandchildren.

It is one of the most recent of the techniques. The oldest examples found in museums and private collections date to the beginning of the 1800s. It developed almost simultaneously from two distinctly different roots. The first, "shepherd's knitting," is a form of thread manipulation used to make dense, warm woolly mittens in the northern European climates. The second is "tambour embroidery," a chain-stitch embroidery on fabric brought to Europe in the early 1800s from Turkey and the Middle East.

It developed quickly into one of the most ubiquitous of needlecrafts because rapid developments in printing techniques made cheap, fast distribution of patterns and examples possible through magazines and craft books.

Godey's, Munsey's, Priscilla, Workbasket, and magazine articles from the mid 1800s to the mid 1900s provided an endless stream of ideas for gifts, novelties, and warm, cozy things to brighten every home.

The most intricate, imaginative and complex designs and pieces were made in the mid to late 1800s. In addition to the expected home and fashion items like mittens, gloves, capes, jackets, collars, cuffs, hats and caps, tablecloths, doilies, antimacassars and doilies, patterns were offered for everything from pen wipes to wastebaskets to earmuffs for horses to lampshades.

By 1900, homemakers had other crafts and occupations to keep them busy, and were rapidly losing interest and patience in doing intricate handwork.

In the 1930s and early 1940s, homemakers still made tablecloths and crochet was still popular but designs were getting simpler, and more repetitive.

When crocheted tablecloths, bedspreads, afghans, doilies, or blouses become popular, the Chinese, Philippine, or other craft markets begin to make more crocheted items to supply the demand.

Crochet very often is combined with other materials and techniques. Crochet was worked directly around the edge of handkerchiefs, pillow cases, and table linens. It was used as a form of glue to hold rickrack, ribbons, and fancy machine woven tapes in decorative lace-like patterns.

How to recognize generic crochet

Generic crochet is based on drawing twisted loops of thread through other loops, which means each stitch is comparatively large and heavy.
- Each single crochet stitch is seed-like or knot-like.
- Individual double or treble stitches look like pillars of twisted threads.

Chain stitched bars will have a line of little interlocking chevrons like the chain it is named for. This row of interlocking chevrons also will appear along one edge of each bit of crocheted fabric.

Features to note
- To bring a high price in the marketplace, crochet has to be in the form of clever, attractive things, in condition good enough to display or use.
- The fiber and quality of the thread or yarn significantly affect the value. Long staple and tightly spun cotton thread gives lace designs better definition and stands up better to wear. Good quality silk thread in brilliant colors also adds to nineteenth century purses, and woolen yarns in attractive shades and combinations are best for afghans.
- The best pieces are those where the maker strayed from the printed pattern and began to innovate. The innovations, from "The Last Supper" to a picture of a fountain from the San Francisco World's Fair worked in fine white thread as filet crochet make the most interesting collectibles.
- Large pieces of Irish crochet, such as jackets and dresses, in elaborate designs with lots of innovative raised work are interesting to collectors.

For more information:
Palauden, Lis; Crochet, History and Technique. First published in Denmark, 1986. Interweave Press, English language copyright, 1995.

Each individual crochet stitch is large, and usually looks like a pillar of twisted threads.

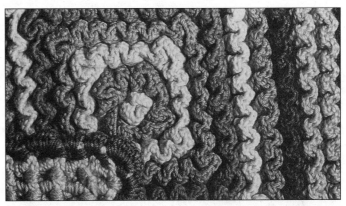

Textured effects are achieved in crochet by working one layer over another. In this mid 20th century pot holder, a square gridwork was crocheted, then tight rows of double crochet were added to create the ruffles. The distinctive pillar-like stitches and chevron-like edge of crochet are partially obscured by the tight stitching.

Types of Crochet

Tunisian Crochet
Also known as Afghan stitch

A double stitch worked in two passes. The establishes a row of loops on a tool that resembles a single hooked knitting needle. In the second pass, another loop is drawn through the first, and the stitch is dropped off the end of the long hooked needle

Shepherd's Knitting
- The knot-like single crochet stitch is almost the only stitch used to make the dense fabric known as shepherd's knit.

Wools that fulled, felted, and shrank into dense waterproof fabrics made this fabric important for mittens, jackets, and even boots.

Novelty Crochet
Crochet very often is combined with other materials and techniques. Crochet was worked directly around the edge of handkerchiefs, pillowcases, and table linens. It was used as a form of glue to hold rickrack, ribbons, and fancy machine woven tapes in decorative, lace-like patterns.

Hairpin and Broomstick Crochet
In hairpin and broomstick crochet, large loops are formed over a simple tool, such as a two-pronged fork or hairpin, or large knitting needle or a broomstick, and fastened with crochet stitches into decorative patterns.

Typically, in hairpin lace, long, loopy braids are made then joined with crochet or sewing stitches. Row after row of loops are twisted and joined with crochet stitches in broomstick lace.

Traditional granny square is worked in double or treble stitches, with any leftover yarns that could be found in granny's knitting basket. Many squares were assembled into afghans.

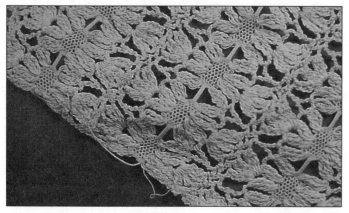

Long, rangy treble crochet stitches form petal-like strands around the center row of turtleback or medallion machine tapes.

A thick crocheted cord forms the meandering curves in Romanian point lace. Needleweaving or needle the fillings.

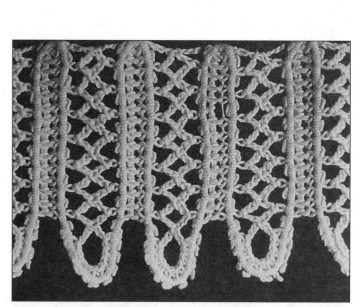

Short zigzagging chain stitches secure a pre-made machine tape in long curves to form this lace.

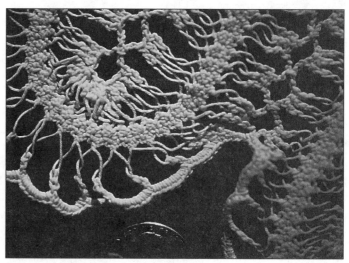

Broomstick lace.

Mid 19th century Irish crochet imitated needle lace.
• Raised work decorates flower centers.
• Picots decorate the bridges connecting motifs.
• Little openwork patterns decorate clothwork in stylized flowers.

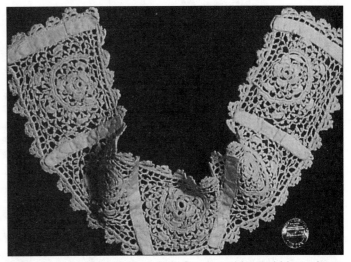

The most common form of Irish Crochet, this could have been made anywhere from China and the Philippines to Europe.

Irish Crochet

Irish crochet is an expressive, creative textural form of crochet originally developed in the early 1800s to provide income for victims of the potato famine.

The designs were so original, attractive, and fashionable, they quickly were adopted around the world. German and Scandinavian pattern books quickly popularized the style across Europe; Chinese and other inexpensive labor was exploited into the twentieth century to fill market demand. Consequently, it is impossible to say where any individual piece was made, or when.

In general, however, the finest thread and most delicate, intricate designs were made in the early nineteenth century, and heavy, layered examples fit the fashion in the later nineteenth century. Often, the best way to date Irish crochet is by the style of the dress, cape, jacket, or collar made from it.

Filet Crochet

Filet crochet is a form of dense, lacy open fabric with grid-like designs.
• The technique consists of nothing more than chain stitch and double crochet stitches.
• The value of the piece depends entirely on the design, and the value and usefulness of the item.

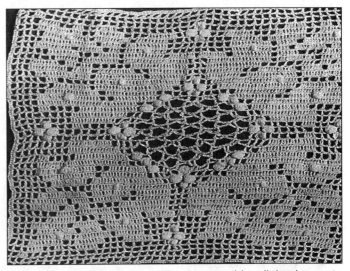

Raised baubles and a decorative center adds a little pizzazz to the basic filet crochet gridwork in this 19th century square.

Knitting

Hand Knitting

Knitting is an ancient method of building a fabric by drawing a continuous thread or yarn through a series of connected loops. It can be used to form a wide variety of fabrics from fine lace to heavy sweaters.

Endless different textures and patterns can be worked into the knit fabric by drawing the thread through the front or back of each loop, by skipping loops, drawing loops through each other, or infinite combinations of other manipulations.

How to recognize generic knit

Knitting consists of a continuous length of yarn drawn through a horizontal row of loops. When each new loop of yarn is drawn through the existing row of loops in the same direction, front to back or back to front, a fabric of even texture will be produced. The front, or "knit" side will have little chevrons arranged in lengthwise rows called "wales." The back side will have crosswise rows of interlocking curves. This is called the "purl" side.

The most basic stitch in knitting is called the garter stitch. Almost everybody is wearing something knitted in the garter stitch at all times: socks, underwear, sweaters, T-shirts.

Decorative effects are worked into knitting by working into the back instead of the front of the loop, skipping a loop, knitting twice into the same loop, etc.

Features to note

The quality of the materials

- Look for long staple, first quality virgin wool, silk and wool blends.
- Look for luxury fibers: cashmere, pashmina, angora, fine silks.
- Look for yarns with thick and thin areas, tweeds, variegated colors, textures that enhance the fabric.
- Lace knits should be long staple, relatively tightly twisted threads. Short staples will shred.

Artistry

- Look for rich colors and intricate detail. Look for details that are not obvious, but that add subtle complexity.
- Look for complex patterns with interesting textures.

Technique

- Yarns carried across the back of the work should not show between the stitches on the front.
- Yarns carried across the back should not be so long they snag or fray.
- Yarns carried across the back should not be so short the cause the front to pucker.
- Knitting should be fairly elastic. Neck holes, wrist bands, and other edges should be reasonably elastic and not baggy.

Imaginative design and technique

Combinations of texture, intricate stitching, and color changes make highly artistic knits. The appearance will change depending on whether the yarn is drawn through the front or back of the loops in each row of knitting.

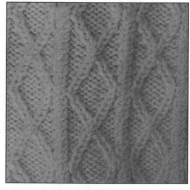

A decorative knit mixing both knit and purl stitches to create texture. Raised rows of stitches that cross the knitted surface typically are called cables.

The purl stitch, or the back side of a basic garter stitch.

The knit stitch, or the right or front side of the garter stitch.

Types of Knits

Textured knits

The possibilities for artistry in knitting are texture, variety of fancy stitching that introduces patterns of holes, raised and textured areas, and patterns of cables, lines, and geometric textures.

This is the whole family of Aran decorated knits. Because the textural pattern is so complex with the stitches

appearing to travel over the surface, they generally are a solid color.

Knitted Laces

The basic knit and purl stitches are well camouflaged in the intricate openwork design of knitted lace. Most often, these are worked in fine thread. Edgings on pillow cases and bed linens, dating from the nineteenth century well into the early twentieth, are the most common form of knitted lace

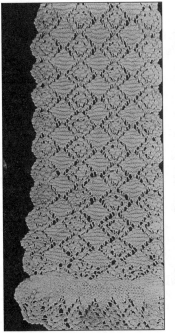

This lace knit tie, about four inches across, probably dates to the late 19th century.

Detail of lace knit, showing basic knit purl stitch.

Stranding or **Fair Isle**. Yarns of the unused color can simply be carried behind the work. They are occasionally twisted with the working color to keep floats short.

found in U.S. attics and flea markets. Knitted tablecloths and large doilies are a tradition in Eastern Europe, and still are readily found today. Edgings on pillow cases and bed linens are the most common form of knitted lace.

The most collectible of all the lacy knits are the Russian Orenberg shawls. These legendary shawls, often five or six feet square, are worked in exceptionally fine cashmere yarn with intricate lacy patterns. Sometimes these are called "wedding ring" shawls, because they often are fine enough to be drawn through a wedding ring.

Colored knits

Color is introduced into knitting by using several different yarns at the same time.

Some garments or caps are knitted continuously, in the round, on circular needles. Others are knitted one row at a time. The knitter turns and changes directions at the end of each row.

If more than one color is used, the knitter has to figure out how to get from one color block to the next, and what to do with unused color yarns in the meantime.

In the stranding, or Fair Isle technique, the knitter carries several yarns along at the same time, letting the unused ones carry across the back of the work until they are needed again. This makes a heavy, warm knit because of all the yarn carried across the back.

In the Intarsia technique, the knitter drops one color and picks up another as needed. To prevent a hole from forming where colors change, the knitter twists the two yarns together before proceeding with the new color.

Neither technique is better than the other. The design usually dictates which will work better. Many artistic designs use both in the same piece.

Intarsia generally works better for pictorial designs, patterns with distinct geometric blocks of color, like argyles or checkerboards. Fair Isle generally works better for patterns

Intarsia. To change colors in Intarsia, yarns simply are twisted, the new color is picked up and the unused is dropped.

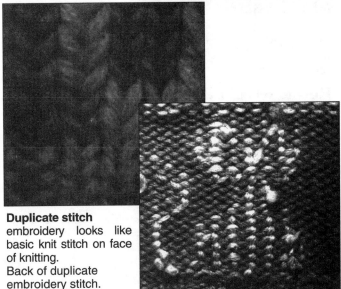

Duplicate stitch embroidery looks like basic knit stitch on face of knitting.
Back of duplicate embroidery stitch.

like Norwegian ski sweaters, with patterns introducing dots of color at short, regular intervals.

Another neat trick for putting in small intricate patterns is simply to embroider a color design over the knitting in loops that trace the pattern of the original knit. This is called duplicate stitch. Often it is impossible to tell that the design was not knit into the fabric without looking at the back side.

Sometimes the fastest and easiest way to work a colorful design into knitting is simply to embroider the design over the stitches. This can be done using the technique called duplicate stitch embroidery. The knit can be done quickly by machine, or by an unskilled knitter.

Machine Knitting: Warp and Weft

First a reminder: warp is lengthwise, weft is crosswise. Handknitting works row by row across the piece. The first machine to produce a knit fabric was developed in 1584, and was used for stockings.

This machine, like knitting machines available today for home use, imitates hand knitting by working back and forth across the rows. Dozens of hooked needles draw loops through an entire row of loops in one motion. This is called weft knitting, because it mimics the back and forth, crosswise motion of weaving.

Machines can knit circular tubes of fabric, which can be cut to form flat yardage or made up into sweaters and other garments, or they can knit back and forth on flat beds.

Many of the power-driven knitting machines do a type of knitting different from the hand version. Instead of working loops across the row, the machine zigzags sideways only two or a few loops, in what is known as warp knitting. This is the technique used to produce many knitted lace fabrics.

Plain machine weft knit fabric is nearly indistinguishable from hand knit.

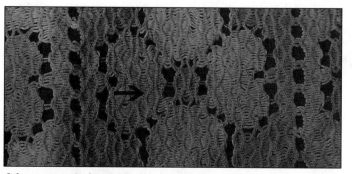

A lacy warp-knitted fabric where the machine knitting consists of lengthwise chains. To form the dense areas of the design, weft or crosswise threads are laid in as fillers.

Needleweaving And Darning

Filet and Burato

One of the oldest and simplest forms of lacemaking is to darn a design over the square gridwork of a knotted or woven net. The origins of this form of lacework are lost centuries ago.

How to recognize filet & burato

- The background is a gridwork. In filet, the background is a hand-knotted net. In burato, the background is an open leno weave.
- The designs are almost always geometric, governed by the square gridwork of the background net.

Features to note

- Fine quality threads and yarns.
- Design is very important, because the technique is so simple. The oldest examples, dating from the seventeenth century, often had whimsical beasts, fish, and figures woven over the gridwork.

Many nineteenth century examples had elaborate decorative embroidery stitches worked over the gridwork and the darned clothwork. Raised needlewoven details added to the texture.

Needleweaving in drawnwork

When weft threads are withdrawn from a fabric for decorative drawnwork, loose threads are left. These are decoratively bundled and woven with a needle and thread.

If both warp and weft threads are withdrawn, a square hole is left where they had crossed. Threads often are laid across the hole and decoratively secured with needleweaving. Except for the fact that the origin was a woven fabric, the technique of filling the space is very similar to Tenerife and nanduti.

Tenerife and nanduti

Needleweaving over a framework of threads radiating like the spokes of a wheel is the basic concept of a whole world of lace that originated in Spain and its surrounding islands centuries ago. It then worked its way across the sea with early missionaries to the Spanish colonies in South America.

Tenerife, named for the city in the Canary Islands, is the Spanish version. Nanduti, named for the Paraguayan word for web, is the South American version.

In good quality drawnwork, the needleweaving is dense enough to form a secure, strong lace, and the design is complex enough to be interesting.

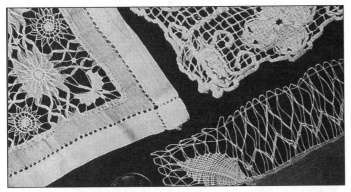

Three examples of needleweaving; left: needleweaving in drawnwork; top, filet; bottom right: nanduti.

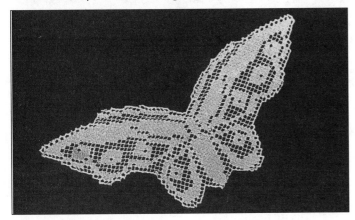

Dense areas in filet lace are formed by darning over a knotted gridwork.

How to recognize tenerife & nanduti

- The background is a network of laid threads. In Tenerife, the background is wheel of threads. In nanduti, the background is not always a circle or wheel, but threads in most of the design radiate from a central point.
- The designs are almost always geometric, because they are governed by the square gridwork of the background net.

Features to note

- Fine quality threads and yarns are important, because the background threads are exposed and will wrinkle, fray and shred.
- Intricate, imaginative, and varied patterns should be worked over the wheels to create a dancing, moving effect and to hold interest.
- Designs worked over the laid background threads should be complex and dense enough to stabilize the background, and prevent fraying and shifting threads.

Knotting

The origin of knotting to build fabric is unknown. Certainly fishermen were knotting nets longer than history records, and it is not a great leap of imagination to think that the technique of knotted netting would be used on other scales for other purposes, and sooner or later would be decorated.

Other decorative forms of knotting have been used for centuries in the Middle East, and each country or area gave it a distinctive name, and slightly different variation. Armenian, oya, Phoenician lace, and bebilla are just a few.

Macramé is another form of knotting thought to have been developed in the Middle East.

Tatting, a form of lacemaking, is the newest of the lot.

Tatting

Tatting is thought to have evolved from eighteenth century techniques of tying knots along a length of string, then stitching the knotted cord to a fabric. Gradually techniques for forming rings and loops were developed, then more techniques for joining the rings and loops to form lacy fabrics.

How to recognize tatting

- The distinctive knot is a double half hitch, which in a magnified view looks like the Greek letter "pi," with two vertical and one horizontal element.
- Design elements consist of bars and loops. They may be decorated with little loops called picots.

Things it's used for

- It is difficult to build up dense clothwork areas in tatting, so most tatting consists of narrow edgings, insertions, and little round medallions.
- Small pieces may be stitched together to form doilies, or occasionally a parasol cover.
- Tatting rarely is used for large items like tablecloths.

Features to note

- The finer the thread and the more intricate the design, the more interesting and valuable the tatting.
- Older forms of tatting, dating to the nineteenth century, were connected by stitching with a needle and thread. Ways to interconnect loops as the lace was made were not developed until the mid or late nineteenth century.

Dense cloth-like areas, formed of concentric rows of knots over thread, are unusual in tatting. Bars and rings covered with knots and decorated with looping picots are more typical. Photo courtesy of The Lace Museum, Sunnyvale, California.

Macramé

The rage of the 1960s that brought jute plant hangers to every home in America originated hundreds if not thousands of years ago.

Macramé supposedly originated when the loose ends of woven towels were decoratively knotted instead of hemmed to prevent fraying and unraveling. Many of the decorative knots used in macramé find companions among the repertoire of sailor's knots as well.

How to recognize macramé

- Many parallel strands of yarn, thread, or fibers are arranged in an assortment of decorative knots.
- Yarns can originate from a large central knot, as in plant hangers, or as the loose warp threads from a woven fabric.

Features to note

- Fine quality threads and yarns
- Wide variety of intricate, complicated knots involving many different strands.

Detail of macramé.

Things it's used for:
- Plant hangers
- Lampshades
- Edges and fringes on table linens, shawls

Armenian Knotting

Also known as Bebilla, Phoenician, Smyrna, or Oya.

The multiplicity of names for this quaint technique is an echo of its age and origin. It was developed in the Middle East hundreds of years ago, and each of the many countries and communities had its own variation and name for the craft.

How to recognize Armenian knotting

- Dense clothwork areas can be built up of closely placed knots. This clothwork has a distinct crisp, crinkled, sharp-edged texture.
- Lacy openwork can be produced by spacing the knots wide apart.

Things it's used for

- Small edgings for shawls, veils, handkerchiefs.
- Doilies and small household decorative items.

Features to note

- Good quality fibers, especially colorful silks and crisp linens and cottons make the best knotted work.
- A wide variety of motifs, especially flowers with raised petals, and decorative geometric patterns are the most interesting.

Narrow edging, less than an inch deep, of small flowers of Armenian lace.

Fabrics: Embellishments

Plain, unfinished fabrics off the loom are called greige, or grey goods. Before they are sent off to the market, any of a nearly infinite array of finishing processes are used to create special effects.

These processes are used to change the appearance, the feel or hand, and the performance. Many of these processes have been used for centuries. Most are fundamental treatments that are hardly noticeable: bleaching, calendering (a flattening or ironing process), beetling (pounding the fabric to add luster, smoothness, and greater absorbency), and embossing to create interesting surface finishes. Fulling expands wool fibers to create a softer, fluffier surface. Learning to recognize the effects of some of these will help you differentiate quality grades in vintage fabrics.

Beyond the basic finishing processes, there are a whole array of possibilities for decorating fabrics. The handful presented in this section will provide a basic reference of what to look for in finished goods in the vintage marketplace.

Pleating

Pleating as a way of embellishing fabrics goes back thousands of years. The Egyptians used hot stones to pleat their cottons. Heavy irons pleated caps and ruffles for fashions from early Europe to the colonies. Fortuny made it his trademark in the early 1900s.

Machine crimped or pleated synthetic fabric, mid 20th century.

Dyeing

Any time between the original processing of fibers to the recycling of old rags, dyes can be used to decorate, enhance, modernize, update, or restore the appearance of textiles.

Fiber Dyeing

Before the fibers are spun into yarns, the dyes have the best potential for complete penetration. This is especially important for many synthetics, which are difficult to dye.

It also is the source of the expression "dyed in the wool" to mean intense or totally committed.

Yarn Dyeing

After fibers, yarns and threads have the best potential for complete penetration of dyes.

Piece Dyeing

Manufacturers can keep undyed fabric, called greige or grey goods, on hand, and avoid the risk of committing to a color that might prove unpopular. They can choose a color and dye the fabric only after the fabric is on order.

Fabric dyed as a piece often can be detected by slight variations in color where the dyes did not completely penetrate between the yarns.

Interesting effects can be obtained when fabric is woven of two or more different yarns. When fibers react to the dye differently, this can result in two or more shades or colors in the finished goods.

Product Dyeing

A fabric may be cut and made up as a dress, shirt, skirt, or other product before it is dyed. With the availability of good home dyes, it is also possible for garments to be colored at home to accommodate changing fashions, or to brighten a faded garment.

It usually is possible to tell when a product rather than the fabric is dyed because everything, including the labels and thread used to sew it, is the same color. It is possible, however, that thread or other parts of the garment will take the dye differently, or resist the dye altogether, depending on the fiber.

Decorative Dyeing — Resist Prints

One of the easiest ways to create a pattern in a dyed fabric is to prevent the dye from penetrating certain areas of the yarns or fabric. This can be done mechanically, by tying strings, or placing tightly wound rubber bands around some areas, to keep the dye from penetrating the yarns or fabric. It also can be done chemically, by painting, printing, or pouring some substance over the fabric to prevent the dye from penetrating.

Batik

Batik is an ancient method of hand-coloring fabrics. Hot wax is poured or painted onto a fabric to form the design. The fabric is then dipped into a dye bath. To build up multiple colors, the fabric is first dipped into the lightest colors, and additional wax is applied to cover and protect more areas.

To complete the process, the wax is peeled off and the residue is dissolved with some sort of solvent. Hand painted details often are added, especially when the batik is done as a fiber art.

Several forms may be collectible:

- Batik is a textile art form that comes and goes in popularity. As with other art forms, the quality and intricacy of the design, the subject matter, and choice of colors determine the value.
- The value of batik yardage fluctuates with the popularity as a decorator or wearable fabric.

Tie-dye

Tie-dye is an ancient hand-coloring process that enjoyed a return to popularity in the hippie heyday of the 1960s.

The fabric or yarns are wrapped tightly with string or rubber bands to keep dye from penetrating. Irregular boundaries and blended or overlapping colors are hallmarks of tie dye.

Multiple colors are achieved by repeating the process several times, each time adding and removing the ties. In the most intricate designs with many colors, hundreds, if not thousands, of tiny knots must be hand-placed.

Several forms may be collectible:

- As long as a single Deadhead lives, someone, somewhere will value the tie-dyed shirts, skirts, and memorabilia of the 60s and 70s.
- Many Asian countries raised tie-dye on silk to an art form. The dyes, however, often are not colorfast. Many beautiful silk shawls and scarves cannot be washed.

Prices of vintage items seldom rise above those still done today.

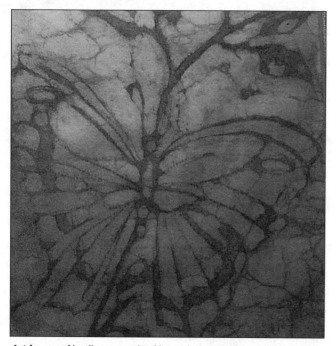

Art forms of batik are worked by painting designs in hot wax on the surface. Dye penetrates to the fabric where the wax layers crack, leaving a crackled, map-like pattern over the surface. Details are hand-painted in.

Tie-dye.

Decorative Dyeing — Discharge Prints

Discharge is in a way the opposite of resist printing. The design is created by bleaching out, or chemically removing the color in selected areas of a darkly dyed cloth.

Chemicals, usually in the form of a paste, are printed onto the dyed fabric. Steam or other chemical treatment then develops the pattern by removing the color where the paste was printed.

The wrong side sometimes provides the clue that tells that a fabric has been discharge printed. The paste sometimes does not completely penetrate the cloth, leaving some color around the pattern on the back side.

Old fabrics that have been discharge printed may be of interest to those restoring old quilts or working on other repairs and restoration projects. Take a close look at the fabric, however, as it may have been weakened by the chemical color-removal process, and over time, will begin to disintegrate, especially in the light areas.

It sometimes is difficult to tell the difference between discharge printing and reserve printing.

Ikat

Ikat is a combination of warp printing and tie-dying in that the design is worked on the threads or yarns before the fabric is woven. The yarns are stretched out prior to weaving, and the artist estimates where the design will appear after the yarns are woven. The parts of the yarns that will create the design are tied in bundles to keep the dye from penetrating certain areas.

The design is almost always a geometric or a stylized figure appearing in the natural, undyed color of the yarns against a solid or striped background. The edges of the design always are hazy, because it is impossible to figure out exactly where the yarns will fall when they are woven. It usually is worked in relatively heavy threads.

Either the warp or weft yarns can be colored — this is called a warp or weft ikat. Both the warp and weft threads can be colored in what is called a double ikat.

A great deal of study, skill, and patience is required to figure out where the yarns will fall to correctly place the design. Ikat is more common in Asian and Eastern cultures.

Several forms may be collectible:

- Indonesian and other Asian blankets, rugs, and heavy textiles with elaborate, multi-color designs, especially with animals, or other figures are especially interesting.
- Geometric and abstract designs often appear in twentieth century folk skirts and fabric for other clothing.

Blueprints are a centuries-old form of fabric decorating from Slovakia in eastern Europe. On the front, or right side of the fabric, the design appears in white where chemicals were printed on the surface to prevent the indigo dye from penetrating.

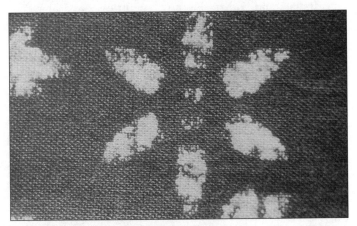

Back, or wrong side of the fabric. Design appears in a shadowy form where some dye has penetrated.

19th century Indonesian blankets decorated with ikat dye. Blurred appearance is distinctive of Ikat dyeing.

Painting and Stenciling

Designs can be hand-painted or stenciled. This provides a relatively fast and easy way to decorate textiles. Canvas type fabrics were stenciled in colonial times to serve as floor coverings; pillows and other household decorative items including skirts, shirts, neckties and other clothing were painted, especially in the twentieth century.

Painting and stenciling have become wildly popular in the second half of the twentieth century. More and better variety in colors, textures, and specials effects, such as raised paints, became available later in the twentieth century.

Several forms may be collectible:

- Painted fabric kits were popular in the early part of the twentieth century, circa 1920-40. The outline was hand embroidered.
- Colonial floor coverings, because they were by design subject to heavy wear, are almost never found. Most colonial stenciling is reproduction. Stenciled and painted fabrics were popular in the early 1900s, especially with Arts & Crafts designs.
- Handpainted neckties from the 1940s, especially those with outrageous or unique designs, are very collectible.

Corner detail from painted khaki fabric. Rose and scrolling leaf design was painted on the fabric, and hand-outlined with embroidery. Piece was dated 1939. Most likely, this was purchased as a kit.

Printing

Warp Printing

An unusual, hazy printed effect is achieved by printing only the warp threads before the cloth is woven. The design will appear only on the warp threads, and the weft or filling threads typically are a white or solid color.

This effect sometimes is imitated with a splotchy, out-of-focus printing on both the warp and filling threads.

Warp printing is not unusual enough to be collectible, but early examples may be of interest.

This process is similar to Ikat, where warp and/or weft yarns are tie-dyed before weaving to place designs into the woven cloth. Haziness in Ikat typically results because the weaver could not accurately predict where the yarns would fall after the fabric was woven. The unprinted filling threads provide the haziness in warp printing.

Block Printing

A design can be printed on a fabric much as a design is printed on a paper with a rubber stamp. A design is carved on a block, or sometimes metal pins are driven into a block in a prettily arranged pattern. The block is dipped in a shallow pan of ink, dye, or paint, and printed onto the fabric. More than one color can be used by stamping several blocks on the same fabric.

This is one of the oldest known methods of decorating fabric. Slight variations in the position of the print on the fabric typically are clues that the fabric was block printed.

Block printing is still used for some fabrics, particularly in Asia. It also was extensively used for printing small things like handkerchiefs and scarves.

Several forms may be collectible:

- Yardage for draperies, pillows, and decorating, especially in Arts & Crafts designs, are especially popular today.
- Large silk scarves and shawls from Africa, Indonesia, India, and other Eastern countries often have spectacular colors and designs.

Asian printing blocks for fabric.

Linen panel with "Kyoto" print by Liberty of London, circa 1910. Photographed by Chrissie DiPietro. Photo courtesy of Paul Freeman, Textile Artifacts, Hawthorne, California.

Direct Roller Printing

In 1783, during the early stages of the Industrial Revolution when fabric production was beginning to be mechanized in earnest, a method of directly printing a pattern onto a continuous length of cloth was invented.

This method is essentially the same as printing on paper. Separate engravings and rollers are used for each color. By overlapping colors, additional colors and shades are produced.

Several forms may be collectible:

- Early fabrics from the eighteenth century often are collectible. Yardage is interesting as an artifact. Fragments are interesting for study, and for repair of old quilts.
- Yardage of designs that started new fashion trends, such as Art Nouveau or the William Morris Arts & Crafts designs, may be collectible.
- Small items, especially handkerchiefs, are collectible.

Embroidering

Embroidery is stitching through a fabric with a needle and thread and creating patterns. It can be as simple as drawing a line by stitching in and out with colored cotton thread, or the entire surface of the fabric can be hidden with intricate patterns of silks and gold.

Some people collect stitches, others collect embroidered things. Some people hardly notice the stitching. They simply want a pretty guest towel, set of pillow cases, or dresser scarf. To them, it is barely relevant whether it is embroidered, printed, or painted. Others look for special, specific combinations of stitches worked in specific kinds of threads.

Every country on earth has its own distinct style of embroidery. Each culture used it in different ways, sometimes for religious purposes, other times for secular purposes — as a fashion statement.

The clues that identify an embroidery as the product of a specific time, place, culture include:

- Choice of base fabric. Any type of woven fabric, including linen, cotton, silk, velvet, burlap, or net has, at one time or another, been embellished with stitchery.
- Type of stitch. There are only a handful of ways of drawing a needle and thread through a fabric. There are endless variations on each technique, and as many different names for a stitch as there are countries on the earth and schools of needlework. Learn to recognize just a handful, and you will be able to make sense of most of the needlework you find.
- Combination of stitches. Only the simplest projects use only one type of stitch for the whole project. Cross stitch is one. Very often, it is used alone on pillow cases, doilies or tablecloths. Geometric designs on huck toweling usually consist of nothing more than threads run through the little dots that float over the surface of the distinctive toweling.

Most often, ethnic and other historic forms of embroidery combine a handful of specific stitches. Oriental embroidery often combines couching and satin stitch; samplers may include a dozen or more fancy stitches.

- Combination of techniques. In the most elaborate embroidered pieces, the embroidery is often combined with other techniques, especially needle lace, needleweaving, drawnwork and cutwork.

- Relationship to the base fabric. The choice of base fabric and type of threads or yarns sets the tone for the work. Some are traditional, other are based on the artistic inclinations of the embroiderer.

Stitching may run higgledy-piggledy in a freeform design over the surface of a fabric. An example is crewel, and most twentieth century home craft embroidery.

Each stitch may be counted, and carefully placed over the intersection of single warp and weft threads. Some examples of this are counted cross stitch, needlepoint, bargello and hardanger.

When embroidery is worked over a net, the result is a lacy fabric. Some famous types are tambour and Limerick.

Features to note

Design

Elegance, whimsy, creativity, and the relationship of design to technique are features that give the most interesting, most collectible embroideries their value.

Technique and Workmanship

Some of the finest embroideries use only the simplest stitches, but they are exquisitely worked. Look for precision in spacing, alignment and length of stitches.

Look also for complex stitches that require skill and imagination.

Rarity

There are some techniques that are rare and highly sought after, but the rarest are superb designs exquisitely worked in complex, difficult stitches.

Condition

The importance of condition depends on the quality of the stitching, whether it is expected to be used or worn, or whether it is an example of a rare, perhaps extinct, culture.

Even the smallest fragment of an ancient Egyptian or Coptic embroidery is valued for its rarity while twentieth century counted cross stitch is so common today it is valued only when perfect, and suitable for framing or use on a pillow.

Inspect both the base fabric and the threadwork for signs of fraying, wear, and stains.

Basic Embroidery Stitches

Running stitch

Stitches running in and out of a fabric are called running stitches.

- A variety of bright colors in plain running stitches sometimes makes up for variety in stitching.
- When the threads are run in and out of a net, the result is lace.

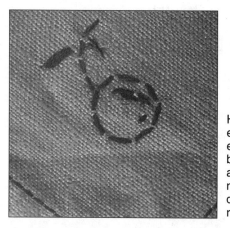

Home-crafted embroidery, especially that done by children and amateurs, consists of nothing more than a design outlined with running stitches.

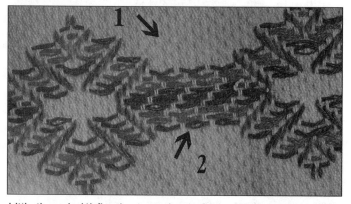

Little threads (1) floating over the surface of huck toweling make it easy to embroider. Running stitches (2) are caught under the floating threads.

The disconnected running stitches can be made into a solid line by interweaving a second thread through the line of stitches. In this example, from a mid 20th century guest towel, a contrasting color was used.

Back stitch

To make a solid line of stitching, the needle must go back into the fabric behind the point it came out. This is called a back stitch.

On the face, or correct side, the stitching is a solid line of slightly overlapping stitches; on the reverse, it looks like a running stitch.

The back stitch is the most common stitch for lines or outlines.

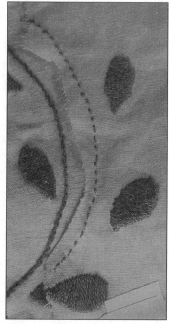

Line of back stitching, left, appears as a solid line. Stitches on the reverse side appear disconnected, like a row of running stitches.

One of the most typical uses for couching is when metallic threads are stitched to the edge of satin stitch to form an outline.

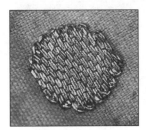

Dense pattern areas can be created by couching several threads right next to each other. The careful placement of the couching stitches creates a basketweave effect.

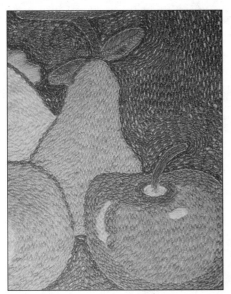

1970s still life. Row after row of chain stitches, worked side by side to create solid, densely colored areas.

Couching

Lines and outlines can be created by laying a thread or yarn on the surface of a fabric, and attaching it with widely spaced stitches. This technique is especially popular in oriental embroideries, where heavy metallic threads are used profusely.

In pre-nineteenth century work, the stitches used to attaching the thread are pulled tightly enough to actually draw the surface thread back into the fabric. This is called reverse couching.

The embroidery was more flexible than with surface couching. The work, however, was much more time consuming, and was almost never used after the eighteenth century.

Chain stitch

The chain consists of a loop of thread caught at the top with another loop to form a chain. The chain ends with the last loop, which is held in place with a tiny stitch.

- It can be found in any type of embroidery.
- The chain also is known as tambour stitch.
- When it is worked on a machine-made net to form lace, it is sometimes called tambour or Limerick tambour lace.
- Dense pattern areas are occasionally built up by working several rows of chain right next to each other.
- The chain stitch was the first stitch to be copied by machine. On the right side of the work, they are almost impossible to tell apart. The machine-worked chain is stitched with either one or two threads.

Chain stitch scrollwork.

Buttonhole or Blanket Stitch

The most common edging stitch is the buttonhole or blanket stitch. Both names come from early common usage as a method to prevent cut slit buttonholes from raveling and fraying, and as a method of finishing off the edges of a woolen fabric to make a blanket. See also needle lace

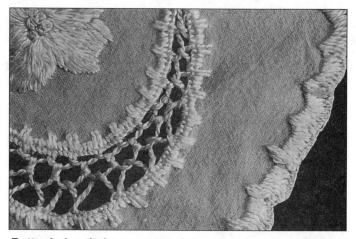

Buttonhole stitches are one of the most common methods of finishing off the edge of 20th century napkins, doilies, and other table linens. Above example is of average quality. Stitches should be extremely close together, and very precise.

Buttonhole or blanket stitch as the edging and decorative scroll on a 20th century cocktail napkin.

Herringbone and Feather Stitches

Slight variations of buttonhole and cross stitches produce endless possibilities for decorative stitches. Two of the most common are the herringbone and feather stitches, used here as the decorative outline on a crazy quilt.

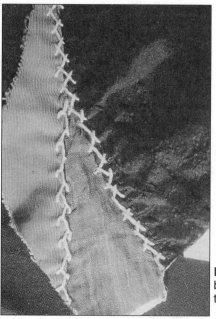

Feather stitch is at bottom left; **herringbone** the right diagonal.

Cross stitch

Cross stitch is simply two stitches crossing each other diagonally. The relationship of the stitch to the fabric is important, and identifies the type of work.

In the most typical form, a pattern of little X's are printed on a fabric. The stitches are taken across the printed X's, wherever they fall on the fabric.

Cross stitch worked on needlepoint canvas. Without a magnifying glass, it is almost impossible to tell the difference between the cross stitch and tent stitch on canvas.

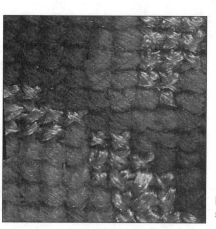

Needlepoint cross stitch.

In counted cross stitch embroidery the design is not printed on the fabric. The embroiderer works from a printed gridwork, carefully counting across and down the threads of the fabric to place the stitches.

In needlepoint, a pattern is printed on a heavy canvas, and the stitches are worked across the threads.

Cross stitch.

Counted cross stitch.

Tent stitch

The tent stitch is a single stitch taken diagonally across the threads of a woven fabric. It is the most common stitch used in petit point, needle point or other canvas work.

In the smallest petit point, the individual stitches are difficult to see without a magnifying glass. Fine needlepoint often is mistaken for a machine made tapestry or woven fabric.

Basket and continental stitches look almost identical to a tent stitch on the front. A close look with a magnifying glass shows a slightly different slant to each stitch. A look at the back would show the stitches were taken differently.

A picture worked in two forms of tent stitch. Larger stitches are worked over both thread of a double weave (penelope) canvas. Four smaller stitches, called petit point, are worked over the same area as one larger stitch.

Satin stitch

Long, side-by-side strands floating across the surface of the fabric to form broad, silky areas are called satin stitch.

Look for precise detail showing how the stitches are taken. Do the stitches cross the design diagonally or straight across? Are the stitches padded to add texture and depth? These qualities define style and quality in embroidery.

Many different techniques are used to raise these stitches above the surface to add dimension and texture. In some cases, a row may be stitched around the perimeter of the area that is to be filled. Or, layers of stitches might be built up, or the thread might be looped around the needle to form a small knot as the thread enters the fabric.

Satin stitch in an early 20th century Arts & Crafts style embroidery, showing the first layer of stitches which gives depth, and a second layer of stitches added diagonally across the first to provide the finished color.

Split stitch

For the split stitch, multi-strand floss thread is used, and each long stitch splits the strands of the floss in stitches already taken on the fabric. This creates a dense, textured area. Stitching through and overlapping earlier stitches makes it possible to create delicate blended shading with many different threads.

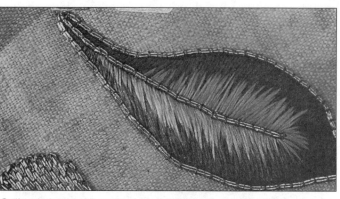

Split-stitched leaf worked in shaded silks in a sampler. Leaf is outlined with metallic thread couched to the fabric.

Long and short and other variations

When very large areas are to be covered with stitching, variations of the satin stitch are used. Long and short, named for the alternating size of the stitches, is one of the most popular variations.

Many variations of the long parallel satin stitches are used. Bargello is one of the most popular twentieth century styles: colors cascade across the surface in long parallel stitches worked in a diagonal progression.

Only imagination limits the possibilities of covering a surface with long silky stitches worked in infinitely changing directions.

Variations of the long parallel satin stitches are one of the most popular stitches in canvas work (needlepoint) because they cover large areas quickly.

Lazy daisy stitch

The lazy ndaisy also is known as the detached chain. It consists of a loop of thread caught at the top with at tiny stitch.

French knots

Decorative raised knots are formed by winding the thread around the needle, then taking a stitch to fasten the loops to the embroidery. The knots can take many forms depending on how many times the thread is wound around the needle.

Lazy daisy stitch and French knots in flower.

Rope work

Long stitches are turned into raised ropes by slipping the needle under and winding another thread around each stitch. Decorative raised ropes were a popular feature of Italian whitework.

Fragment of turn-of-the century Italian whitework with decorative raised ropes.

Detail of 19th century white-on-white drawnwork and embroidery, possibly French. Stitching includes sanding, embroidered drawnwork, and needle lace inserts in the holes, and buttonhole stitching along all cut edges.

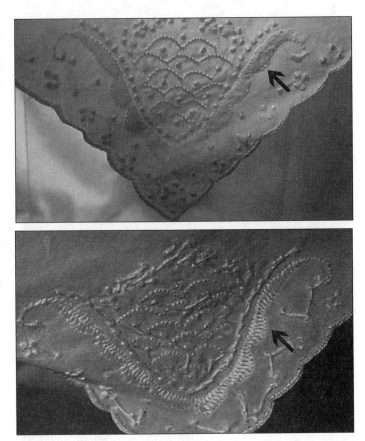

Charming examples of handworked shadow stitch often appear on 20th century handkerchiefs, but are overlooked or ignored because they are so subtle.

Sanding

A delicate texture is added to fine embroidery by completely covering an area—sometimes one that has already been covered with embroidery—with tiny running stitches. This very often is done in whitework (drawnwork, cutwork and embroidery in white on white fabric).

Shadow work

The illusion of a shadow is created in a fine, translucent fabric by completely covering the back of the work with long stitches. The outline of tiny stitches appears on the front, suggesting the shadow was created with an appliqué.

This handwork usually is worked white-on-white, and is so subtle it often is overlooked.

Machine Imitations of Embroidery

By the 1820s, efforts were being made to develop a commercially useful embroidery machine. Josue Heileman's handmachine, patented in 1828, produced work almost indistinguishable from hand embroidery. It embroidered up to twenty motifs simultaneously, which subsequently is the best key to identifying machine embroidery. Each pattern repeat is precisely identical. Each flower petal has exactly the same number of stitches of exactly the same length.

Threads carry across the back from one petal to another, one design segment to another, at exactly the same point.

It is this repetition, with the same motions going on at exactly the same points in the design, rather than the perfection that is the difference between hand and machine. Embroiderers of handwork took great pride in their workmanship, and to our eye today, much of what was done by hand is unimaginably precise. The work of hand embroiderers also was done with great artistry and produced results that appear perfect.

The earliest machine embroideries were carefully designed to mimic the handmade designs of popular contemporary embroideries, especially Broderie Anglaise, Ayrshire, and eyelets.

By the 1860s, machines could bore holes to produce openwork embroideries. By the 1880s, the aetz process, a way of chemically dissolving away the background or substrate from behind the embroidery, was perfected. Dissolving the background released a lock-stitched machine embroidery as a free lace. These today are known as aetz, or the English translation of chemical or burnt laces.

In the 1880s, Schiffli machines were also embroidering on nets and produced reasonable copies of mesh-based laces.

By the end of the nineteenth century, mankind's boundless imagination and creativity was producing an infinite variety of colorful and intricate machine embroideries.

Front view of late 19th century machine imitation of shadow work.

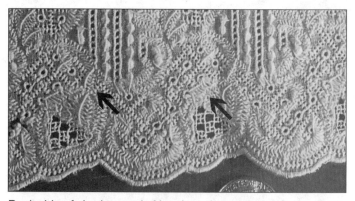

Back side of shadow work. Note how threads carry from point to point at exactly the same place in each part of each pattern repeat. This repetition is almost always a sign of machine work.

Machine chain stitch

From the front, it often is nearly impossible to tell handmade chain stitch from machine. Almost always, however, there are clues on the back that reveal it was machine-made.

There are several different ways machines make chain stitches. Some did it with one thread, others with two.

The uncanny precision of the stitches is one clue to take a closer look. Precision alone, however, does not mean the work was machine done. The finest handmade stitching is sometimes perfect. Notice how the stitches overlap on the sharp turns and scrolls. An embroiderer working by hand most likely would not overlap stitches the way the machine does.

Machine chain stitch is extraordinarily even. Each stitch is precisely the same. The places where the chains make sharp turns and loops, however, are angular and awkward, not at all the way a human would turn a corner when stitching.

Schiffli Embroidery

The schiffli machine is a type of machine invented in the late 1880s that embroiders in a lock stitch. This can be released as lace if the fabric embroidered is chemically dissolved away. This is called chemical or aetz lace. The machine also could embroider on a net, to produce a mesh-based lace.

The stitching is very distinctive. If the stitches are viewed with a magnifying glass, they are irregular and a sort of nervous zigzag. The overall effect is a crisp, if slightly fuzzy lace.

In chemical lace, the design is embroidered on a background that will later be dissolved to release the embroidery as lace.

Drawnwork

A few threads in a woven fabric can be pulled out or squeezed together. Stitching and needleweaving over the remaining threads makes an open, airy design. Both techniques — pulling threads out and squeezing them together — are called drawnwork. Lace as we know it today originated when needleworkers drew out more and more threads. Eventually someone realized it was not necessary to start with a woven fabric. All the stitching and needleweaving could be done over a spare network or skeleton of laid threads.

Nearly every country that needleworks on fabric does some form of drawnwork. The simpler forms were a popular form of home craft.

How to recognize drawnwork

The base is a woven fabric, most often cotton or linen.
- Threads may be withdrawn from the fabric in one or both directions. Look closely at edges of decorative work to see if threads pass from the openwork areas directly through the woven fabric. Edges may be obscured with stitching.
- When threads are withdrawn in both directions, a square or rectangular hole results in the corner. This rarely is left open. Most often it is filled in with needle lace or needleweaving.
- Small areas in the design, such as flower centers, or a background behind motifs may be opened into a decorative gridwork by squeezing threads together, or by pulling some threads out of the fabric. Those remaining will be held in place with stitching.

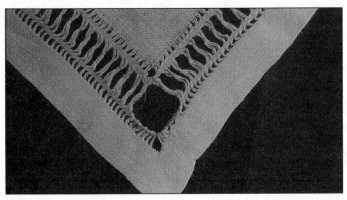

Removing threads in both directions results in a hole in the corner.

Hemstitching can be simple or decorative. The decorative example at the bottom is typical of 19th and early 20th century Italian linens.

Features to note
- Drawnwork leaves single exposed threads that may shred. Fabric should be woven with tightly spun threads of good quality, long-staple fibers.
- Exposed threads should be securely and attractively bundled with needleweaving or stitching to prevent fraying, and should display an intricate, interesting pattern.
- The most interesting drawnwork also is combined with cutwork, needle lace inserted into the holes opened where threads have been withdrawn, and intricate embroidery designs.

Where it is found
- Handkerchiefs often have drawnwork edges or corner designs. Early twentieth century Chinese are especially good.
- Exceptionally fine eighteenth century German and Danish drawnwork known as Dresden was used for scarves, fichus and decorative work on clothing. It is highly collectible even when found as fragments or scraps.
- It is so commonly found in table linens and bed linens that only the most unusual is collectible.

The corner hole that results from pulling threads in both directions typically is filled in with some form of lacework. Most often, threads are stitched across the hole, and needleweaving or buttonhole stitching over the laid in threads creates a bit of lace.

Hemstitching

To define a neat, straight hemline in fine linens and handkerchiefs, a few threads are pulled out just at the hemline.

The stitching that secures the hem draws these threads into neat bundles and makes a decorative line at the hem.

The hemline should be carefully inspected on all vintage linens. Hemstitching has both good and bad points.
- If the threads used to weave the fabric are not good quality, the threads exposed at the drawn hemline will fray, and eventually break.
- If long exposed threads are left in loose bundles, they fray more easily than if the threads have been carefully stitched over.
- Decorative stitching serves two purposes: it provides additional decoration at the hemline, and it covers and protects the threads that have been exposed when the hemline was defined.

Cutwork

One of the easiest ways to make a fabric lacy is to cut holes in it. There are two ways to make patterns: make a design of the cut holes, or remove the background to create a silhouette of the remaining fabric.

Until the nineteenth century, cutwork was hand-worked. Toward the middle of the nineteenth century, machines began to do punchwork, imitating the popular Broderie Anglaise and other eyelets.

How to recognize cutwork

- The base is a woven fabric, most often cotton or linen.
- Designs may be patterns of cut holes, or a design silhouetted out of the fabric.

Features to note

- Intricate designs.
- Edges are carefully and skillfully stitched to prevent fraying. Stitching on edges may be buttonhole, overcast, or hedebo (knotted buttonhole).
- The most interesting cutwork also is combined with drawnwork, needle lace inserts in the cut holes, and intricate embroidery designs.

Where it is used

Nearly every area that produced any needlework did some form of cutwork table linens, bed linens, and clothing. A few of the best-known include:

- Norwegian Hardanger
- Danish Hedebo
- Broderie Anglaise
- Eyelets
- Irish Carrickmacross
- Madiera
- Moravian whitework

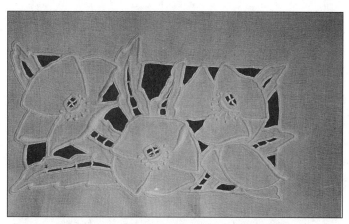

Design is silhouetted by cutting out fabric from behind the design. Edge (detail shown below) has been carefully covered with buttonhole stitches to prevent fraying.

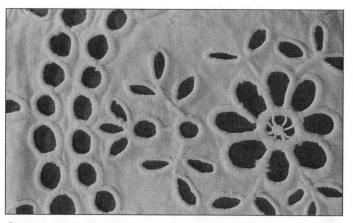

Cut holes form the design in this cutwork. Edges are overcast. Heavy texture suggests several rows of stitching outlined the holes to prevent fraying before they were overcast.

Appliqué

Appliqué is just what it sounds like: one fabric applied over another. There are as many variations as there are fabrics and types of stitching. Hand or machine-made lace motifs may be applied to a net; felt cutouts may be applied to another fabric.

In some cultures a reverse appliqué have worked; the Hmong of southeast Asia is one of the best-known. Several fabrics of different colors are layered, and designs are cut out through one or more layers to produce a multicolor pattern. Cut edges are carefully turned under and stitched.

How to recognize it

- The appliquéd decoration will be on the surface of the fabric. The base fabric will completely cover the decoration.
- Very often, some form of decorative stitching will surround the edges of the applied motif. If the stitches do not show on the surface, often they will appear as an outline on the back side.

Features to note

- If the applied motif has been cut from woven fabric, expect the edges to be either neatly turned under, or completely covered with stitching.
- Look for interesting silhouettes and unusual and carefully shaped motifs. Curves should be graceful and smooth.
- Look for additional embellishments, especially fancy embroidery stitches.

Where it is used

- Quilts, especially Hawaiian style and crazy quilts.
- Laces, especially those where handmade motifs were applied to machine-made nets.
- Ethnic crafts, especially Hmong and Mexican.
- American table linens and pillowcases from the early twentieth century.

Handmade Brussels bobbin lace motifs applied to a machine-made net. This was especially popular in the early and mid 19th century, before machines made patterned laces.

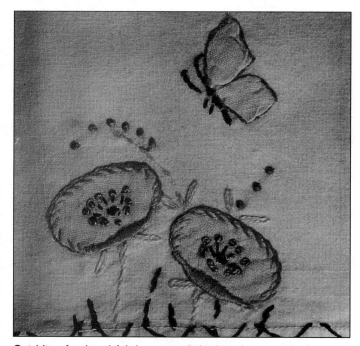

Cut bits of colored fabric were stitched to the towel to form the butterfly wings and small flowers in this tea towel, circa 1920-1930.

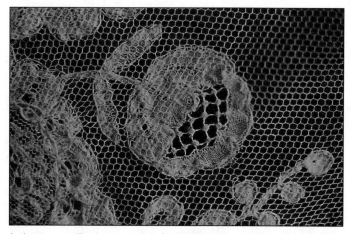

In better quality lace appliqués, the net was trimmed away from open areas by hand to maintain the illusion of handmade lace.

Things

Aprons

Every household has a few old aprons. At Christmas and Easter, when my mother and I roll out the dough for kolache and nut rolls, I still like to wear my grandmother's print apron from the 1930s. Look through the collections of old aprons at every antique mall, and you can trace the history of women for the past hundred years.

Elegant, upper-class women in the seventeenth through the nineteenth century sometimes wore a tablier, or decorative skirt front. Usually made of fine lace, the tablier offered a fashion statement, not any kind of protection from household tasks. The earliest tabliers usually were cut from deep skirt flounces. Most have long since been recycled into oblivion. Late nineteenth century lace tabliers still show up, and make attractive collectibles.

Functional nineteenth century aprons most often were of plain cloth. Prints were very expensive, and were used for the skirts the apron protected. Knit, crochet, or bobbin lace edgings sometimes decorated the "show-off" aprons worn when company was coming. In the nineteenth century, a knit, crochet, or bobbin lace edging was something many homemakers could do. Printed cloth still was too expensive to use for an apron.

By the twentieth century, chemical dyes and roller printing processes had made printed cloth cheap. Even feed sacks were printed by the 1920s, and these materials were used widely for aprons.

✔ Checklist

The parts of an apron are the skirt and bib, waistband and ties, neckties, back ties or shoulder straps, and the back including the pockets and hem. Each part can be functional or decorative.

The changing shape of aprons tells their age. Which of the parts are present, which are dominant, which have been minimized or have disappeared — all these help tell an apron's story.

****

1890s and 1900s

Aprons typically had a bib front, but usually did not have ties at the waist or shoulder straps, presumably to economize on fabric. Aprons were pinned to the front of the dress.

Materials were plain, often unbleached, cotton.

Decoration might include some homemade or store bought lace.

Highly decorative aprons were an important part of European ethnic costumes in the late nineteenth and early twentieth centuries. These embroidered and lace decorated confections were highly valued, and sometimes do surface in the United States.

1920s and 1930s

Aprons frequently had a bib front, ties at the waist, shoulder straps, and a back as well.

Cheerful cotton prints were widely available, and were often used for aprons.

Colorful cotton bias tapes were becoming widely available, and often were used to edge aprons.

Pockets often were designed into the sides of the skirt.

1940s

Large aprons, often just to cover the skirt with no bib, begin to appear in the 1940s.

A wider variety of fabrics, including organdy decorated with colorful bias tape, rickrack, or fabric appliqués were popular.

Checked gingham with little stars embroidered over each tiny square were popular.

A square patch pocket stitched onto the side of the skirt was typical

1950s

This was the heyday of Betty Crocker, the world's most recognized homemaker. The homemaker often had a whole wardrobe of aprons: dressy aprons for company, decorated aprons for each holiday, and plainer aprons for every day.

It was not uncommon to make aprons as presents, as items for church fundraising bazaars, and any other imaginable occasion.

Pockets on this decade's aprons were often very decorative.

1960s

With the emergence of women's lib, aprons became more functional and business-like.

Wrap-around, or bib-front chef-style aprons were beginning to gain popularity.

Carpenter-style pockets along the bottom of the skirt were popular.

Fabrics often were heavy canvas-like blends of cotton and synthetics.

Novelty printed aprons reflected the passion to wear a philosophy or make a statement in clothes. Mottoes, recipes, vegetables and other sayings often appeared on aprons.

Ties often were short, barely long enough to tie. Sometimes aprons were pinned on. Prices typically are $10 to $15.

Aprons from the 1800s were long, to protect floor-length skirts. They were made of white or unbleached fabric. Decoration usually was a bit of homemade lace, or some drawnwork.

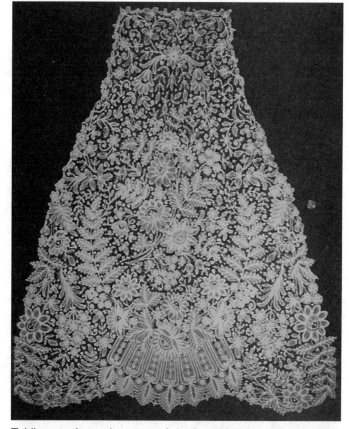

Tabliers, or decorative aprons from the mid-1800s were intended strictly for show, a reprise of an 18th century fashion. This example is of Brussels Duchesse bobbin lace. Price about $1200.

Bib front on this early 20th century red-white and blue print apron has no ties — it was designed to be pinned to the dress's bodice.

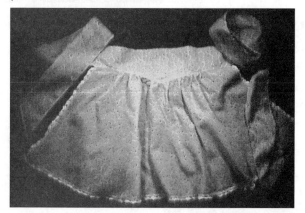

Commercially produced hostess apron in teal fabric with white and black print, and edged with machine lace. Extremely long and wide ties are designed to make a huge bow in the back. Price about $10.

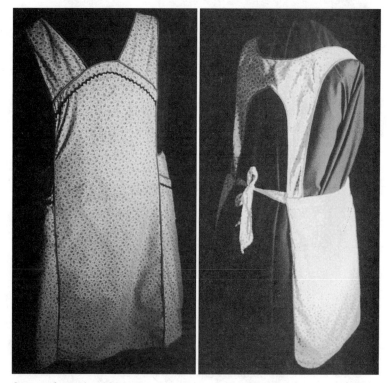

Aprons from the 1930s were homemade in colorful little prints. They were designed to protect the whole dress, and typically included side panels and a back. Prices $10 to $15.

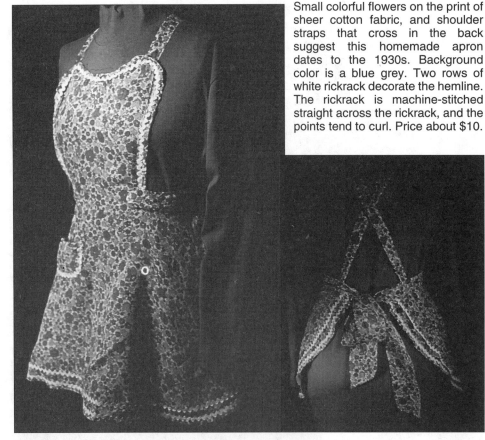

Small colorful flowers on the print of sheer cotton fabric, and shoulder straps that cross in the back suggest this homemade apron dates to the 1930s. Background color is a blue grey. Two rows of white rickrack decorate the hemline. The rickrack is machine-stitched straight across the rickrack, and the points tend to curl. Price about $10.

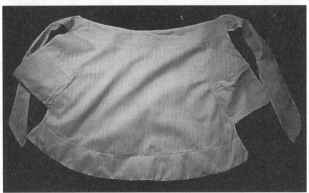

Novelty apron from the 1950s, in blue and red checked fabrics. Side pockets are cleverly hidden on the side, as if they were an extension of the bottom band. Price about $10.

The maker of this handcrafted circa 1930-40 apron must have been both romantic and practical. Cheerful loops and hearts are shaped with rose red rickrack on a sheer white fabric printed with tiny pink and red roses. A close look at the back shows each turn of the rickrack was carefully stitched down by hand. This takes much longer than machine stitching through the middle. Time is saved, however, each time the apron is ironed, because the rickrack does not curl in the wash. Price about $10.

This homemade blue and white checked apron, made in the 1970s in a polyester blend, is a reprise of a craft popular earlier in the 1900s. Quick and easy embroidery stitches create an optical illusion. Each white square is outlined with stitches, and each blue square is covered with a double cross stitch. Price about $15.

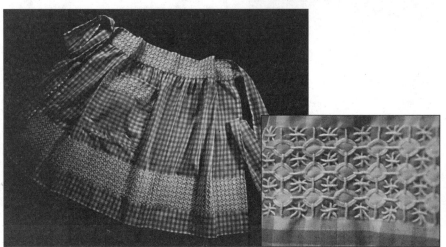

Bridal Veils

The invention of machine-made fine tulle or net at the beginning of the 1800s made it possible for almost any bride of the nineteenth century to have a gorgeous lacy veil.

The most spectacular lace bridal veils date to the mid to late nineteenth century, and were probably influenced by the glorious lace veil worn in 1823 by Queen Victoria. The wedding veil was made of English Honiton bobbin lace appliquéd onto a machine net.

More practical American brides of the late nineteenth century sometimes wore a pair of embroidered net curtains as a veil, and for decades after the wedding, these curtains — sometimes up to ten feet long — would grace the long parlor window of a Victorian or Queen Anne style home.

Many veils made in Europe during the mid twentieth century have simple tape lace motifs appliquéd to them.

✔ Checklist

Shape, size, and overall design significantly influence the value of the bridal veil. Large oval veils currently are very popular. Small square or rectangular veils, such as bonnet veils from the early 1800s, are bargains because they are small and the shape is not popular.

Large point de gaze needle lace veils, with handmade point de gaze mesh background, are among the most rare and valuable. The handmade net, however, is fragile and very difficult to repair.

Quality of the materials and condition of the net is important to check. Quality of cotton net of those made in the late 19th and early twentieth century often was good, and these wash well. Those made around the 1950s often was a very poor quality, and the net often shreds in the wash.

****

Materials

Quality of the thread used to make the net is crucial. Nets made of poor quality cotton thread with very short staples was used in the 1950s, and held together with stiff sizing. When the sizing washes out, the net shreds.

Technique and workmanship

Veils with pretty but poor-quality lace often are priced about the same as veils with lace motifs made with exquisite technique and workmanship.

Look at the clothwork, or dense areas of the design, for even texture, intricate patterns worked into the clothwork, and exquisite shading and shaping.

Look at the fancy fillings for stitches for delicate but crisply and precisely worked buttonhole stitches.

Condition

Look for pinholes, tears, and repairs in the background net. This is the most difficult part to repair.

Stains are very difficult to remove from veils, because the net is so fragile.

Pieces & prices

Rectangular veil or shawl with bobbin lace flowers and bouquets appliquéd on machine net. Mid nineteenth century. About 96 inches by 28 inches. Sold for $1800.

Brussels needle lace flowers appliquéd in scalloped border on machine net, scattered sprigs. Late nineteenth century bridal veil. 74 inches by 69 inches. Sold at auction for $625.

Brussels needle and bobbin lace flowers arranged in bouquets at the corners and in sprays at the border, applied to machine net. Sprigs and spots scattered across the net. 51 inches by 78 inches. Sold at auction for $1530.

Large rectangular veil with bouquet of flowers at each corner, formal posies at border, sprigs and spots scattered across net in fine tambour embroidery. Length 92 inches by 74 inches. Sold at auction for $325.

Late nineteenth century English Honiton bobbin lace appliqué on machine net. Stylized posies at each corner and roses along the border. 75 inches by 73 inches. Sold at auction for $660.

Late nineteenth century English Honiton bobbin lace appliqué on machine net. Spray of flowers at each corner, scattered springs and scalloped border. Length 71 inches by 69 inches. Sold at auction for $238.

Sources

The Honiton Lace Shop
44 High Street
Honiton, Devon, England
EX14 8PJ
To find current web page address on the Internet, search for Honiton Lace Shop.

Red Balloons
Mallory and Jeanette Merrill
10912 Main St.
Clarence, NY
716-759-8999
Vintage lace, clothing.

Karen Augusta
31 Gage
North Westminster, VT 05101
800-OLD LACE
Designer vintage, fine linens and lace. Shows and by appointment.

Paris 1900
2703 Main Street
Santa Monica, CA 90405
310-396-0405
Vintage bridal, and new bridal made with antique lace.

Cornelia Powell
271 B. East Paces Ferry Road
Augusta, GA 30904-4614
706-733-6073
Lace clothing, vintage, and newly made from vintage lace and fabrics. Shop.

Molly Carroll
329 Berryman Drive
Amherst, NY 14226
New York Pier shows and by appointment. Specializing in Irish lace.

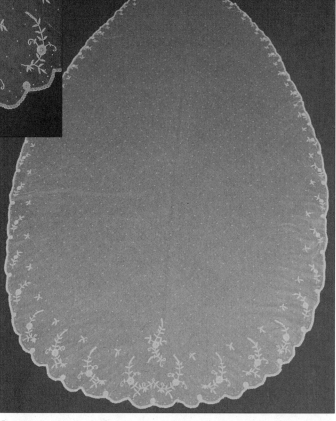

Oval veil, about six feet long, with application of machine-made tape along the edge, and design of simple flower sprigs made from embroidery and cut bits of machine-made tape. The large oval shape makes these veils popular today. They often sell for $300 to $500.

Handmade 19th century Point de Gaze needle lace is considered by many to be the ultimate bridal lace. Large veils entirely of lace with handmade mesh are extremely rare. Prices range upwards of $10,000. Photo courtesy of Karen Augusta, Westminster, Vermont.

Mid 19th century rectangular veil or shawl with floral design hand-embroidered in tambour (chain stitch). Layers of fabric petals are appliquéd over the embroidered flowers. About 72 inches long, 25 inches wide. Sold for about $350.

More than half the surface of this eight-foot-long oval bridal veil is covered with sprays of Brussels bobbin lace. Veils of this quality are difficult to find, and typically sell in the $2,500 to $3,000 range.

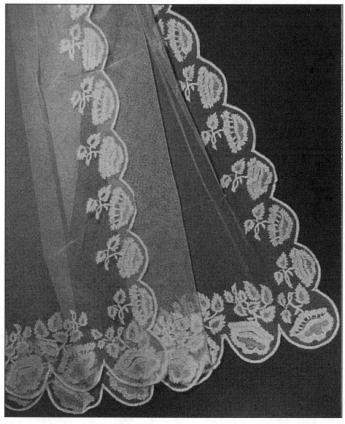

Bonnet veils of the early 19th century were approximately a yard square, and had elaborate hand-embroidered borders of flower sprigs along the bottom and sides. These usually sell for between $200 and $350.

Veil appliquéd over entire surface with handmade Honiton bobbin lace motifs. About 52 inches square. Sold for $1,500.

Dresses

There is vintage fashion, and there is haute couture.

Fashion includes all the styles of any era, from denim to Hawaiian shirts to pink felt poodle skirts. The poodle skirts and Hawaiian shirts of the 1950s, or the denim fashions of the twentieth century are emblems of an era. Their values will fluctuate as the styles are revisited in nostalgia.

Haute couture translates from French to mean "high sewing," and includes all those garments whose quality of design and workmanship truly give them intrinsic worth. The haute couture of past centuries has been rediscovered as the art form it always has been. Even with prices for designer originals rising into thousands of dollars, there should be room for appreciation. Value in these garments is present on many levels. Silhouettes and shapes express the taste and style at unique points in time; they can be appreciated and displayed like fine sculpture. The details of construction that establish the shape and silhouette can be appreciated for their skill, ingenuity, and engineering. Materials almost always are unique, often luxurious.

Embellishments, including lace, embroidery, painting and dyeing often display unique human skill and achievements, whether they are handmade or the products of uniquely crafted and engineered machines. Finally, the association with known designers, models, and perhaps wealthy clients of renowned fashion houses gives haute couture a cultural importance. Vintage couture lets us rub elbows with the famous and the infamous.

In any case, the more haute the couture, the more human thought, imagination, and skill the garment represents.

Reenacting is still growing as a lifetime passion, and subsequently, this is building interest in vintage fashion. Reenactors are putting amazing energy and study into authenticating details of design, workmanship, materials, and techniques of fashion for period costume, especially for the Revolutionary and Civil War periods. Perhaps this energy and quest for detail will translate into more appreciation and demand for original examples, and more support to have museum collections preserved, displayed and made available for study.

✔ Checklist

Features that make haute couture special:

Shaping of the garment is achieved through clever use of darts, seams, and fabric cutting.

Imaginative use of fabrics. Drape, color, texture, finish (matte or shiny). Use of bias, grain, other features of the fabric.

Careful and imaginative matching of plaids and stripes; careful placement of flowers, or other features in prints.

Details of workmanship and technique enhance the shaping, and wearability of the garment.

Topstitching, especially with silk thread, may be used to accent lines and seams.

Buttonholes usually are bound. Seam allowances usually are generous, and finished off as flat fell seams (folded, trimmed, and stitched down so no raw edges show) in sheer fabrics. Edges will be overcast to prevent fraying and raveling.

Special and carefully chosen notions: belt and buckle, buttons, ribbons and lace, embroidery.

Linings can serve several functions. They help hold the shape of the garment, add body, and enhance the color of sheer fabrics.

Facings on lapels, edges of jackets, blouses, or coats help garments hold their shape and affect how the garment hangs and wears.

Many garments were boned (reinforced with stiff whalebone in early garments, fabric-cover metal or plastic stays in later garments) to establish the shape.

Bustles and other structures were sometimes built in to the garment.

Details of haute couture

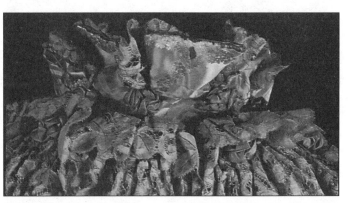

Roses of gold satin ribbon accent the edge between the cape and the standing ruffled collar.

Short opera cape, circa 1900-1905, of gold silk brocade and lace. Style and details of construction make it very special. Condition of the silk is not good: note fraying along the bottom edge.

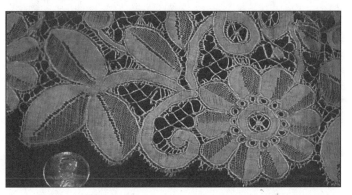

Only a very close look reveals that the showy lace is machine-made, not handmade. The regular grain of the weaving is typical of machine lace. In handmade, the threads would follow the curves of the design. Edge picots are cut and frayed threads. Threads in handmade lace would emerge from the clothwork, twist, and return in continuous loops.

Cracks and shattering in the silk reveal the buckram fabric that supports and shapes the cape.

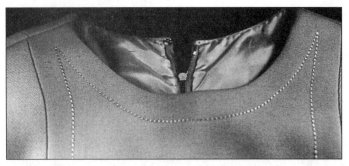

Topstitching, especially in glossy silk threads, was used to accent the lines of shaped garments, and to add detail to pockets, cuffs, and other areas of fine garments. Linings help garments keep their shape over many wearings.

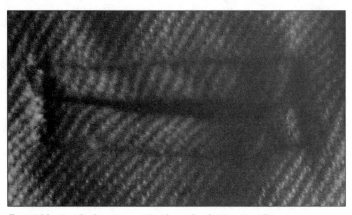

Bound buttonholes were used on the better quality garments.

Expect meticulous shaping, good quality buttons and other notions, and special details, like these lined, turned pockets in couture garments.

Zippers are meticulously put in and topstitched by hand in fine couture garments.

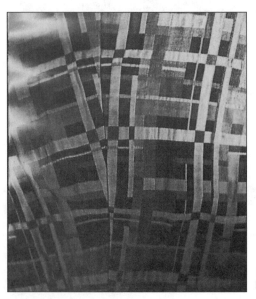

Plaids and stripes were carefully matched in better quality garments.

Women's fashions

1700s
Shapes: Enormous skirts, with yards-wide panniers, hoops, and other support structures.

Fabrics: brocades, velvets, elaborately printed chintzes.

Early 1800s
Shapes: Revolutionary change in fashion with the end of the Ancien Regime and the beginning of Napoleon's Republic in France. Dresses abruptly change to figure-clinging muslins. Waist moved just below the bustline in the empire look. Scoop necklines, short puffed sleeves.

1840-1860
Special shape: Waistline moves back to the waist, skirts become more and more voluminous. Hoops getting bigger and bigger to support formal gowns. Ankles that were visible again disappear under floor-length skirts.

Huge leg-of-mutton sleeves gradually give way. By mid century, dresses are worn off-the-shoulder with ruffled lace berthes for evening, buttoned up to the neck with tiny round lace or white cotton embroidered collars for day. Huge ten-foot long rectangular or triangular shawls worn with the enormous skirts.

1870-90
Special shape: Skirts become flatter in the front, elaborate bustles in the back. Huge gigot (leg-of-mutton) sleeves come back as the century turns.

Key names: Charles Frederick Worth

Fabrics: Opulent

Pieces & prices

Worth afternoon gown, mid 1870s. Fawn silk faille, high waisted bodice buttoned with four self buttons. Robin's egg blue self bows at waist. Three-quarter length sleeves, trained skirt. Blue front panel overlaid with two-tone fawn fringed swags and pleated panels, two tone ruffles at the sides, skirt front, and train hem. Labeled Worth 7 Rue de la Paix Paris. Some damage and alternations to skirt. Sold at auction for $2,530

Wedding gown, circa 1890s. Two piece, candlelight satin. Gigot (leg-of-mutton) sleeves, softly pleated high mousseline collar, long train. Good condition, some dirt. Labeled Macheret Paris New York. Sold at auction with matching pumps for $575

Worth ivory satin ball gown, circa 1890s. Pointed bodice and trained skirt heavily embroidered with flowers, plumes, and foliage in pearlescent beads and sequins, rhinestones, and paillettes. Bodice trimmed with lace flounce extending over the shoulders as sleeves, with beadwork appliqués and strands of rhinestones with drop tassels at the shoulders. Bodice lace in fragile condition, minor splitting in skirt. Labeled C. Worth, Paris. Sold at auction for $3,220

Left: Robe l'Anglaise, 18th century, of beige silk damask patterned with large blossoms and leaf forms on sinuous vinery, circa 1740. The dress has been remodeled many times. Currently has long, shaped sleeves, fitted pointed back, and a stomacher front. Silk is worn, darned considerably and is discolored. A rectangular piece is cut out of the skirt front. Sold at auction for $287.

Right: Silk gown, circa 1790. Remodeled from an earlier gown. Fabric is French gold silk moiré faille figured with bouquets joined with tasseled bows set on and within vertical stripes. The gown is high-waisted with a low round drawstring neckline and an interior linen cross-over bodice. The back is sewn in the robe a la Francaise style with two wide pleats at the shoulder, descending to a graceful train. Sold at auction for $1,265. Photo courtesy of William Doyle Galleries, New York.

Wedding dress, late 1850s, of gold and white silk damask, trimmed with black fringe and black velvet ribbon. From the Kent State University Museum collection, a gift of Helen M. Gallese and Sally J. Vyrostek in memory of their mother, Emma Young Matejka of Richfield, Ohio, 1985.5.1.

Evening dress, circa 1805-1812, of sea green and gold pattern-weave silk, embroidered with silk thread, beads, sequins, and pailettes. From the collection of Allen Art Museum, Oberlin, Ohio, 1949 L1995.17.65. Shown worn with a cotton lawn shawl with tambour-embroidery paisley motifs. Kent State University Museum Silverman/Rodgers Collection, 1983-1-1507. Photo courtesy of the Kent State University Museum.

Ball gown by Worth, mid 1870s, of celadon damask intricately patterned with ferns and blossoms. The waist length bodice is sewn at the back with weighted flaps, buttoning in front to a point. Neckline is cut in low décolletage and V-back. Sleeves have elbow length swags of lace. The bustle skirt is arranged with two front plain crisscross satin panels opening to show brocade and tiers at bottom. Has interior bustle structure. Labeled Worth 7, Rue de la Paix Paris, stamped in green/gold. Sold at auction for $10,300. Photo courtesy of William Doyle Galleries, New York.

Robe d'interieur by Charles Frederick Worth, early 1880s, of blue voided velvet woven with sprays of spring flowers in red, green, and brown. Style is a princess line, with satin vestee overlaid with ruffled lace jabot. The skirt is in open robe style, revealing tiers of lace in front. The bodice and skirt are bedecked with pale yellow and taupe satin ribbons. Bustle train and dust ruffle in back. Lining is checkered fabric. Green/gold stamped on white label, Worth 7 Rue de la Paix PARIS. Similar to a gown made for Sarah Bernhardt for her role in Fedora in 1883. Sold at auction for $16,100. Photo courtesy of William Doyle Galleries, New York.

Left: English Victorian reception gown, circa 1880, of deep burgundy silk faille and ivory satin brocaded with pastel flowers, the cuirass bodice fitted over the hips, with long tight sleeves and two weighted back flaps, faux button-down integral vestee forming the V-neck. A separate brocade dickey has a high band collar. The skirt has a single panel draped to one side over a brocade front with pointed hem. The skirt back is of faille, with an interior bustle structure and train. Labeled Sarah Fullerton-Monteith Young/21 (?)street/Grosvenor Square, and handwritten on tapes on the back of inside skirt: Mrs. Roosevelt. Excellent condition. Sold at auction for $3,450.

Right: American ivory satin ball gown, circa 1890s. Two-piece gown is embroidered with roses in silk threads on chiffon medallion inserts surrounded by vinery and scrolls worked in gold bullion. The dress has rhinestone and pearl embellishments. The bodice is pointed in front, with puffed sleeves of chiffon and fine appliquéd point d'esprit. The low, rounded décolletage is accented with green satin puffed bow. Labeled Re----lau 21 East 47th Street/New York/Paris. Some minor smudges on skirt, otherwise excellent condition. Sold at auction for $3,910. Photo courtesy of William Doyle Galleries, New York.

1900-1910s

Special shapes: Slimmer shapes, but elaborate laces and embroidery still in vogue. Bustles, boning, and under support structures begin to disappear.

Key names: Worth, Callot Soeurs

What's New: Everything in evolution. Lots of variety and experimentation. Skirts getting shorter.

Pieces & prices

Worth evening gown with empire waist, black chiffon over satin, with cream chiffon center panel festooned with rhinestone swags and tassels, repeated as dangling ornaments on the bodice and shoulders. Labeled C. Worth, 76727. Condition very fragile. Sold at auction for $1,035.

Paul Poiret gown of ivory satin with tunic overdress of sapphire blue chiffon embroidered in wool with a row of green, black, and white palm trees above a wide plush band. Bodice and hem trimmed with strands of black beads and rhinestones which hang loosely as a necklace. Size 4. Labeled Paul Poiret a Paris. Good condition. Silk underslip and bodice lining shattering, top sleeves altered at ends. Sold at auction for $16,000

Left: Columnar evening dress, circa 1912, of beige chiffon woven with gold metallic sprays. The underbodice and cap sleeves are of lace. Straight skirt is draped diagonally across the front revealing gold lace of the underskirt. The slightly raised waist is encircled in green satin, beaded fringe and tassel trim. Gold lace panel is centered in the back, ending in a square train. Size 4. Good condition, minor tears to the chiffon. Labeled Dumay 32. Rue Godot de Mauroi Paris. Sold at auction for $1,000.

Right: Afternoon gown of teal blue chiffon and satin. The bodice is embroidered with silk flowers, and sewn with spotted net bretelles. The skirt has a diagonal swath of satin in front, ending in a diagonal floating back panel decorated with woven straw oval buttons. Size 6. Labeled 7 Place Vendome Paris/Nice. The maker is illegible. Dressmakers located at the Place Vendome when this dress was made included Martial & Armand and Cheruit. Schiaparelli later took that location. Fragile, and some discoloration. Sold at auction for $900. Photo courtesy of William Doyle Galleries, New York.

Circa 1900s dress of white Battenberg (tape) lace shows the exaggerated pigeon-breasted and bustled shape popular at the turn of the century, but silhouette is softer, dress is less elaborate than just a few years earlier. Collar is tight and high, accenting the neck. Battenberg, a dramatic and bold lace, was reaching the height of its popularity. Photo courtesy of Just Faboo, Midway, Kentucky.

1920s

Special shapes: Straight sleeveless shift. Waist drops to the hips.

Key Names: Callot Soeurs, Chanel, Fortuny

What's New: Short skirts. Draping. Lots of beads.

Fabrics: Chiffon, beading

Pieces & prices

Fortuny gold velvet cardigan style coat with elbow-length sleeves. Gold stenciling in Middle Eastern inspired motifs around edges and down center back. Stylized cones at the shoulders and hem. Labeled Mariano Fortuny Venise. Good condition, some alterations. Sold at auction for $1,495.

Fortuny Delphos dress in Champagne pleated silk with Venetian glass beads. Very good condition, some loosening of the pleats. Sold at auction for $2,415.

Fortuny Delphos sleeveless dress in rose pleated silk. Glass beads on silk cord at sides, stenciled belt. Good condition, minor discoloration. Sold at auction for $1,000

Red satin Oriental style pajamas. Sleeveless shell with white chinoiserie embroidery and heart shaped pocket, wide legged pants with white dragon embroidered godets. Labeled C.A. Faetery. Very good condition. Sold at auction for $201.

Green satin Oriental style pajama ensemble. Cardigan jacket, self-belt for bodice, pants embroidered with pagodas and bridges. Good condition. Sold at auction for $373.

Beaded evening chemise with long sleeves, low self-belt. Black silk crepe with all-over diagonal leaf bead design in red, blue, and gold. Floral band down left side. Size 12-14. Very good condition. Sold at auction for $287.

Beaded sleeveless chemise party dress in apricot georgette with slightly flared skirt. Beaded all over from the waist in silver leaf pattern accented with large white beaded flowers. Size 6. Very good condition. Sold at auction for $345.

Black satin dress with rows of brown buttons down the sides, appliquéd with ivory net stylized foliage at neck and hem. Size 6. Good condition. Sold at auction for $230.

Circa 1927. Callot Soeurs sleeveless Chiffon frock in ivory chiffon embroidered in ivory silk floss and pearls with Chinese-inspired peonies and other flowers. Dress inset with blonde lace panels and lace on pointed flounce on slip hem. Slip labeled Callot Soeurs Paris Made in France, Nouvelle Marque Deposee. Handwritten label on reverse 99241. Dress in good condition with minor tears, slip has damage. Sold at auction for $850

White lace dresses were a classic from the early 20th century. Each is a special confection of white-on-white embroidery and lace. Very often, the waists, armholes, and sleeves make them too small to wear today without extensive remodeling.

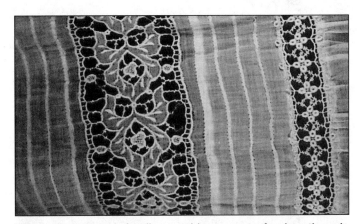

These are extremely fragile — nothing except a few lacy threads hold them together. Look carefully for damage and repairs. Offered for $100.

Left: Black velvet beaded chemise, early 1920s, embroidered at the hem and across the front with bright pink and fuchsia flowerheads. Two free-floating beaded bands descend from the shoulders to the hem in the front and back. Size 12. Sold at auction for $460.

Center: French dance dress, mid 1920s, of black chiffon with rhinestones forming a swan's head at the front and back of the flared full skirt. The bodice is fitted and sleeveless. Size 4. Sold at auction for $690.

Right: French chemise dress, early 1920s, in a slender tubular shape, with long sleeves. The waist drops to the hips, with gathers at the sides. Black velvet, with a folkloric pattern of arches at the hem worked in coral brown seed beads. Size 12. Labeled Robes Isis/Paris/Made in France. Sold at auction for $632. Photo courtesy of William Doyle Galleries, New York.

Back view of a gold velvet coat by Fortuny, cut in a kimono style with V-neck at the back. Velvet is stenciled with Persian-inspired patterns including a row of leafy trees above a wide band of foliage at the hem, and roundels of foliage at the shoulders and sleeves. The front opening is lined with vines. Lined with celadon silk satin. Labeled Mariano Fortuny Venice. Minor spots on the front. Sold at auction for $3,200.

Fabric behind the coat is a muted blue cotton or linen twill attributed to Fortuny, stenciled in gold and silver in a Baroque mirror-image pattern of scrolling acanthus leaves, palmettos, and blossoms. The border is a geometric pattern. Approximately 2 yards, 43 inches wide, sold at auction for $1,200. Photo courtesy of William Doyle Galleries, New York.

Two-piece sports dress of linen, probably Wiener Werkstatte, mid 1920s. A white middy overblouse and a dress with pleated skirt. The dress and trim on the blouse of red and white geometric pattern; the blouse front decorated with appliquéd crisscrossed flags. Labeled Made in Vienna. Sold at auction for $1,955. Photo courtesy of William Doyle Galleries, New York.

1930s

Special shapes: The body reemerges, with clinging, draping shapes, sarongs.

Key names: Jean Patou, Schiaparelli, Fortuny

Pieces & prices

Chanel ivory satin jacket, slightly tapered at the waist, with wide pointed collar, long puffed and shaped sleeves, cuffs sewn sabot style. Size 6. Labeled Chanel. Good condition, some discoloration on cuff. Sold at auction for $1150.

Black gauze evening frock embroidered with sprays of pink carnations. Bodice gathered into front frill; short puffed sleeves. Self belt. Black taffeta petticoat with coral band at the bottom. Very good condition. Sold at auction for $345

Left: Evening gown from the 1930s designed by Jean Patou. Slim columnar gown is sewn in alternating green and black pleated gores ending in points at the bodice and hem. Labeled Jean Patou Paris with the handwritten number 29113. Minor discoloration and holes at the hemline. Sold at auction for $2,300.

Right: Long black sleeveless sari dress by Schiaparelli, 1935. The edges of the black crepe fabric are edged with bands of fuchsia beads and gold triangular paillettes. Size 6. Grosgrain ribbon label: Schiaparelli 21 Place Vendome Paris Eté 1935 #40982. The dress originally belonged to international socialite Eleanor Medill Patterson, whose family founded the New York Daily News. It later was owned by Austine Hearst, wife of William Randolph Hearst, Jr. Sold at auction for $10,350. Photo courtesy of William Doyle Galleries, New York

1940s

Special shapes: Emphasized shoulders, fitted waist, V-neck, Waist is firmly at the waist.

Key names: Adrian, Hattie Carnegie, Lilli Ann, Sybil Connolly, Schiaparelli

What's New: Women's wool suits. Dior's "New Look" at the end of the 40s.

Pieces & prices

Lilli Ann black wool dinner suit jacket. Single-breasted, fastening with rhinestone buttons and self-loops. Yoke of bunched wool studded with rhinestones. Size 6. Labeled An Original from Lilli Ann of San Francisco. Very good condition. Sold at auction for $373.

Traina-Norell black wool jacket with Peter Pan collar. Fitted at the waist with wide inset band, flaring to hip length. Size 6. Labeled Traina-Norell New York. Excellent condition. Sold at auction for $431.

Adrian Spring suit in shell pink wool. Fitted hip length jacket applied with self-semicircular bands at front and back yoke, with mother of pearl buttons with overlapping gilt-metal mounts. Size 6. Labeled Adrian Original. Good condition, some holes. Sold at auction for $316.

Left: Adrian black gabardine suit from the late 1940s. The hip-length jacket is defined at the waist and midsection with self-bands, wide pointed collar and pockets accented with like bands crisscrossed. Straight skirt. Size 10. Labeled Adrian In British Samek Material, Julius Garfinckel & Co. Washington D.C. Very good condition. Sold at auction for $1,400.

Center: Nubbly black and white weave dinner suit by Lilli Ann, late 1940s. Hip-length jacket flares into a peplum at the hips. Left side of notched neckline extends into diagonal self-strap anchored with rhinestone buckle. Straight skirt. Size 10. Labeled an original from Lilli Ann of San Francisco. Very good condition. Sold at auction for $450

Right: Lilli Ann black wool spring suit from the late 1940s with hip-length fitted jacket with peplum. Oversized bertha collar decorated with scattered white, silk-covered buttons. Straight skirt. Size 10. Labeled an original from Lilli Ann of San Francisco. Very good condition. Sold at auction for $250. Photo courtesy of William Doyle Galleries, New York.

Left: Chiffon evening gown by Adrian in shaded-in russet, slate, forest green, and smoke with coral accents at shoulder and waist. One-shouldered bodice is draped asymmetrically and bisected diagonally with a chiffon twist. Size 6-8, labeled Adrian Original. Very good condition. Sold at auction for $2,700.

Right: Black crêpe de chine cocktail dress with sweetheart neck, ruched taffeta upper bodice and short wing sleeves extending under the arms in pleated Vs. Back is low and curved. The skirt is straight in front with taffeta peplum at the waist, overlaid at the back with tiered pleated taffeta panels. Size 6. Labeled Adrian Original. Very good condition, with minor alternations. Sold at auction for $1,955. Photo courtesy of William Doyle Galleries, New York.

1950s

Special shapes: Hourglass shape strapless gowns, fitted waist with huge gathered skirts. Boat neckline.

Key names: Charles James, Christian Dior, Mainbocher, Balmain, Givenchy.

What's New: Lots of petticoats.

Pieces & prices

Charles James black velvet sheath evening gown, 1954. Body hugging strapless sheath with enormous ivory faille hooped pannier flounce. Flounce is embroidered with cascades of gold and silver beads. Size 4. Hand signed satin ribbon label: Charles James '54. Very good condition, minor marks on velvet. Sold at auction for $12,500

1960s

Special shapes: A-line, sheaths.

Key Names: Rudi Gernreich, Balenciaga, Gucci, Chanel, Norell, Valentino, Yves St. Laurent.

What's New: Hippie culture, psychedelic colors, outrageous and daring. Pucci colorful, swirling geometric prints. Courreges vinyl dresses, coats, boots.

Pieces & prices

Norell red poppy-printed silk dress with exuberant long-stemmed pink and purple flowers. Sleeveless with slight extension at the shoulder, skirt gently gathered at waist. Size 6-8. Labeled Norman Norell for I. Magnin & Co. Sold at auction for $550.

Pucci hot pants, 1966, in shades of pink and yellow silk jersey, and pink organdy cover-up with printed silk twill cuffs, both labeled Emilio Pucci Florence - Italy. Sold at auction for $431.

Mini dress, hip length and sleeveless, of emerald green crochet decorated with iridescent multifaceted beads, the scoop neck decorated with fringe of beads. Size 4-6. Labeled Made in Italy. Sold at auction for $345.

French disco knit top, long sleeved, of gold Lurex, covered with shiny dangling gold disks. Sold at auction for $373.

Norell classic sailor ensemble, mid 1960s, of navy wool crepe. Boxy middy top with black silk bow, and knife pleated skirt. Labeled Norman Norell/ New York. Sold at auction for $345.

Chanel navy wool suit, with Eisenhower style jacket, molded gold buttons, interior gold chain, with slightly flared bored skirt. Sold at auction for $402.

Evening gown by Pierre Balmain in ivory satin embroidered with gold bouillon, beads, sequins, rhinestones, and other paillettes in a complex floral pattern worked densely on the bodice and scattered on the skirt. The strapless bodice is cut out on one side to follow lines of the floral design. The skirt is asymmetrically draped, the back sewn with an enormous bouffant bow ending in long wide streamers to form a train. Size 2. Labeled Pierre Balmain Paris. Very good condition, possible alterations at waist, one dark area on streamer. Sold at auction for $3,000. Photo courtesy of William Doyle Galleries, New York

Left: Rose silk faille cocktail dress by Yves Saint Laurent for Christian Dior, spring/summer of 1958. Camisole bodice is tightly fitted at the waist, and extends into a bouffant skirt supported by six layers of crinolines. Self fabric roses at each side of the skirt front. Size 6. Labeled Christian Dior Pairs Printemps-Eté 1958. Model number is illegible. Originally the property of Mrs. Nat King Cole. Sold at auction for $3,000.

Right: Cornflower blue silk cocktail dress by Yves Saint Laurent for Christian Dior, fall/winter collection of 1958. The sleeveless bodice has a low scooped neck. The slightly raised waist is accented with a wide flat bow of self fabric. Bouffant skirt is gathered at the hem into a balloon. Size 6. Labeled Christian Dior Paris Automne-Hiver 1958. Model number is illegible. Originally the property of Mrs. Nat King Cole. Sold at auction for $6,000. Photo courtesy of William Doyle Galleries, New York

Sleeveless A-line paper dress, 1960s, printed with a version of Campbell's Soup labels. Inspired by Andy Warhol's art. Labeled Souper Dress/No Cleaning - No washing - It's Carefree/Fire Resistant Unless Washed or Cleaned. To Refreshen, Press Lightly With Warm Iron. 80% Cellulose, 20% Cotton. Sold at auction for $1,840. Background is a length of cotton fabric printed with an exact reproduction of Campbell's Tomato Soup label, including the central gold medallion. Length 90 inches, width 45 inches. Sold at auction for $230. Photo courtesy of William Doyle Galleries, New York.

Two-piece evening gown by Emilio Pucci, consisting of a straight wrap skirt and sleeveless shell top with cutout neckline. Fabric is distinctive Pucci print, with curvilinear geometric spirals, brackets, and heart shapes in shades of purple, gold, black, and yellow. The design is outlined and partially filled in with colored beads and sequins. Silk lining has "Emilio" woven in. Size 8. Labeled Emilio Pucci Firenze. Slight discoloration, otherwise excellent condition. Sold at auction for $3,750. Photo courtesy of William Doyle Galleries, New York.

Sources for Vintage Clothing

The list of vintage clothing books is too extensive to include here. Ask a dealer or check your local library for books on specific aspects and eras.

Newsletters

Molly Turner, Editor and publisher
Vintage Gazette newsletter
Molly's Vintage promotions,
194 Amity St., Amherst, MA 01002
Phone 413-549-6446
merrylees@aol.com
Inform subscribers on what's new in vintage fashion. Lists textile shows, auctions, fashion history, what's being presented in books, museum shows, exhibits. Articles on history of fashion.

Vintage!
John Maxwell
c/o Federation of Vintage Fashion
1187 Beach Park Blvd
Foster City, CA 94404
707-793-0773
maxwell@wco.com
Tabloid-size quarterly newsletter. Illustrated articles on vintage fashion, care and cleaning, identification, plus a comprehensive calendar of vintage textile and fashion shows across Canada and U.S..

Dealers

George Waldman
Waldman Appraisal Co.
22311 Ventura Blvd. Suite 117
Calabasas, CA 91364-8073
Phone 818-591-8073
Fax 818-591-2073
Vintage Clothing

Leslie Vitanza
Peregrine Galleries
508 Brinkerhoff Ave.
Santa Barbara, CA 93101-3441
Phone 805-963-3134
Vintage clothing

Brian and Stephanie Morehouse
894 S. Bronson Ave.
Los Angeles, CA 90005
323-939-2240
By appointment. Appraising, and consulting buyers and sellers for rugs and tapestries, ethnic textiles. Couture and fashion, general textiles.

Janene Fawcett
Vintage Silhouettes
1301 Pomona St.
Crockett, CA 94525
Phone 510-787-7274
Men's and women's vintage clothing and accessories, 1850s to 1950s.

Holly Hess
Janet Russell
Atelier Polonaise
4610 1/2 Park Blvd.
San Diego, CA 92116
Phone/fax 619-291-8700
Authentic period and bridal apparel.

Kathryn Mancini
Ages Ahead
Palo Alto, CA
Phone 415-327-4480
Fax 415-326-2573
Vintage clothing and bridal.

Janice Stockwell
The Stage Stop
4330C Clayton Road
Concord, CA 94521
Phone 510-685-4440
Men's and women's vintage and collectible clothing.

Paris 1900
2703 Main Street
Santa Monica, CA 90405
Phone 310-396-0405
Shop; vintage clothing, bridal, textiles, linens and lace

Urban Mermaids
1807 Divisadero at Bush
San Francisco, CA
Phone 415-775-7774
Vintage clothing, glitz, drag, and unusual pieces from the 1950s to 1970s.

The Paper Bag Princess
8700 Santa Monica Blvd.
W. Hollywood, CA 90069
Phone 310-358-1985
www.PaperBagP.com
Vintage couture and designer resale.

Teresa Dunn
5146 Grandview Court
Tallahassee, FL 32303
Phone 904-562-5681
Victorian white clothing; doll trimmings.

Reminiscing Vintage Fashions
1579 Monroe Drive, Box 200
Atlanta, GA 30324
Phone 404-815-1999
dgkg123@aol.com
Quality vintage fashions by mail.

Nancy Cordero
AdVintageous
101 Glenlake Avenue
Park Ridge, IL 60068
Phone 847-823-8451
Wearable Vintage, 1920s to 1950s. Shows and by appointment.

Cindy Warrington
The Blue Parrot
Springfield, IL
Phone 217-793-2986
Vintage clothing for men and women. Hats, early 20s to 50s vintage. Shows and by appointment.

Ophelia's
125 Marion St.
Oak Park, IL 60301
Phone 708-386-9194
Vintage Clothes.

Vintage Adventure
403 11th St.
Rockford, IL 66111
Phone 815-227-1892
Vintage clothing and bridal gowns.

Hollis Jenkins Evans
Past Perfect
1520 So. 2nd St.
Louisville, KY 40208
Vintage and collectible clothing; mail or by appointment only.

Robert Walker
Just Faboo
107 East Main St.
P.O. Box 3913
Midway, KY
(Lexington area) 40347
Phone 606-846-5606
1780-1920 High quality vintage fashions, paisleys. Large shop, shows, and by appointment.

Garbo's Vintage Clothing
Covington, KY
Phone 606-291-9033
Specializing in Men's Wear

Sodou, Kathy
Mason Antiques District
208 Mason St.
Mason, MI 48854-1128
Phone 517-676-9753
Vintage clothing dealer

Donna Hicks
Aldon Antiques
Kalamazoo, MI
Phone 616-388-5375
Linen, lace, white apparel for ladies and children. Shows and by appointment only.

Barbara VanWeinen
Nobody's Sweetheart
953 East Fulton St.
Grand Rapids, MI 49503
Phone 616-454-1673
Shop, wide range of vintage clothing and textiles.

Cathy Taylor
Victori
126 South Holmes
Shakopee, MN 55379
Phone 612-928-9061
info@victori.com
Antique and vintage clothing 1800 up to 1940 and fashion collectibles. Special pieces shown by appointment. Shows. Does lectures and demonstrations.

Stacy Gley
Marilyn of Monroe
39 Godwin Avenue
Ridgewood, NJ 07450
Phone 201-447-3123
Vintage designer clothing.

Remmey Galleries
30 Maple Street
Summit, NJ 07901
Phone 908-273-5055
www.Remmeygalleries.com
Occasional vintage fashion, haute couture, and textile auctions.

Barbara Boyce
Another Time
3164 State Street
Caledonia, NY 11423
boyceTime@aol.com
Phone 716-538-9730
Shop, all kinds of textiles for kitchen, fashion, and the home.

Jean Ellis
Sussex Antiques
P.O. Box 796
Bedford, NY 10506
Phone 914-241-2919
Victorian Christening gowns, linens and lace; vintage fashion. Shows only and by appointment.

Jennifer Grambs
Jennifer Grambs Collection
New York City, NY
Phone 212-737-0798
jennylan@aol.com
Classic vintage clothing.

Jean Hoffman
207 East 66th St.
New York, NY 10021
Phone 212-535-6930
Bridal veils, paisleys, lace handkerchiefs. Extensive collection of top quality vintage wedding dresses, petit point bags.

Mallory and Jeanette Merrill
Red Balloons
10912 Main St.
Clarence, NY
Phone 716-759-8999
Shop with exquisite and rare vintage linens, lace, clothing, lingerie, hats, paisleys, unique Victorian textiles and textile arts.

Rosse, Betty
Gallerie Enchantment
Hammondsport, NY
Phone 607-569-2809
Shop: vintage clothing, hats, etc.

Jana Starr
Jana Starr Antiques
236 East 80th St.
New York, NY 10021
Phone 212-861-8256
Shop. Vintage white dresses, lots of old lace and textiles.

Sid Warshafsky
240 Overlook
Woodstock, NY 12499
Designer clothes; lace, linens. By appointment.

Heritage Antiques
42 W. Main St.
Angelica, NY 14709
Phone 716-466-3712
Vintage clothing.

Metropolitan Antiques
110 West 19th Street
New York, NY
Phone 212-463-0200
Call for information on shows and auctions of vintage fashion, textiles, textile and lace sample books, and other related materials.

Cynthia Barta
2568 Kendall Road
Shaker Heights, OH 44120-1141
Phone 216-281-1959
Shows and by appointment. 1940s to 1970s men's and women's clothing and accessories featured at Suite Lorain antique mall, 7105 Lorain Avenue, Cleveland, OH.

Linda Bowman
Legacy
12502 Larchmere Boulevard
Cleveland, OH 44102
Phone 216-229-0578
Shows and by appointment. High style vintage clothing from 1920 through 1960.

Shirley and Tom Wolf
Stitches in Time
61 Truax
Plymouth, OH 44865
Phone 419-687-2061
wolf@stitchesintime.com
Shop, shows, and by appointment. Wide range of vintage clothes, bridal, hats, etc. from 19th century on.

Reflections of the Past
P. O. Box 40361
Bay Village, OH 44140
Phone 440-835-6924
Web site only. Vintage clothing, textiles, linens, lace.

Elizabeth Hine
Hinesight
Phone 717-396-9527
717-393-9132
Fine vintage apparel and textiles.

Winston McKenzie
McKenzie Galleries
7026 Old Katy Road, Suite 161
Houston, TX 77024-2110
Phone 713-863-1213
Fax 713-863-1216
Costumes and textiles.

Adair Appraisals
1311 Devon Glen Dr.
Houston, TX 77077-3211
Phone 713-861-7711
Fax 713-496-6234
Vintage clothing, by appointment only.

Karen Augusta
31 Gage
N. Westminster, VT 05101
Phone 802-463-4958;
800-OLD LACE
Designer vintage, fine linens and lace. Shows and by appointment.

Winston McKenzie
McKenzie Galleries
7026 Old Katy Road, Suite 161
Houston, TX 77024-2110
Phone 713-863-1213
Fax 713-863-1216
Costumes and textiles.

June Adair
Adair Appraisals
1311 Devon Glen Dr.
Houston, TX 77077-3211
Phone 713-861-7711
Fax 713-496-6234
Vintage clothing, by appointment only.

Dixie Elmore
Rt. 1, Box 211
Washington, WV 26181
Phone 304-863-5460
Vintage clothing, hats, clothing 1800-1945. Linens, lingerie, assorted trims. Shows, and by appointment.

Tracey Jones
Retrofit, Pilgrim Antique Mall
W156 N 11500 Pilgrim Road
Germantown, WI 53022
Phone 414-774-6041 (Home)
Shop 414-250-0260
Men and women's vintage clothing, soft goods, textiles. Stalls in Germantown and Grafton malls. Shows and by appointment.

Pat O'Brien
Flapper Alley
1518 N. Farwell
Milwaukee, WI 53202
Phone 414-276-6252
Shop, mail order, and by appointment. Nineteenth century vintage fashion, linens and lace.

Hats

Even though fewer women wear hats today than have in the past, vintage hats are enjoying something of a resurgence in popularity. The finest of designer hats are sculptural delights, and can be used as colorful decorator accents in any room.

Between the reenactors and decorators, and collectors of novelty and historic hats, prices can fluctuate radically.

Even the prospect of $25 to $100 should attract the attention of anyone about to dispose of hats at a garage sale or estate sale. Anyone with vintage hats in their attic that are clean and in good condition should consider consulting a textbook or an expert on hats.

✔ Checklist

There are really only two parts to a hat: the crown and the brim. By accenting one or the other, and changing the angle that a hat perches on the head, the milliner can create an infinite variety of effects from the ridiculous to the sublime.

Design

A hat is a form of sculpture, and the choice of materials, the shaping, the colors, and the embellishment all work together in the perfect hat. Hats that are definitive of their times usually are the most popular with collectors. A big-name designer often adds to the value, but good design still commands attention.

Fabrics

The choice of fabrics changes with the season and with fashion.

The typical spring and summer fabric choices are straw or raffia, silk, cotton, and lace. Typical winter choices for fabrics are felt, plush fabric, satin, velvet, suede, and fur.

Depending on the fashion, and the size and shape of the hat, certain fabrics have been more popular in different eras. Felt is one of the most enduring materials for a hat, because it is pliable, easily shaped, and easy to decorate with dyeing, painting, embroidery, ribbons, or any accent imaginable.

Embellishments

What milliners have done over the past years in using textiles as a sculptural medium is amazing. Anything and everything has been perched on a hat.

Interesting feathers, birds, flowers, ribbons, or other novelty decorations can be valuable in their own right, even if a hat is in poor condition.

Condition

Hats are nearly impossible to clean satisfactorily because it is next to impossible to guess what dyes, stiffeners, sizings, or other materials were used to color, shape, and decorate hats. The safest and best approach is to go for hats that are still in very good condition, and don't require cleaning.

Materials in good condition are supple, resilient, and lively. Materials in poor condition tend to be brittle, stiff, dry, and inflexible. Fading often is a sign that the material, as well as the color, has deteriorated.

Holding a hat up to the light can serve as a form of X-ray to detect repairs, moth holes, tears, and patches.

Details of the decorations reflect the imagination and creativity of the milliner. Petals on the large colorful flower on this hat were made of a transparent felted fabric over silk. Photo courtesy of Red Balloons, Clarence, New York.

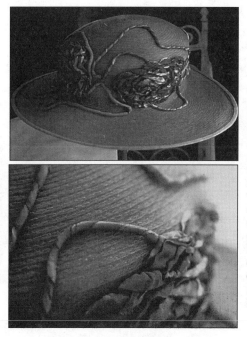

Shape of the hat, the nuances of color, and the imagination skill and creativity of the milliner all make this hat a success. Like a clever sculptor, the milliner has coiled silk ribbon in variegated shades of pink, red, and orange around the crown, and formed a large cabbage rose on this hat. Photo courtesy of Red Balloons, Clarence, New York.

Pieces & prices

Lilly Daché brown felt hat, circa 1930s, with small crown and large upturned brim, heraldic crest worked in gold thread. Labeled Lilly Daché Pairs New York 78 East 56th St. Good condition. Sold at auction for $92.

Hattie Carnegie, 1940s, natural straw hat with pearl band trim. Sold at auction for $34.

Lilly Daché brown felt fedora from the 1940s, with beige grosgrain band, labeled Lilly Daché Paris New York 78 East 56th St. Very good condition. Sold at auction for $46.

Lilly Daché hat, circa 1950s, of light blue straw with half-brim of navy velvet trimmed with wired self-bow. Labeled Lilly Daché New York. Very good condition. Sold at auction for $34.

Head-hugging Masquerade hat by Schiaparelli, 1950s, covered with shocking pink pleated chiffon decorated with bird-shaped spangles and a black velvet mask at the back. In original box. Labeled Schiaparelli Paris. Sold at auction for $258.

Hattie Carnegie cocktail hat, 1950s, of black smooth plush with black osprey feather spray. Labeled. Sold at auction for $23.

Shocking pink pillbox from the 1960s, of silk satin with propeller-like decorations, labeled Emme Inc., New York. Good condition. Sold at auction for $57.

Halston black rose hat from the 1960s, chignon-sized, of woven black straw, with black satin streamers. Labeled Made to Order Bergdorf Goodman on the Plaza - New York. Sold at auction for $143.

Black silk crepe bonnet, circa 1850-69, decorated with black grosgrain ribbon. From the Collection of the Allen Art Museum, Oberlin, Ohio, Gift of Mrs. Howard T. Fewell, 1953, L1995.17.47. Photo courtesy of Kent State University Museum.

American spoon bonnet, circa 1857-64, of dark straw, decorated with green and brown striped silk taffeta ribbons, and black velvet. Kent State University Museum, Gift of Mrs. Richard Silver in memory of Constance Roosevelt Andrus and Laura Gladys Roosevelt, 1994.48.19.

Circa 1900 helmet style silk hat. Large petals covering the crown of the hat are in turn covered with tiny flocked flowers in various shades of pale and deeper shades of lavender. Crown is topped with a cluster of silk roses. No label. Some deterioration of the fabric. $150. Photo courtesy of Nancy Pratt, Vintage Furs and Apparel, Libertyville, Illinois.

Large-brimmed lacy horsehair hat, circa 1918. Made by M. Hoye in Mendota, Illinois. $125 to $150. Photo courtesy of Nancy Pratt, Vintage Furs and Apparel, Libertyville, Illinois.

Selection of 1920s boudoir caps of silk, tulle, ribbon, and crochet lace. Ruffled silk ribbon flowers, imaginative use of dimension in the crochet flowers, and other details make these exceptional. Prices range from $60 to $120. Photos courtesy of Red Balloons, Clarence, New York.

Purple felt hat with bird wings and feathers in tropical colors. Made by Bo-Vee, a Chicago milliner in the 1920s. Mint condition. $200. Photo courtesy of Nancy Pratt, Vintage Furs and Apparel, Libertyville, Illinois.

Fuchsia ostrich feather pompom covers a small felt pod, black felt ring holds this 1940s hat on the head. No label. $40. Photo courtesy of Nancy Pratt, Vintage Furs and Apparel, Libertyville, Illinois.

Christian Dior turban from the 1950s, of olive mohair with mauve and pink feathers. $100. Photo courtesy of Nancy Pratt, Vintage Furs and Apparel, Libertyville, Illinois.

Sources

Books

Langley, Susan, *Vintage Hats and Bonnets 1770-1970*, Collector Books, Paducah, Kentucky, 1998.

Smith, Desire, *Wearable Fashions 1920-1965*, Schiffer, 1998.

Dealers

Nancy Pratt
203 Sunset Drive
Libertyville, IL 60048
Phone 847-367-8456
Shows and by appointment. Also exhibiting at Volo Antique Malls II and III, Volo, IL. Does lectures on hats and clothing, 1890s through 1940s. Vintage furs, apparel, and hats.

Mallory and Jeanette Merrill
Red Balloons
10912 Main St.
Clarence, NY
Phone 716-759-8999
Shop with exquisite and rare vintage linens, lace, clothing, lingerie, hats, paisleys, unique Victorian textiles and textile arts.

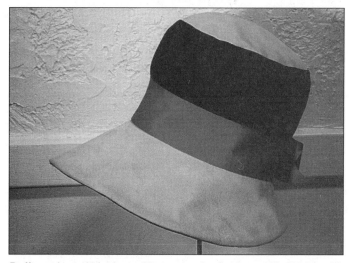

Buff suede and black wool jersey hat by Schiaparelli, 1960s, with red grosgrain ribbon band. $150.

Cindy Warrington
The Blue Parrot
Springfield, IL
Phone 217-793-2986
Vintage clothing for men and women. Hats, early 20s to 50s vintage. Shows and by appointment.

Lace Accessories

Lace collars, scarves, and fichus from the nineteenth century onward are plentiful. Depending on the fashion cycle, these can be in demand or impossible to sell. The market right now is in flux. There is some slowly growing interest in lace for fashion. The most popular lace accessories are small, cape-like pelerines and fichus, and large impressive collars. Those who want wearable collars seldom care if the lace is handmade or machine, as long as the design is great and the condition is very good.

Lace collectors are extremely selective. Only the most unusual examples with superb or unusual stitching and special designs will catch their eye and make them open their purses. It has been a buyers market for so long, with so few informed dealers that collectors have developed the patience to wait for the magic find: when a dealer who has no knowledge of what they have offers a superb piece at a great bargain.

Average quality collars are much more difficult to sell. Those made of coarse thread, with boring designs and sloppy workmanship are almost impossible to sell at any price. They have stitching that doesn't interest collectors, and are not pretty enough to be usable or wearable.

With growing interest in reenactments, the market condition could, however, change dramatically at any time.

✔ Checklist

Thread

Good, quality lace depends on thread choice. The thread should be tightly spun of long staple fibers so it is firm and strong. It should be even, and not slubby.

Thread should be heavy enough to make a well balanced lace that does not appear stringy and loose, and is light enough to define the design without looking dense.

Design

Look at the overall design of the piece. Was the lace designed for the space, or was a space simply filled with scrolling tapes or a mixed assortment of motifs?

Follow the lines of the design in the lace. Odd or errant lines and abruptly cut edges in a motif often mean the lace is remodeled, or assembled from bits and pieces of old lace.

Learn to recognize what motifs are common and which are unusual for different styles of handmade lace.

Technique and workmanship

Look closely at each feature of the lace: clothwork, outline or edge of each motif, mesh or bars, and ornamental stitches, to see how the lace itself was made. Because lace accessories still are comparatively modestly priced, prices for collars made of very fine handmade lace often are nearly the same as prices for machine-made or ordinary quality lace.

Use a good magnifying glass. The fine details that define good handmade lace are not always visible to the naked eye.

Condition

Hold the lace up to the light. Follow the lines of the lace. They should appear logical and graceful. Abrupt shifts or ends in the line often signal repairs, alterations, or patchworks.

Stains that go clear through the fibers and appear dense and deep brown usually mean the fibers are damaged, and the stain will not come out without leaving a hole. If the lace is assembled from small motifs, it may be possible to replace a few stained ones. If the lace is made of continuous threads, it is more difficult to repair.

Tears and breaks in the thread are difficult to repair, especially when the thread is of poor quality. The breaks are a sign of shredding.

Fichus

Fichus were scarf-like accessories. They are long in the front, and rounded like a small cape or large collar in the back. They were particularly popular at the beginning of the nineteenth century, worn over fine figure-hugging muslin dresses with deep scoop necks, and were worn nearly to the middle of the nineteenth century, as sleeves and skirts began to puff out.

Early 19th century fichu of fine white cotton muslin, decorated with machine-embroidery and drawnwork, and edged with 2 inches of handmade Valenciennes lace. 10 inches deep at center back, 54 inches long. Excellent condition. Sold for $450.

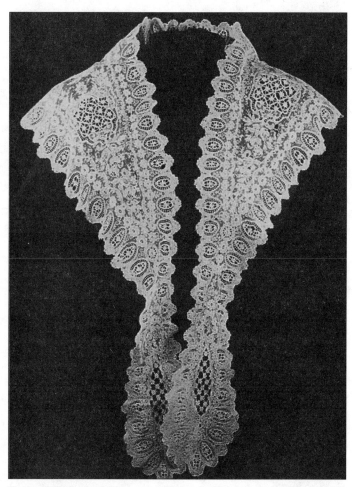

Early 19th century fichu, combining bobbin and needle lace. 13 inches deep at center back, over 65 inches long. Excellent condition. Sold for $485.

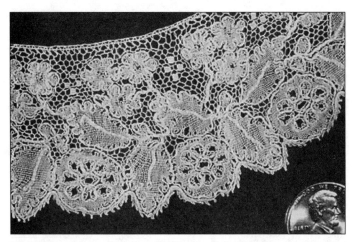

Mid-19th century handmade Bucks Point bobbin lace collar. Quality of the lace is good, and collar might attract a collector if the price were under $100.

Two handmade Bedfordshire bobbin lace collars. Both are ordinary quality, typical of the mid 19th century when lacemakers were cutting corners, speeding up work, and simplifying designs while trying to compete with machines. These would sell today for under $50.

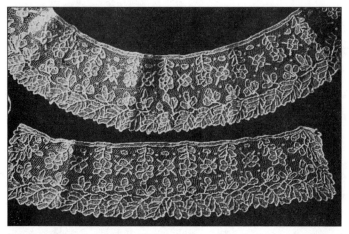

Design of this handmade Point de Gaze needle lace collar is not exceptional enough to attract a collector, and too fragile to wear. That makes it difficult to sell. Tears also detract from the value. About 2 inches deep. Would sell for $45 to $100.

Collars

From about the middle to the end of the nineteenth century, small round collars were an everyday accent on plain day dresses. Necklines in the mid nineteenth century were small, and often are too small and tight to be worn by women today. Often, however, they are suitable for children's dresses.

Larger collars and berthes were used for more formal wear.

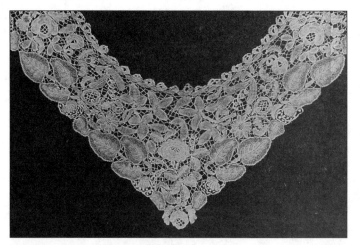

Honiton collar, with design of shamrocks, roses, and thistles. About 6 inches deep at center back, and about 28 inches long. Sold for $275.

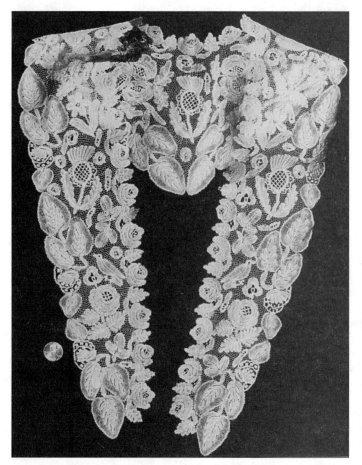

Honiton collar, mid-19th century. Design of roses and flowers, with a small bird on each lapel. 6-1/2 inches deep at center back, 48 inches long. Excellent condition. Sold for $425.

Circa 1900 collars

High, tight collars are the style known as chokers and were popular from the end of the nineteenth into the beginning of the twentieth centuries.

Most often, they are found with bad cases of ring-around-the neckline because they were so high and so tight. They rarely were made of good quality lace, however, and usually are no great loss.

Tape laces, Irish crochet, and other hand-crafted laces were typical.

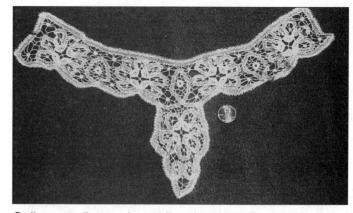

Ordinary quality tape lace collar, circa 1900. Design consists of little more than swirling, looping tapes. Workmanship and technique are very ordinary — just a few stem-stitch wheels and looping stitches. Prices for simple tape lace chokers seldom go above $25.

Good quality tape lace collar, circa 1900. Tapes are fine quality, complex design imitated Belgian Bruges bobbin lace flowers, leaves, and scrollwork. Filling stitches are varied, decorative, and structurally sound. Should sell for about $100.

Berthes

Lace berthes were long lace pieces designed to be worn off the shoulder. When laid flat, they form more than a complete circle, typically a circle and a half. They were especially popular in the mid nineteenth century, when elegant evening gowns with deep necklines and bare shoulders were in vogue.

They are popular today because they are so long, and can be worn many ways, including tied loosely as a scarf, or ruffled down the front of a V-neck dress.

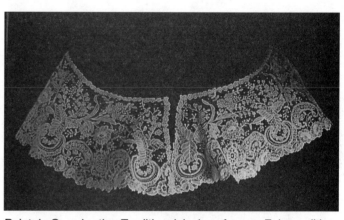

Point de Gaze berthe. Traditional design of roses. Fair condition, some tears in the mesh. 6 inches deep, 90 inches long. $425.

Mid-19th century berthe. This example is typical Brussels Mixed lace, combining Duchesse bobbin lace flowers with inserts of Point de Gaze needle lace roses inside the bobbin lace scrollwork. Ecru, excellent condition, 6 inches deep, 50 inches long. $425.

Bruges bobbin lace berthe, mid 19th century Belgian. Scrolling design with stylized flowers, and hexagonal background of braided bars decorated with thorn-like picots is typical. White, excellent condition, 7 inches deep, 42 inches long at top edge. $425.

Plastrons and stomachers

Triangular lace decorations known as stomachers were popular in the seventeenth and eighteenth centuries. They were worn between the waist and breast. In the late nineteenth century, they were worn higher, just below the neckline, and were known as plastrons.

Very few seventeenth century lace stomachers survive today. Nineteenth century plastrons, often in sets with matching cuffs, are not uncommon in the market today. A complete set dating from the late 1800s also might include a high, choker-style collar and a pair of cuffs. Circa-1900 plastrons were worked in needle lace in designs copied from the seventeenth century, and sometimes are mistaken for earlier lace.

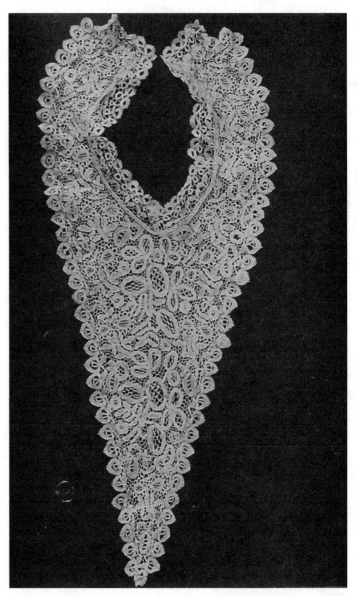

Honiton choker collar combined with plastron, circa 1900. Design is busy and disorganized, motifs are poorly formed, nearly unrecognizable flowers and leaves. $125.

Paisley Shawls

At the end of the 1700s manufacturers introduced large, soft woolen shawls decoratively woven with colorful patterns that were worn as a head covering or shoulder mantle. These were imported to Europe and the United States from Kashmere in India. The name Kashmere or cashmere shawl applied both to the source, and to the fine woolen fiber used to make them.

Fabulously beautiful and equally expensive, these hand-woven shawls became an indispensable accessory for the very rich. As with any high priced status symbol, these shawls were quickly targeted by manufacturers. Weavers in Scotland, Turkey, and France quickly began competing with India for this lucrative market, each using their own distinct weaving methods.

Some shawls were woven as complete, continuous pieces of cloth. More often, they were made in sections, then joined. The seams often are nearly invisible. Other shawls were made from individual motifs that were assembled on a solid ground, still others have been remodeled after sections were rescued from worn shawls and reused.

The finest shawls, made for the high-fashion market, evolved as fashion changed, and generally adhered to classic styles, designs, and shapes. Cheap knockoffs are far more unpredictable and more difficult to place and date.

Until a nineteenth century shawl is unfolded in front of you, it is difficult to comprehend how enormous many of these shawls are. The mid nineteenth century shawls were designed to be worn instead of a winter coat over the huge hoop skirts, and they are larger and heavier than many king-sized blankets. Because they are so large, it is difficult to find a suitable use or display space for them today. Probably for that reason, they are far undervalued and unappreciated today.

The early nineteenth century Indian Kashmiri shawls, truly made of cashmere wool, are especially undervalued. Because they have been relatively low-priced for several decades, many have been cut up and reused as fabric for coats, skirts, and capes.

The Parts of the Paisley Shawl

1. Field (reserve): the central, usually undecorated area in the center of the shawl.

2. Vertical border

3. Horizontal borders: outer horizontal, main border, and inner horizontal borders.

4. The border that encircles the center field is called a gallery. This may consist of two parts, a wider outside border, and an inner border called a secondary or counter gallery.

5. Corner motifs.

The shawls almost always are edged with a fringe. On long rectangular shawls, the fringe appears on the two horizontal edges. A square shawl sometimes has fringe on all sides.

Pointy-ended oval motif usually is called a paisley motif, a name taken from the town of Paisley in Scotland, renowned for manufacture of shawls. This motif also is known as a pine, pine cone, or "boteh," from the Turkish, or "buta" from the Persian.

Example shown is an early 19th century French shawl, with a cream wool center. Cones, flowerheads, and medallions are worked in green, red, blue, and yellow. 39 inches by 57 inches. Sold at auction for about $650. Photo courtesy of Phillips Auction, London.

✔ Checklist

Fibers

The original shawls, known as Cashmere or Kashmir, were named for the fine goat's hair fiber used to make them. Cashmere is extremely fine and soft; softer and finer still is Pashmina.

The European drawlooms and continuous-weft weaving technique put considerably more stress on the warp threads than the Indian handlooms. Fine wool would shred in this process, so European shawls were usually made with silk warps, or wool-wrapped silk.

Weaving techniques

Many shawls were woven as a twill, where warp and weft threads pass over and under two threads, or three over three threads and under one, resulting in a weave with barely perceptible diagonal lines.

Many Indian shawls made from the middle of the nineteenth century are made of a patchwork of small twill-tapestry pieces sewn together, a technique known as "tilikar." This method was faster and cheaper than weaving a continuous shawl because several weavers could be working at the same time.

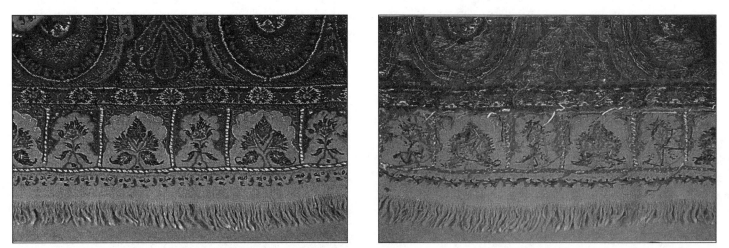

Indian twill tapestry shawl, 1983.1.2233. Indian (Kashmiri) shawls were woven by hand using a tapestry technique. The weft threads did not continue from edge (selvage) to edge. Different color yarns were wrapped around small shuttles or bobbins, and woven only in the small area that called for each specific color. This technique is called espoliné. A tiny ridge, often visible only with a magnifying glass, shows up on the back side where colors change. Photo courtesy of the Kent State University Museum, Kent, Ohio.

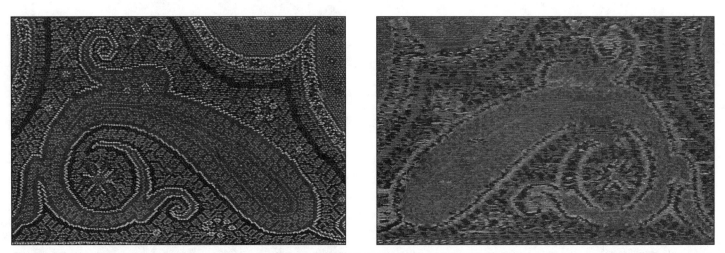

European shawls were woven with continuous weft threads. When a color was not used in the design, it was carried or floated across the back. This technique is called au lancé. The floats often were trimmed off after the shawl was finished. Thus, the back side of the shawl often is fuzzy with trimmed threads. Photo courtesy of the Kent State University Museum, Kent, Ohio. 1986.126.2.

Design

The design of the shawls took several basic forms:

A burnous shawl was designed to be worn like a cape without folding. The plain reserve area was placed along one side.

In a filled ground shawl, the entire shawl was covered with ornamental patterns. There was no plain central reserve.

Harlequin shawls had horizontal edges decorated with patterned rectangles.

Lopsided shawls had only one main border.

A Medallion shawl was typically square, with one large medallion in the center, and a quarter medallion in each corner.

Striped shawls had small motifs, often tiny paisleys, arranged along colored stripes.

Turnover shawls were designed to be worn folded. Wide borders were sewn on two sides at right angles, two narrow borders were sewn on reversed, so they showed their right side when the shawl was folded into a triangle.

The basic design element that defined the paisley shawl was the distinctive pointed oval known variously as the paisley, pine cone, pine, boteh (Turkish) or buta (Persian).

The number, size, and arrangement of these motifs often help date the shawls.

Circa 1800-1810

Central plain solid color field extremely large.

Pine cone motifs quite small, often ten to a side.

Circa 1810-1820

Corner ornaments introduced after 1810.

Gallery introduced.

1820-1830

Number of pine cones reduced in number, usually eight to a side, and increased in size.

Secondary gallery introduced about 1825.

1820-1830

Center field continued to reduce in size.

Horizontal edges typically finished off with narrow multicolor band.

Circa 1830-1840

Horizontal edges evolve into ornamental rectangles of different colors called a harlequin.

Circa 1840-1850

Harlequin edges become several inches deep, and composed of highly ornamented rectangles.

Huge pine cones (paisleys), sometimes over a yard long, pivot around a very small plain center.

Shawls often as wide as 65 inches.

Pieces & prices

Early 19th century Paisley shawl with bright red central area with feathery floral and foliate forms. End design with three large cones in maroon, blue, and pink. Length 9 feet, width 21 inches. Very good condition. Sold at auction for $150.

Paisley shawl woven with large palmette and wide border in shades of red, olive, black, and white. Black star center. Good condition, fragile center. Length 64 inches, width 69 inches. Sold at auction for $250.

Paisley shawl, French, 1860s. Woven with enormous swirling cones in shades of red, blue, green, and gold. Black star center with two fleurs de lis. White woven signature. Length 11 feet, 2 inches, width 64 inches. Very good condition. Sold at auction for $1000

Embroidered Kashmir shawl, mid 19th century. Intricate pattern of elongated swirling cones and palmettes in a rainbow of colors, with a black star center, harlequin borders. 76 inches square. Some damage, holes, repair. Sold at auction for $260

Square Paisley shawl, mid 19th century. Design of palmettes at each corner, quatrefoil black center, woven in red, green, and black. Peaked harlequin border. 70 inches square. Very good condition. Sold at auction for $200

Double-sided Paisley throw, 20th century. Silk and wool in shades of rust, brown, black, and gold. 68 inches by 71 inches. Excellent condition. Sold at auction for $250

Paisley shawl, mid 19th century. Design of arches in shades of red, gold, blue, and white with a large black center, harlequin border. 70 inches by 70 inches. Fair condition, some holes. Sold at auction for $300.

Left to right: French Paisley shawl, circa 1860s. Enormous swirling cones in shades of red, blue, green, and gold, and small star-shaped black center with white signature. Two fleurs de lis off the center. 11 feet long, 64 inches wide. Very good condition. Sold at auction for $1,000

Scottish Paisley shawl, mid 19th century. Unusual red and white center, borders of swirling paisleys in shades of deep purple and green, feathery flowers encroaching on the center. 10 feet long, 5 feet wide. Very good condition. Sold at auction for $2,200.

Indian Kashmir fold-over shawl, mid 19th century. Two wide and two narrow borders at right angles woven in a wide range of muted colors around a large central black reserve. One enormous cone brackets one corner. Embroidered flowers around the reserve, and in the harlequin borders. 6 feet by 68 inches. Did not sell at auction. Photo courtesy of William Doyle Galleries, New York City.

Red wool square turnover shawl, with single motif applied to the corner. Condition very good. Offered for $120. Photo courtesy of Another Time, Caledonia, New York.

Shawls shown on easels behind figures, left to right: Square "lopsided" shawl with ivory field. Europe, possibly France, late 1820s to early 1830s. Pieced, woven au lancé in a 3/1 twill. The floats across the back have been trimmed. Both warp and weft are wool. Part of the Shannon Rodgers Collection, 1986.97.39.

Square European shawl, circa 1835-1845, with light blue field. Wool warp and silk or cotton weft, pieced, woven au lancé in a 3/1 twill. The floats across the back have been trimmed. Part of the Silverman/Rodgers Collection, 1983.1.1550.

Square European shawl, late 1820s to 1844, with corner-ornamented ivory field. Wool warp and weft, woven au lancé in a 3/1 twill. The floats across the back have been trimmed. Part of the Silverman/Rodgers Collection, 1983-1.1.1542. Photo courtesy of Kent State University Museum

Left to right: Tilikar (pieced) shawl, Kashmir, India, mid 1960s. Tapestry weave in a 2/2 twill, with wool warp and weft. Outer borders are embroidered. Collection of the Allen Art Museum, Oberlin, Ohio, gift of Catherine H. and Laura M. Dwight, 1949, L 1995.17.1037.
Long tilikar (pieced) shawl, Kashmir, India, circa mid 1860s to 1870s. Tapestry weave in a 2/2 twill, with wool warp and weft. Outer borders are embroidered. Kent State University Museum, Silverman/Rodgers Collection, 1983.1.1544.
Long tilikar (pieced) shawl, Kashmir, India, circa 1855-1870. Tapestry weave in a 2/2 twill, with wool warp and weft, and embroidered outer borders. Collection of the Allen Art Museum, Oberlin, Ohio, gift of Clarence Ward, 1950, L 1995.17.727.
Long tilikar (pieced) shawl, Kashmir, India, circa 1855-1870. Tapestry weave in a 2/2 twill, with wool warp and weft, and embroidered outer borders. Kent State University Museum, Silverman/Rodgers Collection, 1983.1.1541. Photo courtesy of the Kent State University Museum.

Sources

Book

Rossbach, Ed; The Art of Paisley, Van Nostrand Reinhold, 1980, New York

Collections

Chicago Art Institute
Textile Department
Michigan Avenue
Chicago, Illinois

Kent State University Museum
Kent, OH 44242-0001
Phone 330-672-3451
Fax 330-672-3218

Val Arbab
Box 684
La Jolla, CA 92038-0684
619-453-4686
FAX 619-457-3647
Expert.

Dealers

Robert Walker
Just Faboo
107 East Main St.
P.O. Box 3913
Midway, KY (Lexington area) 40347
Phone 606-846-5606
justfaboo@aol.com
1780-1920 high quality vintage fashions, paisleys. Large shop, shows, and by appointment.

Mallory and Jeanette Merrill
Red Balloons
10912 Main St.
Clarence, NY
Phone 716-759-8999
Shop with exquisite and rare vintage linens, lace, clothing, lingerie, hats, paisleys, unique Victorian textiles and textile arts.

Laura Fisher
1050 Second Avenue, Gallery 84
New York, NY 10022
Phone 212-838-2596
Antique quilts, hooked rugs, paisleys, coverlets.

Jean Hoffman
207 East 66th St.
New York, NY 10021
Phone 212-535-6930
Bridal veils, paisleys, lace handkerchiefs. Extensive collection of top quality vintage wedding dresses, petit point bags.

Auctions

William Doyle Galleries
175 East 87th Street
New York, NY 10128
Phone 212-427-2730
Fax 212-369-0892
www.doylegalleries.com
Doyle holds occasional couture and textile auctions which almost always include some paisleys.

Phillips International Auctioneers
101 New Bond Street
London, W1Y OAS
Phone 44-171-629-6602 (textile department)
New York phone for catalogs and sale information 212-570-4830 Regular sales of textiles, about 6 per year, include European band, spot, and European and American needlework samplers from the seventeenth through the nineteenth centuries.

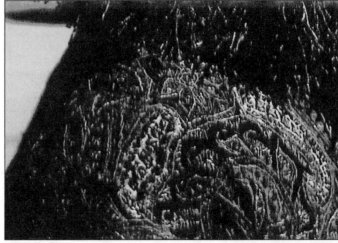

Paisley woven fabrics often were cut up to make coats, capes, and other garments. This long coat-like paisley cape, however, hangs straight in the front, and is bell-shaped in the back, designed to fit over a circa-1870s dress. It is not a remodeled paisley shawl, but a garment made for its time. Woven in red, shades of brown, blue, and green wool and silk. Offered for $3,200. Photo courtesy of Just Faboo, Midway, Kentucky.

Children's Dresses

Children's dresses, especially baby dresses, are especially popular because they can be used to dress dolls, and because they are small enough to display easily. In spite of their popularity, prices still are very reasonable when the quality and prices of vintage are compared with the quality and prices of new baby dresses.

✔ Checklist

Fabrics

Very fine cotton fabrics, often the weight of handkerchiefs, often are used for nineteenth and early twentieth century children's dresses.

Technique and workmanship

The handworked detail on vintage baby dresses, both homemade and commercial, often includes meticulous tiny tucks, microscopic embroidered flowers, and perfectly finished seams, edges, and hems. The fine sewing often makes these tiny vintage garments truly couture.

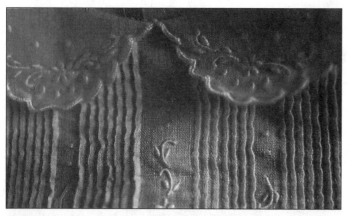

Edges, such as collars, cuffs, and hems, often are finished off with nearly microscopic, nearly perfect handmade buttonhole stitches. Subtle hand stitched details, like tiny tucks, and white-on-white embroidery, often decorate baby clothes.

Seams on many baby dresses were trimmed, folded, and stitched, a type of seam sometimes called a flat fell seam. Often, all edges are finished off by hand to keep the fine delicate fabric from fraying. Detail shown here is where the puffed sleeve joined the shoulder seam on a baby dress.

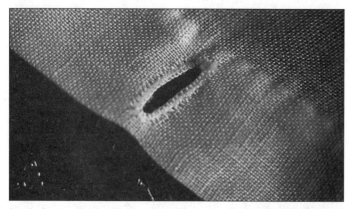

Look for meticulously handmade button holes, each carefully edged with buttonhole stitches. Note the precise and almost invisible hand stitching that secures the folded edge.

Edges and corners on hand-worked baby clothes often are extremely neat and precise.

Early 20th century baby dress of fine handkerchief-weight cotton. Dress front is decorated with fine drawnwork and embroidery. Edges are hand finished with buttonhole stitches. Offered for $25. Photo courtesy of Aldon Antiques, Kalamazoo, Michigan.

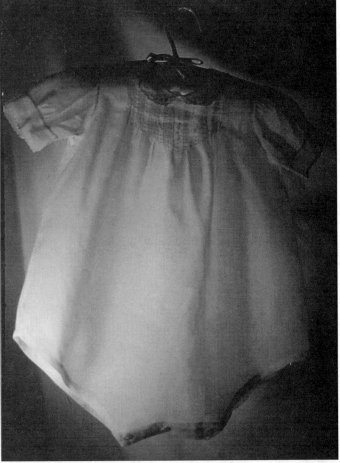

Baby dress, possibly for a boy, designed to be buttoned between the legs. The front of the dress has a cluster of tiny embroidered flowers. Collar is finished off with buttonhole stitches, front of bodice is decorated with tiny tucks. Edges are carefully mitered, and finished off. Photo courtesy of Aldon's Antiques, Kalamazoo, Michigan.

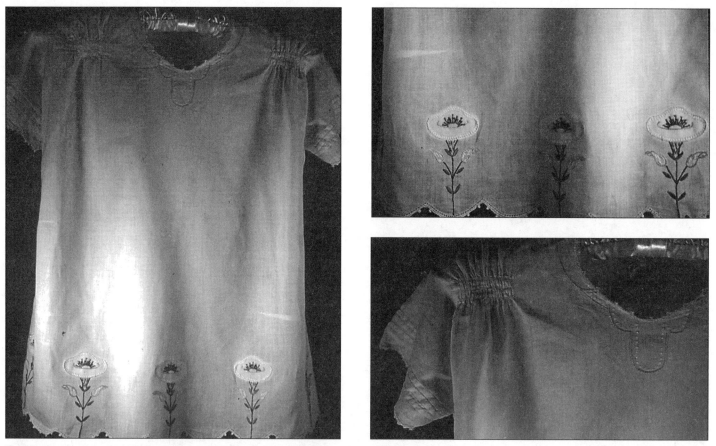

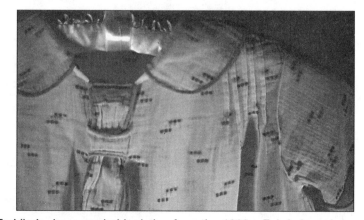

Toddler's dress, probably from the 1930s. Skirt is decorated with appliqué flowers in pink. (Note the similarity of these flowers and appliqué flowers on table linens of the same era.) Dress is shaped with darts on each side, and with a cluster of gathers at the shoulders. Offered for $25. Photo courtesy of Aldon's Antiques, Kalamazoo, Michigan.

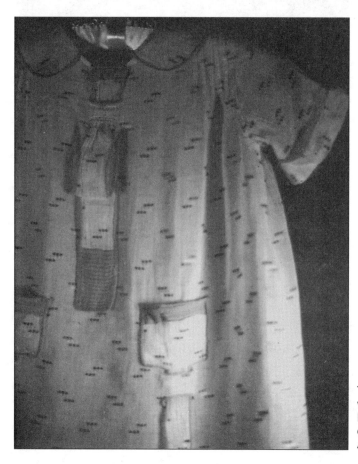

Toddler's dress, probably dating from the 1930s. Fabric is a sheer white cotton dotted Swiss with teal blue, yellow, and tangerine dots. Dress, pockets, and tabs are decorated with rows of tiny tucks and edged with tangerine bias tape. Offered for $35. Photo courtesy of Aldon's Antiques, Kalamazoo, Michigan.

Christening Gowns

Christening gowns have not yet been discovered as a collectible. Many families have a special one that is handed down through the generations, and never goes outside the family. Other times it becomes fashionable to have a special dress made from the bride's wedding gown fabric.

It was not until the late eighteenth century that a special gown-like garment was used for Christenings. Prior to that, a heavily decorated mantle was wrapped around the baby. Some of the most valuable and collectible Christening outfits are the little shirts, decorated with shoulder inserts of Hollie Point lace, that were worn under the mantle. This subtle lace is made with a tiny knotting stitch, and minute designs appear as patterns of holes in a knotted background.

Long white dresses that we recognize today as Christening gowns really came into being at the beginning of the nineteenth century. The most spectacular and valuable of these were the Ayrshire gowns, elegant confections of white drawnwork, cutwork, and embroidery on a fine, nearly transparent cotton fabric.

Family Christening gowns hold great potential as special heirlooms and collectibles because they so often are homemade, and are related to such a special event in life. Individual family dresses should be documented, especially with notes of who made the dress and when, and pictures of the babies that have been Christened in the dress.

✔ Checklist

Materials

Fine, nearly transparent cotton was traditional fabric in the early 1800s. Later in the century, heavier cottons were used.

In the twentieth century, the fashion to make Christening gowns of other materials, such as satin, velvet, and other pieces of wedding gowns was fashionable.

Look very carefully at each element of the gown including the sleeves, bodice, and skirt panels. It is not at all uncommon for gowns to be remodeled with the styles of the time or taste of the owner. One of the most common alterations was to add long sleeves to a cap-sleeved gown from the early 1800s, retaining the caps to use as cuffs.

The difference in fabric may be only a slight difference in weight, texture, or shade of white. It is not uncommon for the difference to only be visible with a magnifying glass.

Embellishments

Early nineteenth century Christening gowns were decorated with hand embroidery. Ayrshire embroidery is especially valuable. It consists of fine floral gardens of embroidery, mostly in satin stitch and drawnwork. It's often decorated with embroidery, and in the flower centers, clusters and ladder-like trails of small cutwork holes with tiny bits of needle lace in some of the cutwork holes. Broderie Anglaise, consisting of bold patterns of cut holes edged with overcast stitch, was worked by hand until the end of the nineteenth century.

Lace trim often included handmade Bucks Point bobbin lace, often called baby lace, and handmade Valenciennes bobbin lace. Both typically used small patterns suitable for baby dresses. Just as it was fashionable to appliqué lace onto machine net for adult fashions, bobbin lace and needle lace motifs were stitched onto net for Christening gowns. As soon as fully patterned laces were developed in the middle of the nineteenth century, they were used to decorate Christening gowns.

Embellishments cannot be trusted as a way of dating a gown, because they often were added as part of remodeling. On the other hand, however, trimmings that don't match up in time with the rest of the materials can be a good indication of remodeling.

Shape and style

Shape of bodice, neckline and method of fastening, length and type of sleeves, placement and style of waistline and/or yoke all are important clues to the date, and provide clues as to whether any remodeling has been done.

In the early 1800s, up until about 1840, the style was for short sleeves or only a small cap sleeve, a wide neckline, a triangular front on the bodice.

Skirts in the early nineteenth century were exceptionally long, often from 39 to 42 inches long.

A robe front, or wide panel gathered into a point at the center of the waist, and surrounded on both sides by inch-wide embroidered or lace trimmed "wings" was popular from the first part of the nineteenth century to the middle. The panel was often heavily embroidered, or was made up of carefully hand stitched rows of lace and embroidery.

Skirts gradually got shorter as the nineteenth century progressed.

The triangular front on the bodice gradually disappeared after the middle of the nineteenth century.

Bodices at the end of the nineteenth century were shortened to more of a yoke, the waist moved up to chest level.

After the turn of the twentieth century, all styles were used, as homemakers began making dresses based on historical styles as well as remodeling vintage gowns.

The most common twentieth century style was a standard waistline placement, with a skirt about twelve to fifteen inches long. Long sleeves became more popular than short in the twentieth century.

Workmanship

Hand-stitching on early gowns was microscopic and perfectly uniform. It boggles the mind, and often is mistaken for machine because of its perfection.

Skirts were gathered into perfect microscopic pleats in early nineteenth century dresses.

Sewing machines were invented in the mid nineteenth century, and by the end of the 1870s, were readily available to nearly every homemaker.

Many early baby clothes, including Christening gowns, had strings or little cotton ribbons in the neckline and at the waist to adjust the size for different babies. These were typically hidden in casings and seams.

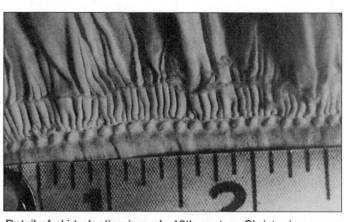

Detail of skirt pleating in early 19th century Christening gown. Handstitched pleats were often about an eighth of an inch in depth, and about twenty per inch.

Mid 19th century Christening gown with triangular bodice and robe front hand-sewn of little strips of handmade Valenciennes lace, and hand-embroidered whitework. Side wings trimmed with handmade Valenciennes. Some small tears between piecework. Owner will not part with this dress for less than $850.

Piecework panel in skirt front.

All lacemaking, embroidery, and piecing was meticulously done by hand.

Pieces & prices

Late nineteenth century Christening ensemble consisting of an ivory silk coat decorated with embroidery, cream braid, and machine lace. Gown is of ivory cotton with Broderie Anglaise and topstitiching. Sold at auction for $115.

Victorian Christening ensemble, circa 1890s. High-waisted open-front gown and detachable capes of ivory silk rep with padded and quilted lining. Both pieces trimmed with chemical lace and pleated China silk ruffles. Good condition, some discoloration. Sold at auction for $150.

Mid to late twentieth century home-sewn Christening gown, some machine stitched tucking, trimmed with narrow machine made lace. $45.

Sources
Dealer

Phillips International Auctioneers
101 New Bond Street
London, W1Y OAS
Phone 44-171-629-6602 (textile department)
New York phone for catalogs and sale information 212-570-4830 Regular sales of textiles, about 6 per year, often include children's clothing, and Christening gowns.

Between the 19th and 20th centuries, Christening gowns got much shorter. The skirt on the longer one, late 19th century, 39 inches long, is attached to a short yoke-style bodice. It is decorated with several rows of machine-made lace, embroidery, and tucking at the bottom of the skirt. Long sleeves are trimmed with machine lace. The shorter, early 20th century, also is attached to a yoke style bodice, and is about 30 inches long.

Circa 1940 Christening gown, made by the author's mother, and worn by the author, her sister, and her nieces and nephew. It is trimmed with numerous tucks and narrow machine lace. Slip was made from the same fabric, and trimmed with matching lace. Tucks on the slip are designed to show through the transparent material of the dress, but not compete in decoration. Dress is not for sale.

Heavily damaged and repaired Christening gown, purchased for $25, is fascinating for the stories it suggests and tells. Notes that accompanied the gown read: "My mother, and all of grandma Pratte's children, all of the Myers' children, starting with me, and my children were baptized in this dress," and: "The note was written by Maria Myers Moses, who was born in 1885. Her mother (Matilda Pratte Myers) who is referred to in the note, was born in 1965."

The question then becomes, does this make sense? Do the material, design, and workmanship fit with that time? The fabric is very fine cotton. Although the style is not the same as a mid 19th century high fashion commercial gowns shown elsewhere in this section, it is not inconsistent with homemade mid 19th century clothing.

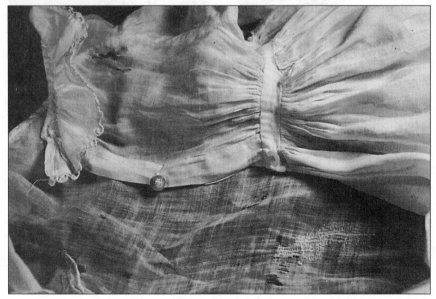

Features: The front and skirt are made from a single piece of cloth. The skirt is gathered in the back, and attached to the two side sections of the bodice back. Although there is heavy damage, it seems apparent that the skirt originally was precisely hand pleated using the typical 19th century technique. Drawstrings at the waist suggest it was somehow gathered to fit different sized babies.

There is extensive, and careful hand-darning of the fabric where it has worn and torn.

The sleeves are long, with seams at each side. The ruffle at the neckline is badly stained. This is not surprising since babies spit up and drool, and the first thing to be stained is the neckline.

The crochet and tape lace attached to the bottom is actually too heavy to fit gracefully with the rest of the fine dress fabric. It is consistent, however, with crochet and folded ribbon designs offered in Godey's and other fashion magazines of the mid to late 19th century, and also would be consistent with a homemade, home-designed dress. The dress, including the seams and rows of decorative tucks in the skirt, were stitched by hand.

Net Christening gown decorated with machine tapes and embroidery, a technique often called Princess lace. This was especially popular at the end of the 19th and in the early 20th century. Dress is from the collection of The Lace Museum, Sunnyvale, California.

Christening gowns are notoriously hard to date with any reliability. Handmade motifs of English Honiton bobbin lace are applied to a machine-made net in this Christening gown. The triangular bodice front was typical of early 19th century Christening gown styles, but Art Nouveau flavor of the lace motifs is more typical of the late 19th or early 20th century.

Skirt front of Ayrshire gown, circa 1830-1840, with extensive whitework embroidery on center robe front and wings. Embroidery includes cutwork with needle lace inserts. Triangular bodice front, short sleeves, skirt 39 inches long. Sold for $585.

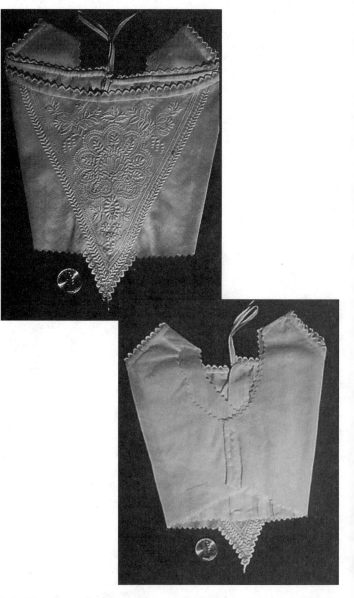

Bodice front of Ayrshire gown.

A bodice for a Christening gown that was never used, dating from the first half of the 19th century. Embroidery technique is Ayrshire. According to tradition, the pointed bodice front indicates the dress was for a boy. If the dress was used later for a girl, the point would be tucked into a slit in the waistband. Sold for about $100.

Left: Robe l'Anglaise, 18th century, of beige silk damask patterned with large blossoms and leaf forms on sinuous vinery, circa 1740. The dress has been remodeled many times. Currently has long, shaped sleeves, fitted pointed back, and a stomacher front. Silk is worn, darned considerably and is discolored. A rectangular piece is cut out of the skirt front. Sold at auction for $287.

Right: Silk gown, circa 1790. Remodeled from an earlier gown. Fabric is French gold silk moiré faille figured with bouquets joined with tasseled bows set on and within vertical stripes. The gown is high-waisted with a low round drawstring neckline and an interior linen cross-over bodice. The back is sewn in the robe a la Francaise style with two wide pleats at the shoulder, descending to a graceful train. Sold at auction for $1,265. Photo courtesy of William Doyle Galleries, New York.

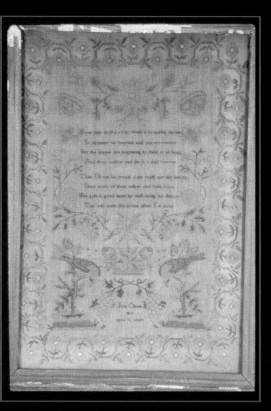

Needlework sampler, probably English, stitched "Jan Oliver 1825 aged 13 years." Upper panel has pious verse surrounded by border of flowers and butterflies. Lower panel has bird and flower design. Floral border. Fading, minor staining. 19.2 inches by 12.8 inches. Framed. Sold at auction for $546. Photo courtesy of Skinner, Inc., Boston, Massachusetts.

19th century American hooked rug with design of two black horses and naive flowers in taupe background, with a straited border of black, rust, blue, purple and brown yarns. Minor fading and wear. 28 inches by 48-1/2 inches. Sold at auction for $518.

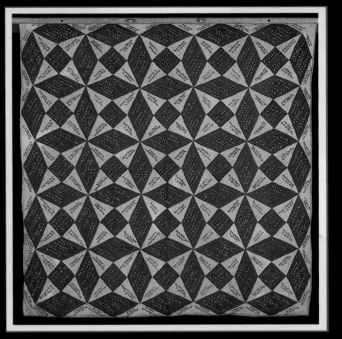

Embroidered names, signatures, initials and regiments of Civil War soldiers add greatly to the value of this pieced star and block quilt. Reverse is worked in a feather star variation in similar shades of red, off-white, and blue, and includes more names and initials. Sold at auction for $4,887. Photo courtesy of Butterfield and Butterfield, San Francisco, California.

Mid nineteenth century Jacquard woven cotton coverlet with central star, spreadwing eagles, and fruit and flowers. 76 inches by 79 inches. Sold at auction for $725. Photo courtesy of Butterfield and Butterfield, San Francisco, California.

Full-sized mannequins in period dress accent the enormous size of early Victorian paisley shawls. A full description is given in the Paisley Shawl section. Photo courtesy of Kent State University.

Ball gown by Worth, mid 1870s, of celadon damask intricately patterned with ferns and blossoms. The waist length bodice is sewn at the back with weighted flaps, buttoning in front to a point. Neckline is cut in low décolletage and V-back. Sleeves have elbow length swags of lace. The bustle skirt is arranged with two front plain crisscross satin panels opening to show brocade and tiers at bottom. Has interior bustle structure. Labeled Worth 7, Rue de la Paix Paris, stamped in green/gold. Sold at auction for $10,300. Photo courtesy of William Doyle Galleries, New York.

Fine cotton dress length of fabric, probably made in India, embellished with embroidery for the bodice, sleeves, and skirt. Style suggests it was done early in the 20th century. Embroidery on these dress lengths often is extraordinary. They are attractive for use in bridal or other couture uses.

Baby dress, possibly for a boy, designed to be buttoned between the legs. The front of the dress has a cluster of tiny embroidered flowers. Collar is finished off with buttonhole stitches, front of bodice is decorated with tiny tucks. Edges are carefully mitered, and finished off. Photo courtesy of Aldon Antiques, Kalamazoo, Michigan.

Robe d'interieur by Charles Frederick Worth, early 1880s, of blue voided velvet woven with sprays of spring flowers in red, green, and brown. Style is a princess line, with satin vestee overlaid with ruffled lace jabot. The skirt is in open robe style, revealing tiers of lace in front. The bodice and skirt are bedecked with pale yellow and taupe satin ribbons. Bustle train and dust ruffle in back. Lining is checkered fabric. Green/gold stamped on white label, Worth 7 Rue de la Paix PARIS. Similar to a gown made for Sarah Bernhardt for her role in Fedora in 1883. Sold at auction for $16,100. Photo courtesy of William Doyle Galleries, New York.

Most sought after and highly valued examples of Normandy work are those that include round French white-on-white embroidery, cutwork, and needle lace motifs about the size of dinner plates. These likely once were French cap backs. Other laces in this example include hand-embroidered machine net laces, handmade Valenciennes, Bucks Point, Lille, and other bobbin lace. A large tablecloth of this quality would sell for $1,500 to $2,500.

English Victorian reception gown, circa 1880, of deep burgundy silk faille and ivory satin brocaded with pastel flowers, the cuirass bodice fitted over the hips, with long tight sleeves and two weighted back flaps, faux button-down integral vestee forming the V-neck. Excellent condition. Sold at auction for $3,450.

American ivory satin ball gown, circa 1890s. Two-piece gown is embroidered with roses in silk threads on chiffon medallion inserts surrounded by vinery and scrolls worked in gold bullion. Sold at auction for $3,910. Photo courtesy of William Doyle Galleries, New York.

Handmade 19th century Point de Gaze needle lace is considered by many to be the ultimate bridal lace. Large veils entirely of lace with handmade mesh are extremely rare. Prices range upwards of $10,000. Photo courtesy of Karen Augusta, Westminster, Vermont.

Wedding dress, late 1850s, of gold and white silk damask, trimmed with black fringe and black velvet ribbon. From the Kent State University Museum collection, a gift of Helen M. Gallese and Sally J. Vyrostek in memory of their mother, Emma Young Matejka of Richfield, Ohio, 1985. 5.1.

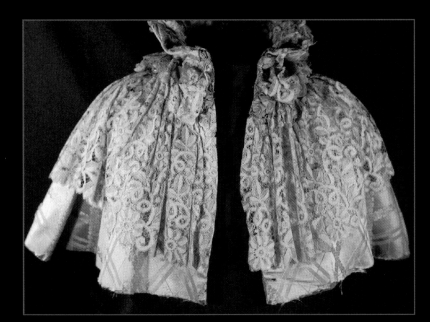

Short opera cape, circa 1900-1905, of gold silk brocade and lace. Style and details of construction make it very special. Condition of the silk is not good: note fraying along the bottom edge.

The inside story: Mid nineteenth century "dresses" typically were assembled from separate pieces, including a skirt, short-sleeved bodice and long-sleeved jacket. Long, narrow tape-like pockets held whalebone stays that shaped the garment. Dozen of hooks and eyes fastened the bodice before the zipper was invented at the end of the 19th century. Fabric on this bodice silk crepe de chine brocade. Photo courtesy of Stitches in Time Plymouth, Ohio.

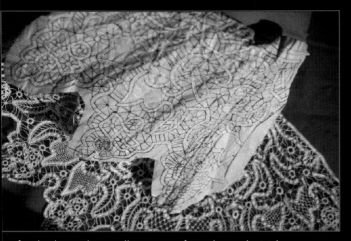

Unfinished tape lace collar project from the early 20th century was not found with enough tape to complete the collar according to the original design. There was, however, enough to fashion a suitable matching corner, and make a wearable collar. The collar, when complete, was worth approximately $150.

Woven silk bookmarks with detailed little pictures and sentiments bring prices of between $40 and $100 when featured at special auctions devoted to Stevengraphs.

White lace dresses were a classic from the early 20th century. Each is a special confection of white-on-white embroidery and lace. Very often, the waists, armholes, and sleeves make them too small to wear today without extensive remodeling. These are extremely fragile — nothing except a few lacy threads hold them together. Look carefully for damage and repairs. Offered for $100.

Left: Columnar evening dress, circa 1912, of beige chiffon woven with gold metallic sprays. The underbodice and cap sleeves are of lace. Size 4. Good condition, minor tears to the chiffon. Labeled Dumay 32. Rue Godot de Mauroi Paris. Sold at auction for $1,000.
Right: Afternoon gown of teal blue chiffon and satin. The bodice is embroidered with silk flowers, and sewn with spotted net bretelles. Sold at auction for $900. Photo courtesy of William Doyle Galleries, New York.

Amish pieced cotton "Bar" design, 20th century. Worked in reds, teal blue, purpl and black on a quilted teal blue ground. 81 inches by 84 inches. Sold at auction for $1,035. Photo courtesy of Butterfield and Butterfield, San Francisco, Californi

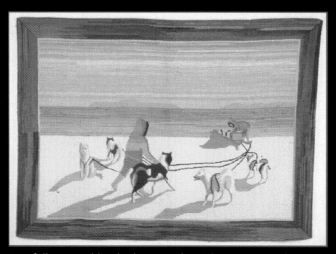

Paisley woven fabrics often were cut up to make coats, capes, and other garments. This long coat-like paisley cape, however, hangs straight in the fron and is bell-shaped in the back, designed to fit ov a circa-1870s dress. It is not a remodeled paisle shawl, but a garment made fo its time. Offered f $3,200. Photo courtesy of Just Faboo, Midway, Kentucky.

Grenfell pictorial hooked rug, early 20th century, made in Newfoundland or Labrador. Design of two people with dogsled, minor fading, staining , and minor losses. Label on reverse. 27-1/4 inches by 39 inches. Sold at auction for $2,185. Photo courtesy of Skinner Auctions, Boston, Massachusetts.

Geometric American hooked rug, dated "Jan 19, 1927" with all-over pattern of stars. Minor losses, wear, and fading. 19-1/2 inches by 39-3/4 inches. Sold at auction for $633.

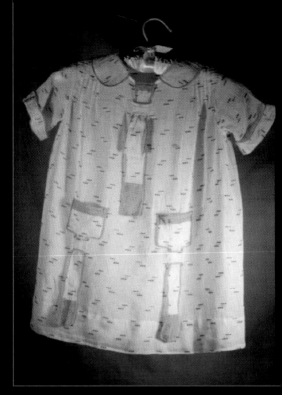

Toddler's dress, probably dating from the 1930s. Dress, pockets, and tabs are decorated with rows of tiny tucks and edged with bias tape. Offered for $35. Photo courtesy of Aldon Antiques, Kalamazoo, Michigan.

Filet lace tablecloth, probably made in Czechoslovakia in the 1930s. Flowers have been re-embroidered to add dimension. $125 to $150.

Toddler's dress, probably from the 1930s. Skirt is decorated with appliqué flowers in pink. (Note the similarity of these flowers and appliqué flowers on table linens of the same era.) Dress is shaped with darts on each side, and with a cluster of gathers at the shoulders. Offered for $25. Photo courtesy of Aldon Antiques, Kalamazoo, Michigan.

Left: Evening gown from the 1930s designed by Jean Patou. Slim columnar gown is sewn in alternating green and black pleated gores ending in points at the bodice and hem. Labeled Jean Patou Paris with the handwritten number 29113. Minor discoloration and holes at the hemline. Sold at auction for $2,300.

Right: Long black sleeveless sari dress by Schiaparelli, 1935. The edges of the black crepe fabric are edged with bands of beads and paillettes. Size 6. Grosgrain ribbon label: Schiaparelli 21 Place Vendome Paris Eté 1935 #40982. The dress originally belonged to international socialite Eleanor Medill Patterson, whose family founded the New York Daily News. It later was owned by Austine

Machine tapestry, with designs of figures, animals, courtly couples, and other scenes of yesteryear make poplar pillows. Prices range from $25 to $75, depending on the colors, and detail of the tapestry.

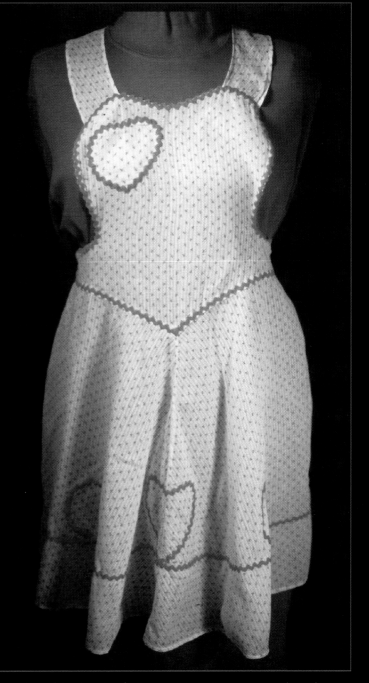

The maker of this handcrafted circa 1930-40 apron must have been both romantic and practical. Cheerful loops and hearts are shaped with rose red rickrack on a sheer white fabric printed with tiny pink and red roses.

Sassy commercially produced novelty aprons from the 1950s. A red checked skirt on a painted doll lifts to show lace-trimmed petticoat. Petticoat lifts to show underwear. Price $50. Photo courtesy of Just Faboo, Midway, Kentucky.

Woven silk pictures were widely manufactured from the mid nineteenth through the early twentieth centuries. Color and detail and general attractiveness of the picture often affect the price as much as manufacturer and date.

Fish pillow was needlepointed in the 1970s by the author from a childhood crayon drawing by her niece, Elizabeth Poder Michael. Afghan, known as the "Parrot" afghan, was crocheted by the author in wild bird colors. Photo courtesy of Elizabeth Poder Michael.

Boudoir caps in the 1920s were fabulous confections of lace and ribbon, and are highly collectible today. Prices typically hover around $100 for attractive examples in good condition. Photo courtesy of Red Balloons, Clarence, New York.

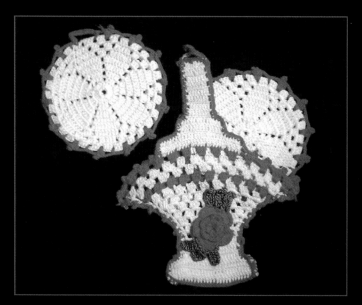

Potholders in a basket holder, probably circa 1940s. Especially during that era, potholders were a popular way for homemakers to express creativity and make gifts for friends. They have yet to be discovered as collectibles, and prices are still low, rarely going above $15.

Tape lace, popularly known as Battenberg lace, was a wildly popular home craft from the late 1880s through the latter part of the 19th century. They make dramatic wearables, and have regained popularity today. Prices for attractive examples with an attractive, coherent design and unusual stitches range from $100 to $150. Photo courtesy of Last Chance Antiques, Kalamazoo, Michigan.

Children's handkerchiefs often came in boxed sets, ideal for gift-giving. This mid 20th century set would sell for $20 to $35. Photo courtesy of J.J. Murphy.

Left: Rose silk faille cocktail dress by Yves Saint Laurent for Christian Dior, spring/summer of 1958. Camisole bodice is tightly fitted at the waist, and extends into a bouffant skirt supported by six layers of crinolines. Originally the property of Mrs. Nat King Cole. Sold at auction for $3,000.

Right: Silk cocktail dress by Yves Saint Laurent for Christian Dior, fall/winter collection of 1958. Size 6. Labeled Christian Dior Paris Automne-Hiver 1958. Model number is illegible. Originally the property of Mrs. Nat King Cole. Sold at auction for $6,000. Photo courtesy of William Doyle Galleries, New York.

Details of the decorations reflect the imagination and creativity of the milliner. Petals on the large colorful flower on this hat were made of a transparent felted fabric over silk. Photo courtesy of Red Balloons, Clarence, New York.

Soft cotton feedsacks from the 1930s with their cheerful little prints are very popular with today's quiltmakers and seamstresses. Photo courtesy of Ronald Bennett.

Sleeveless A-line paper dress, 1960s, printed with a version of Campbell's Soup labels. Inspired by Andy Warhol's art. Labeled Souper Dress/No Cleaning - No washing - It's Carefree/Fire Resistant Unless Washed or Cleaned. To Refreshen, Press Lightly With Warm Iron. 80% Cellulose, 20% Cotton. Sold at auction for $1,840. Background is a length of cotton fabric printed with an exact reproduction of Campbell's Tomato Soup label, including the central gold medallion. Length 90 inches, width 45 inches. Sold at auction for $230. Photo courtesy of William Doyle Galleries, New York.

Evening gown by Pierre Balmain in ivory satin embroidered with gold bouillon, beads, sequins, rhinestones, and other paillettes in a complex floral pattern worked densely on the bodice and scattered on the skirt. The strapless bodice is cut out on one side to follow lines of the floral design. The skirt is asymmetrically draped, the back sewn with an enormous bouffant bow ending in long wide streamers to form a train. Size 2. Labeled Pierre Balmain Paris. Very good condition, possible alterations at waist, one dark area on streamer. Sold at auction for $3,000. Photo courtesy of William Doyle Galleries, New York.

Two-piece evening gown by Emilio Pucci, consisting of a straight wrap skirt and sleeveless shell top with cutout neckline. Fabric is distinctive Pucci print, with curvilinear geometric spirals, brackets, and heart shapes in shades of purple, gold, black, and yellow. The design is outlined and partially filled in with colored beads and sequins. Silk lining has "Emilio" woven in. Size 8. Labeled Emilio Pucci Firenze. Slight discoloration, otherwise excellent condition. Sold at auction for $3,750. Photo courtesy of William Doyle Galleries, New York.

Linen damask was the rage for table linens and hand towels at the turn of the 20th century. The exquisite white-on-white designs are subtle for today taste, and many fabulous examples are available at bargain prices.

Circa 1900s dress of white Batten-berg (tape) lace shows the exagge-ated pigeon-breasted and bustled shape popular at the turn of the century. The silhouette is softer, and the dress is less elaborate than just a few years earlier. Collar is tight and high, accenting the neck. Battenberg, a dramatic and bold lace, was reaching the height of it popularity. Photo courtesy of Just Faboo, Midway, Kentucky.

Afghans

Any home that lives by the maxim: "Love people and use things ....not love things and use people" will have at least one homemade, treasured afghan. Very likely these will never become collectibles. They were made to keep people warm and cozy, and even in the age of central heating, they are indispensable for snuggling during the winter and sitting on the porch on chilly summer nights.

✔ Checklist

Size

As more and more adults reach six feet, it is more and more important to be sure any vintage afghans you are considering will cover the intended warmee from chin to toe. Because afghans typically were homemade of available materials in the first place, it would not be inappropriate to add on a few rows in a congenial yarn and color to make a vintage afghan big enough.

Embroidering on a note telling who added on and when would add value to a favorite family afghan.

Materials

Ordinarily, we would say look for good quality wool and other natural fibers. However, rules of good quality materials do not fit this category. Afghans, more often than not, were made with love and with the hope that they would be used. We cannot fault those who chose to use polyester and other synthetic yarns, because they certainly are washable and durable.

Using leftover yarns for afghans was traditional. When bringing an afghan into your family, look for interesting yarns, especially wools, and for interesting mixes of yarns.

Design

The "granny square," crocheted from leftover yarns, and the ripple or wave patterns in knit or crochet are some of the most traditional of patterns.

Look for variations that add dimension, texture, or color to these typical patterns.

Workmanship and technique

Most often, techniques are simple crochet or knitting.

Importance and congeniality

It is up to each family to establish the importance and congeniality for their own afghans. Make notes, or better yet, embroider names and dates, on afghans that tells who made it, when, and why.

Pieces & prices

Afghans are not considered collectibles, and rarely are offered at antique shops. They most often are found at garage sales, and prices barely reflecting the value of the yarns, let alone the workmanship.

Granny square afghans typically sell for $25 to $30; elaborate cable knits in off-white for $50 to $85.

Traditional granny square afghan. Choice of wicked orange, hot pink, beige, and brown betray its 1960s origins, and will forever limit its value.

Knitted woolen afghan in cable and textured stitches. Slight shrinking and felting testify that it was much used and well loved. Current size 62 inches by 48 inches. Made in the 1960s by Ethel Wegner and her daughter, Elizabeth Lonze.

Blankets

A blanket is simply a piece of cloth, but who can say the word without also thinking "security." Blankets offer us warmth, comfort, and for many centuries, a way of expressing ethnicity, roots, and history.

Some old blankets, especially American Indian, and many ethnic blankets are handwoven works of art and are well worth collecting. Most old blankets may not be collectibles, but to anyone furnishing a cottage, boat, or second home, they are well worth taking a second look at, especially at garage sales. Many old blankets are pure wool, and are of much better quality than any synthetic offered is stores today. A good soaking and hand washing can bring them up to any sanitary standards, especially if they're only going to be used for camping and cottages.

✔ Checklist

The essence of any blanket is the large flat woven surface. The weave is the first clue that identifies date and place of origin. Most are plain weave, but there may be some form of overshot or waffle weave that adds texture. Layers, or any texture that traps air in little pockets makes the blanket warmer.

Often two sides are selvage, or the edge as it was finished on the loom. The edge of the blanket, especially that on plain weave blankets, may be secured with large, widely spaced buttonhole stitches, also known as the blanket stitch for exactly this reason. The top and bottom may be finished off with a wide ribbon, usually satin, to keep the edge from fraying, or the edges may be fringed.

****

Design

The weave of the blanket may identify the origin. This is especially true of handwoven blankets. Overshot is a type of weave that is worked relatively easily on a fairly inexpensive two-harness loom, and consequently was popular in early American homesteads, especially pre nineteenth century.

Stripes were especially popular in American Indian blankets, and in South American serapes.

Ikat and other combinations of dyeing and weaving were more typical of East Asian and African blankets.

Condition

Look for fraying along the edges. Sometimes only the blanket stitch is frayed, and this is easily repaired. Sometimes only the ribbon covering the top and bottom edge is frayed. Good old fashioned satin ribbon is harder to find, but it can also be replaced.

Moth damage to old woolen blankets is one of the biggest sources of damage. This requires reweaving.

Depending on the fiber, blankets often can be carefully hand-washed or dry cleaned.

Pieces & prices

Amish blanket of grey homespun wool, plain weave, blanket stitch along edges. First half of the twentieth century. Single bed size offered for $32.

Navy blanket in cream wool, in a dense plain weave. Single bed size. $35.

Army blanket in brown wool, in dense plain weave. Single bed size. $35.

Stadium blankets rarely are carried to football games today, but a good old-fashioned school blanket can make a novel gift for an old school chum. The gold printed crest in this black wool Purdue University blanket dates it to the 1960s or earlier. After that, Purdue introduced new graphics for the crest.

Hudson's Bay Blanket, cream white with red, black, yellow, and green stripes; four point blanket. First half 20th century. These blankets typically are fulled, a process of fluffing the fibers so they are approaching a soft, loose felt. Double bed size, offered for $150.

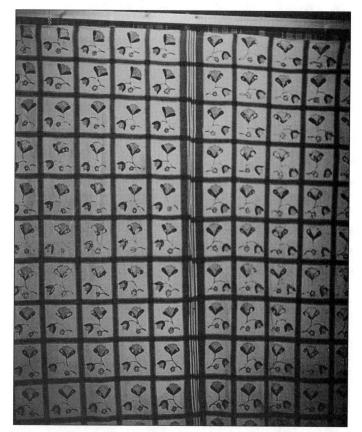

Handwoven Ikat dyed Indonesian blankets, worked in red, white, and black. Probably 19th century. Prices range from $500 to $700. Photo courtesy of Eye on Design, Hinsdale, Illinois.

19th century wool blanket, handwoven in a twill weave in two narrow widths and joined with a center seam. Background color is pink; windowpane stripes are blue. Blanket is embellished with embroidered flowers. Overall size 63 inches by 72 inches. Design and embellishments as well as age make it highly collectible. Photo courtesy of Textile Conservators, Chicago, Illinois.

Handwoven wool blanket from Northern Europe. Weave is warp-faced with a fine weft. Center stripe is bright cherry red; additional stripes are red, blue, tan, yellow, and olive. Photo courtesy of Textile Conservators, Chicago, Illinois.

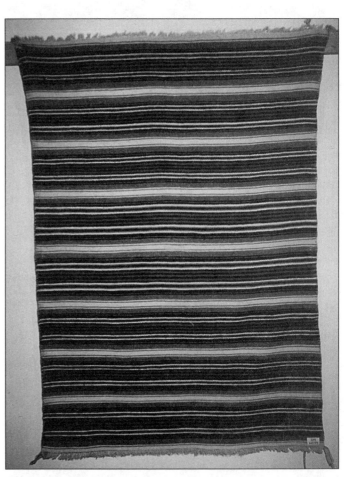

Rio Grande blanket handwoven in blue, brown, black, grey, and natural wools. 64 inches by 49 inches. Photo courtesy of Textile Conservators, Chicago, Illinois.

19th century twill weave plaid blanket handwoven in blue wool and natural off-white cotton. Blanket was woven in two sections, and joined with a center seam. Photo courtesy of Textile Conservators, Chicago, Illinois.

Coverlets

Coverlets are one of the earliest forms of American weaving, dating to the eighteenth century. The earliest examples were an integral part of Colonial life, when the colonists were growing, retting, scutching, and spinning their own flax into linen yarns; and growing, shearing, carding and spinning their own wool into yarn. A four-harness loom, often homemade from hand-hewn timbers, was found in many early cottages, and was used by homemakers for weaving. Blankets, and geometric overshot coverlets were typical home products.

By the 1830s, the jacquard mechanism, a high-tech, expensive innovation, put weaving into the hands of professional weavers, and made elaborate woven pictorial coverlets available to average homemakers. Early jacquard designs often are mind-bending collections of pictures and mottoes that celebrate the technical marvel of the new weaving mechanism.

Jacquard woven coverlets were most typical of the period from the 1830s to the Civil War in the 1860s. The war limited the availability of cotton, linen, and wool for coverlets. After the war, some limited hand jacquard weaving picked up again, but power weaving in fully mechanized factories essentially eliminated the market.

Because coverlets were almost entirely produced before chemical aniline dyes were available, indigo and natural linen and wool colors were most prevalent. Other subdued hues came from vegetable and natural dyes. Red was produced from the cochineal beetle or madder roots; brown from red oak, hickory, and walnut husks; yellow from leaves and flowers.

Today, old handwoven coverlets are prized for their charm and are a cozy reminder of a bygone, self-sufficient pioneering lifestyle. They are, however, seldom used except as occasional decorations. These heavy, linen-and-wool covers, essential in drafty cabins and cottages, usually prove much too warm and heavy for today's centrally heated homes. Far too many are being cut up for skirts, jackets, and worst of all, home handicrafts.

✔ Checklist

Fiber

A combination of undyed cotton yarn or linen and dyed wool yarn was the most common in eighteenth and nineteenth century coverlets.

Synthetic materials are a definite clue that a coverlet was really made in the twentieth century, even if a 1800s date is woven into the design.

Colors

Indigo blue wool yarn with white or natural ecru (undyed) cotton or linen is the most common and popular combination. Red typically was made from South American cochineal or imported Asian madder roots. Other homemade dye colors included brown from red oak or hickory; yellow from peach leaves, goldenrod, or black-eyed Susans. Chemical dyes were not available until after the 1860s. Colors that did not come from natural dyes sometimes provide an important clue: coverlets with corner block dates in the 1840s and 1850s might really have been made much later.

Corner blocks

Design blocks sometimes appeared in the bottom two corners of coverlets with borders on three sides; or on all four corners of coverlets with a borders on each of its four sides.

Traditionally the corner blocks contain the year and the date the coverlet was woven, the name of the weaver, and/or a unique symbol that was a trademark of a weaver. Sometimes the corner blocks contained the name of the customer.

Border

A decorative border with patterns about six to ten inches deep typically was used on three sides, and sometimes on all four.

Center seam

Most jacquard coverlets were woven in two parts, then sewn together with a center seam.

Types of Weaves

Overshot

Overshot refers to a type of thick but loose weaving where weft (horizontal) threads pass over, or overshoot, at least three warps. These also sometimes are called floating thread weaves, because the threads float over each other. Overshot weaving was among the earliest of techniques used for American coverlets, dating to the early 1800s. Almost all overshot coverlets were woven in two sections, and joined with a center seam.

Designs almost always were geometric, combining rectangles, stripes, and diamonds. In the earliest overshot coverlets, the weft, or overshot yarns were dark colored, especially indigo or red, and the warp yarns were natural ecru or beige linen or wool. After the 1830s, dark colored warps sometimes were used with multicolored wefts.

Overshot coverlets typically wore out more readily because of the abrasion on the long floating threads.

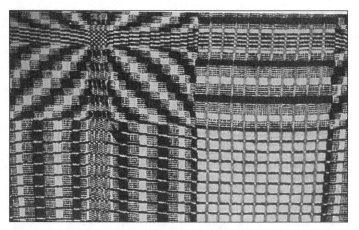

Detail of overshot weave. Weft threads float over three or more warp threads to form a design.

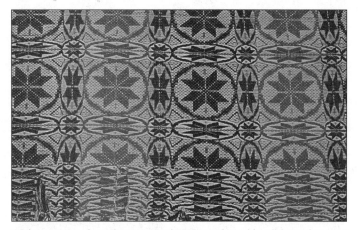

19th century American overshot coverlet with eight point star design, worked in red, natural, and two colors of blue. Some damage to edges. 66 inches by 70 inches. Photo courtesy of Textile Conservators, Chicago, Illinois. Offered for $400.

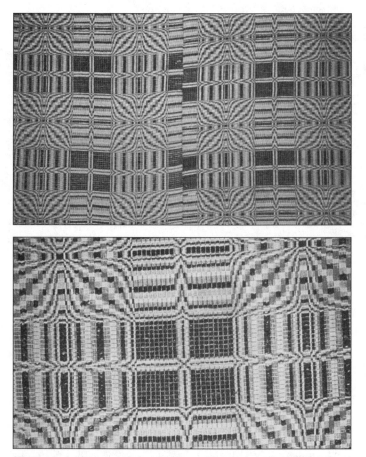

Two panels unevenly joined with center seam in double bowknot with table pattern. Uneven joins are very typical in handweaving, because it is extremely difficult to control the exact positioning of each filling row. Warp is white cotton; weft is blue and rust. 71 inches by 92 inches. Photo courtesy of Textile Conservators, Chicago, Illinois. Offered for $600.

19th century geometric overshot coverlet. Warp is natural, weft is red and orange. 67 inches by 87 inches. Photo courtesy of Textile Conservators, Chicago, Illinois. Offered for $400.

Double Weave

These are extremely heavy coverlets woven with two sets of warps and two sets of wefts. They consist of two separate layers of weaving that intersect and reverse along the outlines of the designs. The coverlets are reversible, and typically are dark on one side and light on the other. Alternative names are double cloth, or pocket weave, named so because of the little pockets that are formed between the layers.

Detail of a double weave coverlet. Coverlet is woven as two entirely separate layers, crossing at the edges of motifs. Little pockets form between large solid color areas, and the layers can be pulled apart.

Double weave jacquard coverlet in indigo and natural, with stylized floral design; border of flowers and urns. Corner blocks include a large shell design. Woven in two panels, precisely joined at the center. 76 inches by 79 inches. Photo courtesy of Textile Conservators, Chicago, Illinois. $600.

Summer-winter

Almost all coverlets are reversible with a dark side and a light side. The term summer-winter, however, usually is reserved for a specific type of tightly-woven, single thickness reversible weave where no yarn overshoots by more than three threads.

Summer-winter coverlets are different from overshot because the yarns do not float as far over the surface, and are different than the double weave in that they consist only of a single layer of weaving.

Jacquard

The term "jacquard" is the name of the mechanism, invented by Jacquard in the early 1800s, that simplified and sped up the weaving of complex designs. This mechanism can be used to produce any type of double-weave, overshot, or summer-winter coverlets. Most often, however, the term is loosely used to describe coverlets with extremely complex floral and pictorial designs.

Pieces & prices

Jacquard colored wool and cotton coverlet, inscribed Emanuel Meily, Lebanon, 1835, P. Bowman. Worked in red, green and blue wool, and off-white cotton. 76 inches x 96 inches. Sold at auction for $430.

Jacquard cotton coverlet, inscribed Suzana Kenyon, Wove, Illinois, 1837. Woven in a summer-winter technique with buildings and spreading eagles woven in the borders. 80 inches x 92 inches. Sold at auction for $430.

Jacquard blue and white woven in a summer-winter field with a lily and floral border. 71 inches x 82 inches. Sold at auction for $288.

Jacquard colored wool and cotton coverlet. Worked in red, blue and teal green wool on an ecru cotton ground. Inscribed "Peace and Plenty, 1845." 86 inches x 70 inches. Sold at auction for $978.

Jacquard coverlet, inscribed A. Kemp and George Becker, 1841, Hanover. Woven in bands of red, green and blue in summer and winter pattern. 83 inches x 85 inches. Sold at auction for $345.

Jacquard cotton and wool summer-winter, mid 19th century. Woven in red, blue and green wool on an ecru cotton ground. 88 inches x 82 inches. Sold at auction for $230.

Jacquard woven cotton and wool coverlet. Inscribed J. Lutze, 1842. Worked in rose, burgundy, mustard and dark blue in a rose and passion flower pattern motif on a natural white ground. 71 inches x 94 inches. Sold at auction for $230.

Jacquard woven cotton coverlet, mid 19th century. Woven in blues, reds and off-white in an overall design depicting grape vines with grape clusters and foliage interspersed with geometric design, birds and butterflies. 80 inches x 90 inches. Sold at auction for $430.

Single weave coverlet, dark orange dominant on one side, natural off-white on the other. Grape clusters and flowers on the border; the name "Hester Pier" and "N Young Wever" are centered on the side of the border, and style more typical of Pennsylvania or New Jersey weavers. Offered for $245.

Small circles and interlocking rings surround groups of small blocks in this 19th century summer-winter coverlet in natural and blue. 75 inches by 96 inches. Photo courtesy of Textile Conservators, Chicago, Illinois. Offered for $400.

Single weave coverlet, with dark colors dominant on one side, and light on the other. Threads do not float over the surface. This weave sometimes is called a "summer-winter" weave.

Sources

Museums

Abby Aldrich Rockefeller
Folk Art Museum
P.O. Box C
307 South England Street
Williamsburg, VA 23187

Alling Coverlet Museum
Palmyra, NY 14522
315-597-6737

Art Institute of Chicago
Christa M. Thurman, Curator
Michigan Avenue at Adams
Chicago, IL 60603

Columbus Museum of Art
480 East Broad Street
Columbus, OH 43215

Illinois State Museum
Jan Wass, Curator of
Decorative Arts
Spring and Edwards Streets
Springfield, IL 62706

University of Maryland
Historical Textiles Database
0202 Tawes

University of Maryland at College
Park
College Park, MD 20742-1215

Lakeview Museum of
Arts and Sciences
Kristan McKinsey
1125 West Lake Ave.
Peoria, IL 61614-5985
309-686-7000
kristanm@lakeviewmuseum.org

Dealers

Gordon Fine
2678 California St.
San Francisco, CA 94115
gordonfineantqiues@att.net

Joyce Rivers
Rivers Antiques
Box 297
East Woodstock, CT 06244-0297
860-974-3578

Elizabeth Olson
Fort Lauderdale, FL 33304
954-764-1726
lizolson@ix.netcom.com
By appointment

Evan Sommerfield
Madison, IN
973-423-2220
By appointment

Maury Bynum
Textile Conservators
215 West Ohio, Suite 600
Chicago, IL 60610
maurybynum@textileconerva-
tors.com

Susan Cimino
3004 State, Rt. 5 South
Little Falls, NY 13365
By appointment

John and Martha Jack
46 Woodbury Way
Fairport, NY 14450-2475
716-223-7142

Elizabeth Kile
Box 221
Red Lion, PA 17356
familyheirloom@mindspring.com

Barb and Tim Martien
Chagrin Falls, OH 44022
440-338-3666
By appointment

Doilies

Somewhere about the middle of the nineteenth century, a London haberdasher was trying to build a little extra profit into his business, and came up with the idea of selling small decorative bits of cloth to place under bowls, atop tables, and anyplace else the Victorians could think of to further clutter their homes. The name of the haberdasher? Mr. Doily, of course.

Ubiquitous might be a better name for that little bit of cloth today. Like parsley on a plate, or powdered sugar on unfrosted cakes, they are the inevitable finishing touch.

These little cloth bits were tailor made for the textile collector. They provide an opportunity to inexpensively collect with a chosen focus. Like collecting coins of a certain subject, a collector can accumulate examples of all the different lacemaking or embroidery techniques. Or, by focusing on any one technique, a collector can collect animals, birds, or flowers. By focusing on time periods, a collector can illustrate the passage of time, and the changing of styles.

No one technique is inherently more valuable than any other. As always, look to the design, technique and workmanship, condition, and rarity to assess value.

✔ Checklist

Materials

Look for the best possible materials — fine, long staple cotton, shimmering silk embroidery threads, lustrous linen. The prices for the best often are not significantly higher than the prices for average quality.

Design

Doilies provide a neat, small, contained space. Within that limited area, look for the most complex, graceful, flowing, harmonious, witty, or charming of pictures.

Workmanship and technique

Whatever the technique — embroidery, bobbin lace, needle lace, crochet — look for examples that demonstrate the more difficult stitches and manipulations of thread.

Look for examples that demonstrate a thoughtful blending of technique and design. The technique should enhance the design, and be unobtrusive, or it should be novel and witty.

Collecting lookalikes can be fun: machine versions that carefully mimic designs traditional in another technique, or crochet that copies a traditional bobbin lace design.

Rarity

Novel use of a technique, an extraordinarily difficult technique, or a particularly good design can signal rarity.

Each technique — crochet, knotting, tatting, bobbin lace, needle lace, and filet — has a few standard basic designs that have been produced year in and year out for nearly a century. The markets are awash in these few designs. Notice what is common, and stay away from those.

The origin of this Daisy Shave doily is a mystery. Could it be an early promotional gimmick? White daisies are embroidered on a dark beige homespun linen. Lettering is in dark golden-yellow thread.

Embroidery

Very subtle details distinguish the finest of hand-embroidered doilies from the average quality:

- The embroidery will be carefully matched, blended or balanced with the background fabric.
- Threads will be long staple, and smooth.
- Colors will be carefully chosen, and beautifully blended and shaded.
- Edges should be carefully hemmed, hand rolled, or neatly and precisely covered with buttonhole stitches.

Scrolling flower stems, and outlines of flower petals are padded to give this early 20th century doily texture and dimension. Roses are embroidered in bright red artificial silk (rayon) thread; stems are gold. Oval doily, about 18 inches across, is edged with crochet. Price about $30.

Machine-made trim is stitched by machine to the edge of this hand-embroidered doily. Most likely, the shaped and edged doily was offered as a printed pattern for home embroidery around the late 1920s or 1930s. Price about $10.

Drawnwork

Drawnwork is one of the oldest forms of lacemaking. Styles have come and gone with alternations and variations over the centuries. Often, it is very difficult to date pieces any closer than a hundred years or so to their actual date of origin because styles and technique have changed so little.

The quality of the underlying fabric is extremely important in drawnwork. Because individual threads are exposed to wear, it is important that the base fabric be woven of long staple, tightly woven threads of good quality.

The embroidery and needleworking does more than decorate the work. It supports and protects the exposed threads. Look not only for decorative handwork, but for sturdy, dense and attractive work.

Threads used for embroidery and needlework should be carefully and thoughtfully matched or blended in color, density, and twist to the threads used to weave the underlying fabric.

Cupids frolicking in this drawnwork doily greatly add to the value. Size about 18 inches in diameter, price about $45.

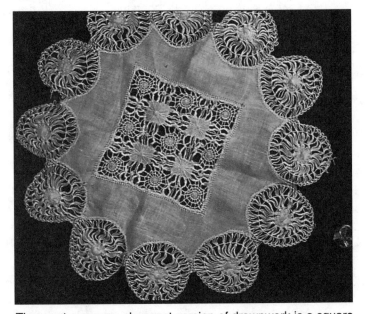

The most common, cheapest version of drawnwork is a square grid with minimal needlework and needleweaving. Edging of tenerife circles is also one of the most common edgings. Price about $5.

Crochet

Crochet is a technique available to anybody with a ball of string and a hook. It appeared on the scene relatively late. The earliest examples found date to the middle of the nineteenth century. But it quickly became something every homemaker was expected to be able to do. After mastering just four basic variations of the same stitch, imagination should kick in, and the lacemaker should be able to imitate designs from a good picture. (Or at least that's what *Godey's* and most other lady's magazines of the nineteenth century tell us.)

What is obvious from the piles of crocheted doilies available at every Wal-Mart and country craft and decorating shop priced at just a dollar or two is that a doily has to be extraordinary to be worth bringing home from the antique mall or garage sale. The search for the rare, unusual, witty, or weird, however, is always rewarded.

Because crochet was a technique so readily worked at home by a clever homemaker, it was used to imitate other more difficult and expensive techniques. Because each individual crochet stitch is so large and distinctive, the imitations always are easy to tell from the original. They are, nevertheless, the most amusing quarry of a doily hunter.

Large doily or centerpiece, about 18 inches in diameter, imitating the meandering tape and wheat ear motifs of Cluny bobbin lace. Made in the 1990s in Russia. Sold for about $45.

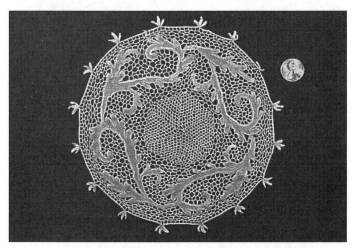

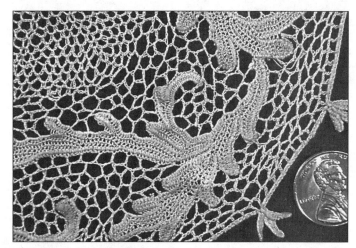

Unusual early 20th century crocheted doily, made in Hungary. Design would be more suitable for needle lace. Detail shows distinctive knot-like crochet stitches in the clothwork, and chain stitching in the background. Doily is part of the collection of The Lace Museum, Sunnyvale, California.

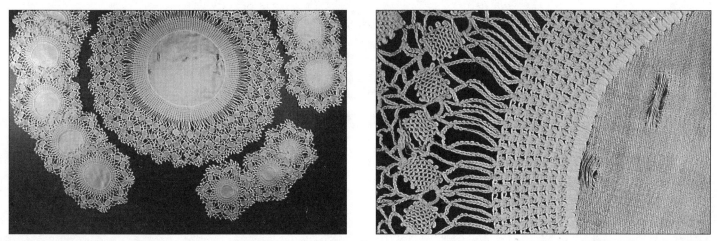

Look carefully at the clothwork center of doilies with crochet edges. Because the crochet was worked directly onto the edge of the cloth, it is nearly impossible to replace a worn out center cloth. Worn centers seriously detract from this turn-of-the-century lemonade set of doilies, coasters, and centerpiece. Price as-is with worn centers, about $10.

Small details, like the cluster of decorative holes in each diamond-shaped flower petal and outside triangle, lighten and add texture to the simple but unusual modern design of this crocheted centerpiece, about 20 inches in diameter. Price about $45.

Some of the more common styles of crochet. These are still made today, and are cheap. Expect to find these styles for about $5 or less.

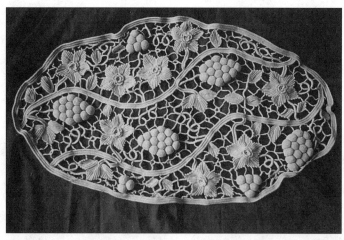

Heavy raised clusters of grapes and raised petals on the flowers make this doily distinctive, and nearly unusable. Uneven workmanship mars the novel doily—it won't lie flat. Part of a private collection, and not for sale.

Needle lace

Needle lace is composed of the smallest, simplest thread manipulation, and offers the greatest possible variety in design. Lacemakers can essentially paint a picture, stitch by stitch. The most interesting and valuable needle lace doilies are those that take the best advantage of this potential. Look for great variety in stitches and texture, shading in the clothwork areas, decorative edges around the motifs, and decorative thorn-like picots along the edges and on the connecting bars.

Graceful scrolling leaves, nicely shaped flowers, and some shading in the clothwork make this a better-than-average doily. Connecting bars are lightened with picots, and are nicely arranged. Price about $45.

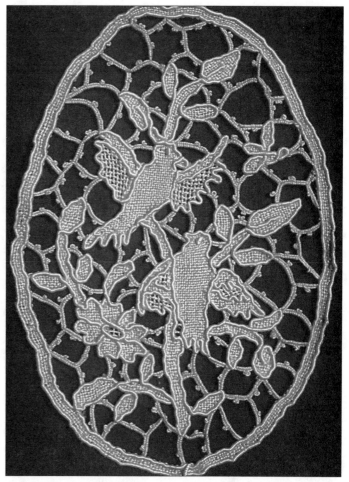

The fluttering birds design catches the eye, but it is the unusual technique used to make this doily that makes it attractive to collectors. The clothwork areas of the design are not worked in the buttonhole stitch typical of needle lace, but instead are needlewoven. Background connecting bars are covered with buttonhole stitches. From the collection of J. Margaret Barber.

Workmanship is very precise but the design is monotonous in this early 20th century Chinese doily. Price about $15.

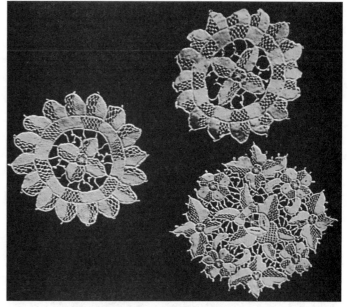

The most commonly found needle lace doilies have this flat pinwheel design. There is no shading or detail in the petals. Short staples and loose spin of the thread give the doily a flat, matte, slightly fuzzy appearance. Price about $3 to $5.

Normandy work

Patchworks of lace sometimes are called Normandy work. They may be homemade, assembled from bits and pieces of old leftover laces. Or, they may be commercially handmade — assembled around the turn of the century from newly made machine laces. Value depends on the attractiveness of the patchwork, the neatness of the stitching, and the value of the lace used in the patchwork.

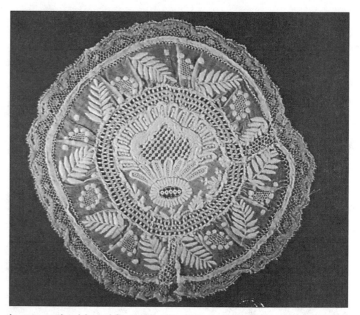

Large embroidered flowers with drawnwork, and cut holes filled with minute bits of handmade needle lace often are a signal that the Normandy work is made from old French cap backs. Even though this doily is not quite circular, it is assembled from interesting old handmade whitework and is therefore interesting to a collector. Price about $25 to $35.

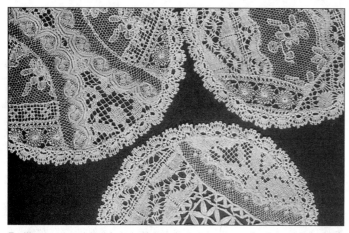

Doilies assembled from odd bits of handmade lace, and stitched together by hand. Each is a different patchwork, but all are made from the same selection of handmade laces, and all are edged with the same handmade bobbin lace. Part of a set of six doilies, six placemats, and a table runner, the set most likely was commercially produced around the turn of the century. Set sold for about $800.

Bobbin lace

Bobbin lace is a form of off-loom weaving. There are only three possible basic thread manipulations: two pairs of threads weaving over and under each other to form woven clothwork; a single pair of threads twisted around each other; and pairs of threads braided together to form bars. Work with enough pairs of threads, however, and these simple manipulations can be combined in an infinite number of ways. Each country in Europe, each of the countries ever colonized by Europeans, and each generation in each of these countries for dozens and dozens of years devised their own style of weaving bobbin lace.

That just begins to give a clue how many different styles of bobbin lace doilies there are to collect.

The Chinese must dearly love butterflies, or they think the rest of the world does, because this style of doily with little butterfly motifs is one of the most often exported. These have been made almost endlessly for the past hundred years, and usually can be found for $1 to $5, depending on the size.

Count the number of threads across the width of the bobbin lace edging on a doily, take a close look at the complexity of the weaving pattern, and it provides a clue how much training and skill was needed to make the doily. This style of bobbin lace, known by various names including Point de Paris or sometimes Flanders lace, is one of the most difficult, and yet is under-appreciated. At any price under $100, it is priced less than its true value.

Technique in this doily includes elements of many techniques popular in Belgium in the 19th century. The flowers and scrollwork were made in separate pieces. The background was filled in as they were gathered together and assembled. Either late 19th or early 20th century. Price about $45.

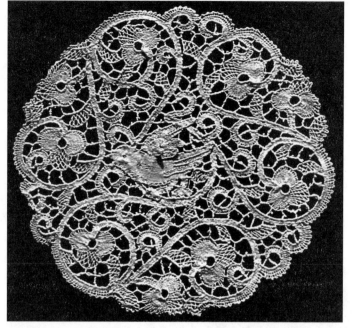

Scrollwork and tri-lobed florets are similar to the Cantu lace doily. The scrolls, however, have a distinctive crinkled edge known as a winkie-pin edge. Many different names are assigned to this late 19th to early 20th century style, including Italian Rosaline and Rococo. Price for this large doily would be about $75.

The little bird fluttering in the center of the scrolling vines would instantly capture a collector. A close look at the technique shows the also has technical virtuosity to offer. By cleverly carrying the threads as ropes along the edge of the scrolls, the lacemaker can make the lace with almost no cut ends to ravel or fray. The ropes along the edge of the scrollwork also add a distinctive dimensional texture to the lace. This bobbin lacemaking technique is often called Cantu. Diameter of the doily is about 6 inches; price about $45.

Simple large, cookie-like flowers, simple scrollwork, and background bars in distinctive double-hexagon pattern all are typical of a Belgian style called Bruges or Bloemwork. This is a very common design, quickly and easily worked, and has been a mainstay of the tourist souvenir counter for the past hundred years. Price about $25 to $40.

Generic style of bobbin lace, sometimes called Saxony Guipure because it was commonly made in the Saxony area of Germany, and it has a background of bars instead of mesh. This is one of the most common kinds of bobbin lace found in flea markets, and one of the fastest and easiest to make. These generally sell for about $5.

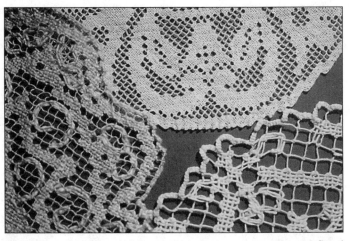

Selection of some of the more common geometric and floral designs. Doilies of this quality level are very plentiful, and usually sell for $1 to $5 each.

Filet

Filet lace is an easily worked technique of darning over a hand-knotted net. The technique is easily and quickly learned, and after a little practice, workers can produce it quickly. To have any value at all, the design must be complex and the thread fine. Designs with animals, mythological figures, cupids or angels, or other particularly charming patterns have the most value.

Machine lace

By the end of the nineteenth century, machines effectively copied filet lace, needle lace, crochet, and many styles of bobbin lace. Machine embroideries and variations of the weaving process were two of the basic types of ways machines imitated laces.

Chemical lace is formed by machine-embroidering a design over a substrate that later is chemically dissolved away, leaving the lock-stitched embroidery as a piece of lace. It makes crisp, sharp designs. Raised edges easily are worked in to the embroidery, to make attractive textured laces. Attractive machine lace doilies are valued relatively highly today.

This imitation of filet lace with its romantic scene of young lovers in a rowboat, would make a great valentine present. Lace is about 6 inches deep. Price about $85.

Chemical lace doily with a clever imitation of the roses and scrollwork typically worked in Brussels mixed bobbin and needle lace. Doily is about 6 inches by 8 inches. Price about $35.

Tape laces (Battenberg)

Almost all tape lace doilies were homemade, crafted from patterns offered in Sears Roebuck's catalog or any of the endless craft magazines and pattern books available to the late nineteenth and early twentieth century homemaker. Because the technique is comparatively simple, and a bit of lacy fabric can be made quickly, it is the most common of the export and souvenir laces.

Tape lace originated as a shortcut version of needle lace. Unless a tape lace doily includes many interesting needle lace and needle weaving stitches, chances are its value is purely as a short-term, use-and-enjoy decoration.

Chemical lace doily with a clever imitation of the roses and scrollwork typically worked in Brussels Mixed bobbin and needle lace. Doily is about 6 inches by 8 inches. Price about $35.

Although the design is fairly monotonous, the buttonhole-stitch covered bars joining the tapes guarantee the doily will be durable, and withstand many washings. Price about $20.

Cutwork

Silhouetting a design by cutting away the background is a simple technique, and one that has been done for centuries nearly everywhere in the world. Identifying the origins of cutwork is difficult, unless the style and technique both are distinctive. Examples of this are the combination of designs of square holes surrounded by precise counted satin stitches typical of Hardanger, or patterns of shaped holes outlined by the distinctive knotted buttonhole stitch in Norwegian Hedebo, and a few other unusual combinations.

Look for precise hand stitching, especially buttonhole stitches, surrounding cut holes, and a firm, tightly woven fabric that can hold the stitches and resists raveling.

Machine-made medallion inserts imitating needle lace add a little interest to this otherwise loopy doily. Price about $15 to $20.

Silhouetted flowers surrounded by neatly hand-worked buttonhole stitches is a fairly common technique. Look for well-formed flowers, precise stitching, and firm fabric. This type of work often is called Madiera, regardless of where is was made. Detail from one of a pair of pillowcases. Price about $25.

Egyptian designs became very popular in the 1920s, following the discovery of King Tut's tomb. Novelty of the design makes it popular today as well. Diameter of doily is about 12 inches. Price about $35.

Hooked Rugs

Hooked rugs began to appear in America in the early 1800s. They were typically small rugs used before the hearth to catch sparks that might damage the far more important and expensive imported carpets that were just beginning to gain popularity as floor coverings. They were easy enough for the simplest craftsperson to make: Find a hunk of burlap, like an old potato sack, and use that as the base. Find some old yarn, or old fabric and cut it in narrow strips, then pull the strips through the backing fabric to form loops on the front. If you want a fluffy rug, cut the loops after the rug is done; if not, leave them as loops.

Because there is so little to the technique, the design and the choice of colors becomes very important. These rugs with an imaginative, original, or charming design are the ones that qualify as folk art and win out at auctions and sales.

✔ Checklist

Materials

Hooked rugs consist of only two parts: the pile, or top, and the backing, or bottom.

Jute and burlap are the most typical backing materials. Early American rugs were made from old gunnysacks, which were originally used to transport dry good to the United States. Homespun hemp, linen and flax also were sometimes used.

The pile might be strips of wool, cottons, extra yarn, old clothes. The scraps and yarns sometimes were dyed a new color.

Design

Folk designs, especially those with animals, birds, figures and homespun symbols are the most valued. Age is not as important as a distinctive, appealing design. By the nineteenth century, commercial patterns were supplied, and little by little originality started to diminish. Edward Sands Frost offered printed burlap for homemade hooking starting in the 1860s. Because copyright was not yet protected, these often were copied, perhaps only with slight revisions, and produced by other companies. By the twentieth century, very few original designs were produced; almost all rugs were made from kits.

Border, motifs, and background all provide clues to the age and origin.

With borders, examine stripes, mottling, curves, etc. How are the motifs shaped? Are they naïve and childlike, or professional? Was the background worked in a solid color, or with mottling and shading?

Workmanship and technique

The term "hooked" rug sometimes is used rather loosely. It applies to rugs formed by pulling lengths of yarn or fabric through the backing, and to rugs formed by stitching the pile to the backing.

True hooked rugs, where the strips of fabric were pulled into the backing were perhaps the most commonly worked. Burlap, gunnysack or other open-weave or loosely woven base was needed in order to make it possible to pull loops through the base. Friction alone held them tightly in place.

Shirred or chenille rugs are formed by hand sewing the pile onto the base, which is usually a closely woven fabric like a linen. There are a few variations on how the pile was produced. Narrow, cut strips of fabric might be gathered up the middle on a thread. These fuzzy, caterpillar-like strips then were hand-stitched to a backing. Other alternatives for shirred rugs were bias-cut strips of fabric folded in half, and then the folded edge stitched to a backing. Narrow (one to four-inch wide) strips of knitting sometimes were folded, and the two edges sewn to the base with the fold up. When the rug was completed, the folds were cut, allowing the knitting to unravel into fuzzy rows. Finally, strips of fabric were stitched in accordion-like folds to the backing.

Look for natural fibers with natural dyes: black walnut, hemlock, butternut and maple, leaves of lily of the valley, madder root, berries and insects.

Rugs with a a sculpted look, where the pile has been cut to various lengths to accent the design, often are called Waldoboro rugs, after the town that introduced the effect and made it popular. Nearly any spelling of the word can be used.

Condition

Condition is extremely important. Nothing holds the rug together except where the loops are held in the backing fabric. Rotten or dried out backings are very difficult to repair.

In good repairs and restoration, burlap or other natural materials will be used to replace parts of the backing.

Avoid rugs with a latex backing covering the base. It certainly was not used in early rugs, and either is a bad attempt at repair, or it's a twentieth century rug. In either case, it eventually dries out and crumbles.

Rug with green Star of David and date 1934 in a brown background. Some imperfections. 30 inches by 17-1/2 inches. Sold at auction for $460.

19th century American hooked rug with design of two black horses and naive flowers in taupe background, with a striated border of black, rust, blue, purple and brown yarns. Minor fading and wear. 28 inches by 48-1/2 inches. Sold at auction for $518.

American hooked rug, dated "Feb. 14, 1922" with a trotting horse. Scalloped border is worked in stripes of black, gray, brown, red, blue, and purple yarns. Minor repair, wear, and fading. 29 inches by 39-1/2 inches. Sold at auction for $1,093.

Late 19th or early 20th century American hooked rug. Scene is a hunter with dog, fox, and bird worked in grey, black, sage, red, and ecru yarns on a cream background. Minor repair, fading, and staining. 28-1/2 inches by 52 inches. Sold at auction for $860.

19th century American hooked hearth rug. Design has field of stars, flowerheads, and geometric motifs worked in purple, blue, green, red, and olive yarns on a sand field; border of diamond shapes. Has some fraying and fading, and is backed. 39 inches by 84 inches. Sold at auction for $2,415.

Late 19th century or early 20th century American hooked rug with a black horse and corner hearts and stars with a striated background of black, pink, and blue yarns. Minor wear, fading, and losses. 40 inches by 49 inches. Sold at auction for $1,380.

Geometric American hooked rug, dated "Jan 19, 1927" with all-over pattern of stars worked in blue, red, green, yellow, grey, and brown yarns. Minor losses, wear, and fading. 19-1/2 inches by 39-3/4 inches. Sold at auction for $633.

Hooked rug, designed and made in the 1930s by Nellie Martin of Gurham, New York (Albany area). Said to be a prize-winning rug at regional fair. Hooked of home-dyed wool strips in turquoise, mustard, olive, and forest green with ecru background. 34 inches by 57 inches.

Early 20th century American hooked rug with design of two lions in exotic landscape, worked in ecru, cinnamon, black, sage, red, and purple yarns on beige background. Minor repair, fading, and staining. 30-1/2 inches by 60-1/2 inches. Sold at auction for $805.

Hooked rug, designed and made in the mid 20th century by Nellie Martin. Design of grape leaves commemorated retirement purchase of upstate New York vineyard. 20 inches by 27 inches.

Late 19th early 20th century American hooked rug showing a heron and butterfly standing amid cattails and water lilies. Waldoboro-type with pile cut to varied heights. Foliate borders, worked in peach, sage, ochre, cream, and amethyst. Fading, minor split and repairs. 27-1/2 inches by 52-1/2 inches. Sold at auction for $431.

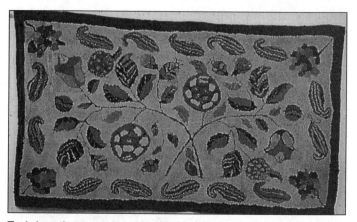

Early hearth rug made in New England in the 19th century. Design of leaves and flowers with boteh (stylized pine cones) motifs around the edge. Design worked in red, green, blue, mustard, and yellow in an ecru background. Border stripes in brown and black. 73-1/2 inches by 43-1/2 inches. Sold at auction for $4,600.

Grenfell Rugs

Dr. Wilfred Grenfell was a young British doctor who started missions in Labrador and Newfoundland in 1892. Convinced that a long-term enterprise was needed to supplement the meager incomes natives earned from fishing and hunting, Dr. Grenfell introduced various handcrafts.

Early in the twentieth century, Dr. Wilfred Grenfell gave a new boost to the rug hooking in Labrador by introducing new patterns, styles, and materials. Although it was not a commercial enterprise and the rugs often are not labeled, they are distinctive. Rugs made in the same style are also called Grenfell.

These rugs are usually small and lightweight, and often look like large, soft needlepoint. Very thin strips of wool and cotton-knit jerseys from worn-out stockings, underwear, and other materials were densely and very evenly worked in neat rows over burlap. Loops are not cut. Designs typically include bears, puffins, icebergs, trees, and other scenes of rural Labrador. Colors usually are muted.

Authentic Grenfells, and Grenfell-style mats are highly collectible.

Series of three Grenfell rugs with winter village and home scenes. Photos courtesy of Textile Conservators, Chicago, Illinois.

Small mat-sized rug worked in colored silks in the manner of Grenfell. Design of bold red rose in scrollwork border in not at all typical of Grenfell rugs. Photo courtesy of Textile Conservators, Chicago, Illinois. Offered for $600.

Canadian hooked rug dating to the 1950s, worked in wool on linen, with design of seagulls in muted tones of brown, grey, and blue. The muted toned and choice of motifs is somewhat reminiscent of Grenfell, though this rug is much later, and worked in different materials. 61 inches by 36 inches. Photo courtesy of Textile Conservators, Chicago, Illinois. Sold for $600.

Sources

Dealers and Experts

Joel and Kate Kopp
Planetarium Station
Box 919
New York, NY 10024
Phone 212-535-1930
Authored a book on hooked rugs, and also collect, buy, sell, and appraise them.

Thomas Woodard
Woodard & Greenstein
506 East 74th St.
New York, NY 11209
Phone 212-988-2906
Gallery specializing in hooked rugs, quilts, coverlets.

Jessie Turbayne
Box 2540
Westwood, MA 02090
Author of several books on hooked rugs. Repairs, cleans, evaluates and appraises.

Maury Bynum
Textile Conservators
Chicago, IL
Phone: 312-329-0097
Quilts, coverlets, hooked rugs, extraordinary vintage textiles. Buy and sell, repair, restoration. By appointment.

Gretchen Noyes
P.O. Box 948
Alexandria, VA 22313
Phone 703-920-0348
Appraisals of antique needlework and textiles, including samplers.

Books

Kopp, Joel and Kate, *American Hooked and Sewn Rugs*, University of New Mexico, 1995
Turbayne, Jessie, *Hooked Rug Treasury*, Schiffer
Turbayne, J, *Hooked Rugs - History and Continuing Tradition*, Schiffer,1991

Turbayne, J., *Hooker's Art*, Schiffer, 1993

Grenfell pictorial hooked rug, early 20th century, made in Newfoundland or Labrador. Design of two people with dogsled, minor fading, staining , and minor losses. Label on reverse. 27-1/4 inches by 39 inches. Sold at auction for $2,185. Photo courtesy of Skinner Auctions, Bolton, Massachusetts.

Auctions

Horst Auctioneers
50 Durlach Road
Ephrata, PA 17522
Phone 717-738-3080
Fax 717-738-2132
Located in Amish country in Pennsylvania, Horst Auctions frequently include samplers and other textiles.

Skinner, Inc.
Bolton, Massachusetts
Miscellaneous auctions frequently include hooked rugs.

Linens

Once upon a time, linen meant any fabric made from flax. That was decades ago, when the only fibers available came from plants, like cotton, flax, and related greenery, and silk and wool from animals. Fast forward to a shopping mall today, and it is almost impossible to find any natural fibers in fabrics meant for the table, yet everything is called linens.

Somewhere around the 1950s, the manufacturers of table textiles convinced us that natural fibers stain, and require ironing. They would give us fabrics that would not stain or need ironing. Those of us who still remember the cool, satiny feel of fine linen and cotton and the look of a beautifully set table are not convinced the manufacturers have done us any great favors.

Today's synthetic fabrics still wrinkle. The problem is ironing them is no longer a pleasure. The wiry, springy fibers fight against the iron, and threaten to melt into goo if treated carelessly. Pure linen turns to luscious satin with ironing.

Use and enjoy all but the most artistic and fragile of the old lacy linens. Although they require washing and ironing, they respond graciously to that effort, and reward us by being sensual, cool, and satiny to the touch — supple, and glistening to the eye.

Damask

Damask is an optical illusion of a fabric. Threads are carried across the surface, producing a silky pattern that contrasts with the background weave. The pattern is reversible — silky flowers appear in a matte background on one side, matte flowers in a satiny background on the reverse. In extremely fine damask, a satiny pattern appears in a satiny background.

Up until about the 1950s, damask was considered one of the essential elements of setting a fine table; the shimmer of the silky pattern set off by candlelight bouncing off the crystal and silver. It traditionally was all a single color, usually white or off-white, but may be a pastel or other color.

Damask, when it was sold in the early twentieth century, was often labeled single or double damask. This term is used in various ways. It often refers to the length of the threads floating over the surface — in double damask the floats are longer. The term double damask also sometimes refers to the thread count. There are many more threads per square inch in double than in single damask.

Almost all damask has floral designs. Figural designs, sometimes commemorating special events, or designs including animals and birds are much more rare, and sometimes sell for higher prices.

Today, damask is one of the best bargains in the antique markets. After the casual wash-and-wear entertaining style, which began in the 1950s, nobody wanted to "do up" the luxurious damask linens. Complete sets with napkins and the original labels often are found in estate sales and garage sales at prices far below what new, no-iron tablecloths sell for.

✔ Checklist

The length of the floating threads is important to note. The more threads the floats pass over, the silkier and more distinctive the pattern will be. On the other hand, longer floats may snag and wear out faster. Short floats pass over just about four threads; in elaborate designs, the threads pass over up to twenty threads.

Look closely at the thread used to weave damask. Because long threads carry over the surface, it is important that the threads be spun of long, even fibers. Short fibers will pull out, and pill and shred faster than long fibers. Linen fibers are by nature longer than cotton fibers, so they naturally make better damask.

Texture is the best way to judge good damask. Pure linen is cool, firm, and creamy to the touch.

The weave should be tight so the threads do not slip. Loose weave wears out faster. Hold the tablecloth and napkins up to the light. Loosely woven fabric will often have uneven, worn-out areas. Holes will show up as if X-rayed.

Tilt napkins up to the light and make sure the designs all match. Because the design is so subtle in damask, it is easy to accidentally mix in a mismatched napkin or two.

The artistry of damask is subtle and elusive. It appears and disappears as the light plays over the surface of the fabric and dances off the floating threads. Perhaps because it is so subtle, it has not attained the level of popularity of the more dramatic embroideries and laces. Vintage damask often is very low-priced in garage sales, flea markets, auctions, and antique malls.

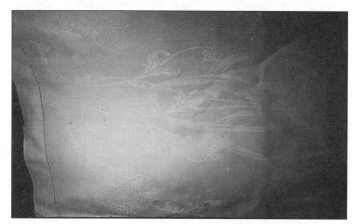

Hand towel of linen damask with Art Nouveau floral and scrollwork design. Offered for $15.

Pieces & prices

Mint condition dinner cloth of Irish double damask with floral design, circa 1950s, with eight napkins, in original gift box marked "Liddels." Cloth 62 inches by 78 inches; napkins 22 inches square. Sold at auction for about $190.

Mid nineteenth century banqueting cloth of fine quality linen damask, commemorating the Crimean War Sebastopol, Sept. 8, 1855, and other battles, the Royal Coat of Arms, medallions with portraits of English, French, Turkish and other commanders with banners and weapons, with oak and acanthus in the surrounding borders. Labeled "Manufactured by D. Dewar Son & Sons, Dunf & London, expressly for Messrs. Hodge & Lowman, Regent Street, London." Tablecloth and seven napkins, each 35 inches by 30 inches, and a table runner, 27 inches by 214 inches, depicting the commanders in oval medallions. Banquet cloth about 208 inches by 106 inches. Probably Scottish. Sold at auction for about $700.

Late nineteenth century dinner cloth of linen damask woven with a central sun motif surrounded by emblems of members of the British Empire, garlands of roses and thistles, marked "Dickins & Jones Ltd. No. 1901." Probably made to commemorate the Diamond Jubilee of Queen Victoria in 1897. Tablecloth about 125 inches by 90 inches. Sold at auction for about $170.

Mint-condition, never finished pure linen tablecloth and set of 12 napkins with a design of roses and leaves. Little shamrocks emphasize the Irish origins. The damask was sold as yard goods. The 12 napkins were woven as yard goods 24 inches wide, with each single napkin pattern separated from the next by a cutting line woven into the yard goods. The two cut sides would be hemmed, the two selvage edges could be left unhemmed. The tablecloth was 72 inches square, the napkins 24 inches square. The set is probably early 20th century, and has remained folded since it was woven. Because linen is not elastic, the center fold probably never will be ironed out. The linen damask has extremely long floats, giving the surface a satin like sheen. Set was purchased at a garage sale for about $25.

Damask luncheon napkins in teal blue and white. Set of 6 for about $15.

Set of three unused linen damask table napkins with Celtic knot and shamrock motifs, fourteen with various Celtic scenes and symbols, a similar tablecloth, thirty-three damask guest towels, and assorted other pieces. Irish. Sold at auction for about $160.

Mid nineteenth century dinner cloth of fine linen damask with heraldic motif surmounted by visor, plumes and eagle, with the motto "Mali Mori Quam Faedori" surrounded by scattered roses, thistles, and shamrock, within a border of scrolling vines and passion flowers. Labeled "Coulsons Manufacrs. Lisburn, Ireland." Sold at auction for about $520.

Late nineteenth century dinner cloth of fine linen damask designed with fish in the Art Nouveau style, with seventeen matching napkins. Some repairs. Cloth about 178 inches by 78 inches, napkins 27 inches by 27.6 inches. Probably Danish. Sold at auction for about $510.

Mid nineteenth century dinner cloth of fine linen damask designed with fleur-de-lis in staggered rows on a spot ground, enclosed in a border of formal stylized flowers alternating with fleur-de-lis, with eighteen matching napkins. Some repairs. Cloth about 180 inches by 62 inches; napkins 40 inches by 33 inches. Probably Flemish. Sold at auction for about $550.

Lavender cotton damask tablecloth with design of large full-blown roses and a trellis, about 62 inches by 82 inches, with napkins 18 inches square. Offered for $35.

Set of eight turquoise and white luncheon napkins, good condition. Some slight fraying. $15/set.

Ivory rayon damask tablecloth, 1930s, colored in shades of blue, yellow, pink, and green. Design is an eighteenth century couple emerging from a carriage. 8 feet 10 inches by 6 feet 2 inches. Twelve matching napkins. Sold at auction for $201.

Golden-yellow and white damask tablecloth from the 1930s, with design of pairs of women reading a book and playing the lute. Hemstitched border. 8 feet 10 inches by 60 inches. Sold at auction for $201.

Embroidered linens

For additional information and detailed photos of specific stitches, see the Materials section.

At whatever point needles were actually invented, it's probable that embroidery was invented a day later. The urge to decorate and create is so deep in the human soul that we cannot imagine anyone stitching two pieces of hide or two woven grass mats together without making a few decorative stitches at the same time. Anyone who picked up a needle at one time or another did a bit of embroidery. The quality can range from homemade linens with a few running stitching to superb-quality, professionally embroidered linens.

Embroidered linens dating back to the sixteenth century occasionally show up in the auction markets, especially in London, and surface now and then in American attics. Most are white-on-white embroidery, while some are quite colorful.

Of course nineteenth and twentieth century embroidered linens turn up most often in the marketplace. So much novel, imaginative, and superb hand-embroidery shows up in the market done by "anonymous" that it is well worth learning to look closely, and to learn to recognize quality work regardless of whether or not it is labeled.

There are a few names that generally indicate good quality:

Porthault is a French linen retailer, renowned since the nineteenth century for commissioning unique, and very high-quality linens, and for early innovations in color linens. Many are superbly embroidered.

Beauvais is a region in France well-known for hand-embroidery, especially chain or tambour stitch embroidery.

Marghab was the name of an early twentieth century linen firm started by an American woman on the Portuguese island of Madeira. Marghab linens were known for subtle yet meticulous workmanship. They were marketed in the United States only through special departments in a few of the finest stores. The firm closed in the 1960s, and many pieces were sent to the Memorial Art Center of the South Dakota State University in Brookings, South Dakota.

✔ Checklist

Design

Look for a complex, interesting, balanced, and flowing design complemented by the choice of embroidery thread, stitches and color. Look for unusual, graceful and delicate shading of flowers and other designs.

Threads

Threads used for the embroidery should be long staple, and have a good twist to keep long satin and running stitches from shredding.

In the finest of embroideries, even the twist of the thread was chosen to enhance the design. A fine silk floss with minimal twist makes satin stitches shimmer like stained glass. Perle cotton thread with high twist adds texture and dimension to embroidery.

Workmanship and technique

The most common, easiest stitches are running stitch, backstitch, and satin stitch. Look for interesting variety.

Condition

Check the color of the thread on both sides to see if there is any fading or discoloration.

Look over the threads carefully for signs of repair, replacement, or patching.

Old threads are unpredictable. The backing and the embroidery often were done in different fibers, and will behave differently in the wash, or with cleaning. Woolen thread embroidered on cotton or linen fabric often was attacked by moths. Silk threads were sometimes unstable. What appears to be a perfect or good quality embroidery may shred and disintegrate in the wash. Colors were notoriously unstable until well into the twentieth century. Old embroideries of any worth or historic value should be seen by an expert before any type of cleaning is attempted.

Huck towels, with elaborate geometric designs embroidered with running stitches, were very popular in the 1940s. The textured fabric is called huck or huckaback. Intricate designs could be quickly and easily worked by running colorful threads through the threads floating across the surface of the fabric.

Better quality embroidered huck towels have embroidery both on the front and back edges of the towel. Look for intricate, complex designs. Different shades of color add dimension. Prices range from about $10 to $15 each.

Early Turkish cotton towel embroidered in silk thread in shades of pink, rose, brown, blues, greens, and gold. The motif, called a "boteh" in Turkish, was the basis for the paisley shape also called a pine, or pinecone. Photo courtesy of Textile Conservators, Chicago, Illinois.

Tablecloth, about 36 inches in diameter, dating to the turn of the century. Padded satin stitches in beautifully shaded colors, often outlined in black thread, was one characteristic of Arts & Crafts embroidery. $45 to $65.

Fingertip towels, about 12 by 16 inches, from the Portuguese Azores, probably dating to the mid 1950s or 1960s. Delicate flower sprigs are hand-embroidered in bright pastels. Fabric is an extremely fine, satiny cotton in a very firm weave. Edges are rolled and stitched by hand; bottom was edged in fine, tight buttonhole stitches. All the towels in this assortment still had their original labels. Each also had two tiny triangular points in a knotted stitch marking the center back. Prices range from $5 to $10.

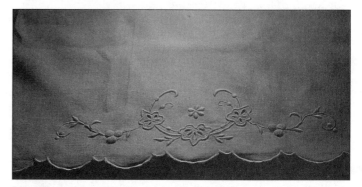

Pillowcases with highly padded satin stitch embroidery. $35 pair.

Guest towel, circa 1940, with cheerful embroidery in bright red, green, orange, purple, and shades of blue cotton embroidery thread on coarse linen, sometimes called crash. Simple stitches include running, daisy stitch, and French and bullion knots. $10 to $15.

Pieces & prices

Porthault white linen tablecloth with Beauvais embroidery of two-tone blue carnation bouquets caught up with a curvaceous ribbon. Size 9 feet 4 inches by 68 inches. Eleven napkins. Sold at auction for $500.

Flower embroidered tablecloth from the 1930s. Butter-yellow linen embroidered with pale blue inner and outer borders of delicate floral wreath and spray designs. Includes some appliqué and drawnwork, 8 feet 6 inches by 64 inches. Twelve matching napkins. Sold at auction for $350.

Linen tablecloth, embroidered in white with wheat ear and daisy bouquets. Hemstitched border, 122 inches by 66 inches. Fourteen matching napkins. Sold at auction for $517.

White linen Porthault tablecloth, 1950s, embroidered with green silk and gold metallic thread in a design of crossed arrows. Bordered with forest green. Fourteen matching napkins. Labeled Porthault Inc. The Linens of Queens. 118 inches by 77 inches. Sold at auction for $690.

Spring green Porthault organdy tablecloth with Beauvais embroidered pink flowers. 144 inches by 72 inches. Twelve matching napkins. Sold at auction for $747.

Bone organdy Chinese tablecloth with birds and flower sprigs embroidered in taupe and beige. 108 inches by 66 inches. Twelve matching napkins. Sold at auction for $575.

Eastern European tablecloth, probably 1920s, with fine line embroidery in red and blue in Wagnerian scrollwork at each corner. Edged with crocheted lace. Six matching napkins. 67 inches square. Sold at auction for $460.

Early twentieth century table cover embroidered in a Turkish tile pattern in red, beige, and black on a beige cotton fabric. 66 inches by 58 inches. Sold at auction for $200.

Cutwork and Drawnwork

For characteristics and other basic information, see the Materials section.

Cutwork and drawnwork often appear together in the same linens; very often they are combined with inserts of other laces. There is a great deal of average quality cutwork and drawnwork on the market. These should be used and enjoyed — more of this type can always be made. When choosing pieces of vintage cutwork and drawnwork for collectibles, or for very special uses, look for the very best quality.

Pieces & prices

Tablecloth, mid-twentieth century, with rectangular linen panels with floral cutwork; linen cutouts joined by large buttonhole-stitch covered bridges. Embroidered and outlined in taupe. 8 feet 4 inches by 64 inches. Eight monogrammed napkins. Sold at auction for $400.

Tablecloth, probably 1920s, with a center section and border of elaborate drawnwork in urn, cornucopia, and scrollwork design. Side panels of fancy stitching. 9 feet 4 inches by 66 inches. Twelve monogrammed napkins. Sold at auction for $350.

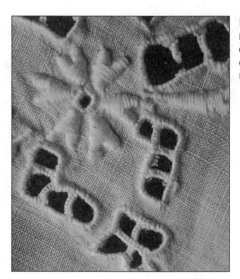

In good quality cutwork, the fabric is firm and woven tightly enough to hold together. Edges may be carefully overcast or covered with buttonhole stitches. Connecting bars should be close enough together to keep the fabric stable, but wide enough apart to sustain the openwork illusion. Connecting bars should be covered with buttonhole stitches; they will not unravel even when broken.

In better quality drawnwork, holes are filled with closely worked and intricate needlewoven or needle lace designs that are both attractive and structurally sound.

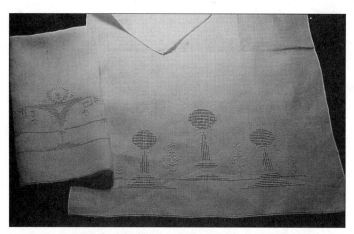

Very fine, lightweight cotton guest towels in drawnwork and embroidery, probably made in China in the 1930s. Prices range from $10 to $15.

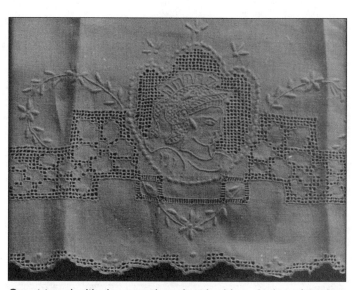

Guest towel with drawnwork and embroidery design of ancient figure. Scallop edge is finished off with drawnwork. $65 to $75.

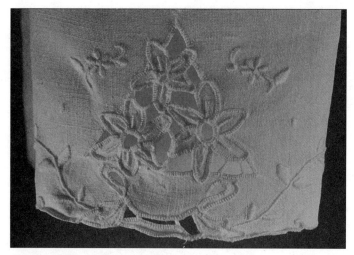

Guest towel with simple floral design silhouetted in cutwork, edged with buttonhole stitches. $15

Hardanger, with its design of square holes surrounded by blocks of satin stitches, is one of the more distinctive and popular forms of embroidered cutwork. Tablecloth, about 25 inches across. $175 to $180.

Embroidery threads in various shades of blue are used to shape the drawnwork patterns in this early 20th century tablecloth, found in a flea market in the Netherlands. About 36 inches square. $45 to $65.

Combinations of lace and embroidery

Once people began making linens lacy by withdrawing threads, cutting holes, and embroidering around and into the cut holes and over the withdrawn threads, the thrill of creativity took over. Some of the most wonderful linens are those that are fanciful combinations of every needlework technique imaginable.

It is easy to be dazzled by a complex design and to overlook the fine details that separate great linens from those that are merely busy.

✔ Checklist

The more cutwork and inserts there are, the more important the basic background fabric becomes. A firm, closely woven fabric is important to hold up under the cutwork and needlwork.

The combinations should enhance each other, and not simply add to the complexity.

Needle lace should be precisely stitched, gracefully shaded, and include interesting stitches.

Bobbin lace should be complex and precisely worked.

Cutwork and drawnwork should be carefully stitched and needlewoven over to support the structure.

Look not only for figures and animals, but for interesting and whimsical scenes.

Pieces & prices

Round cutwork tablecloth with filet lace inserts, circa 1930s. Filet lace inserts depict various scenes of au naturel figures cavorting in nature. Edged with pointed filet lace. Diameter 53 inches. Sold at auction for $450.

Cutwork tablecloth embroidered with grapes, with needle lace inserts depicting figures playing musical instruments at each corner. Deep border of Cluny bobbin lace. 72 inches square. Sold at auction for $172.

Cutwork tablecloth with inserts of needle lace depicting courtly couples in pastoral gardens, probably 1920s. Deep border of floral filet lace. 106 inches by 92 inches. Sold at auction for $1,380.

Spectacular linen round tablecloth, 98 inches in diameter, of cutwork inset with needle lace medallions depicting figures in various activities, filet lace medallions of stags and leaping animals. Sold at auction for $3,220.

Italian napkin with corner detail of bobbin lace, and inner accents of cutwork, needle lace, and embroidery.

Needle lace insert has unusual shape that echoes the shape of the surrounding scrollwork. Cupids on the crescent moon are surrounded by a neatly and carefully worked background of buttonhole stitch-covered bars. Leafy shapes are echoed in the cutwork and in the embroidery alongside the scrollwork.

Early 20th century table linens from the Philippines, with subtle drawnwork and embroidery edged with delicate knotted lace.

Tablecloth has small center of embroidered white linen accented with needle lace medallions. Rectangular, square, and triangular motifs in Cantu bobbin lace, filet lace with reclining figures, and other bobbin and needle lace inserts. A deep edging of bobbin lace with a six-point star mesh background and meandering, stylized floral design completes the tablecloth. 39 inches square. $450 to $525.

Printed tablecloths

From the 1930s to the 1950s, casual tablecloths for everyday use appeared in bright floral and garden prints. With the renewed interest in solid-color fiesta ware dishes, these cheerful vintage tablecloths have been rediscovered.

Overlook a few flaws — a bright, busy floral or fruit pattern can absorb and camouflage a few drips and stains — and take a vintage cotton print to the picnic.

Pieces & prices

Pucci round cotton and polyester tablecloth, probably 1960s, with bright blue, jade, green, white, gray, and purple geometric design. Diameter 70 inches. Six matching napkins. Sold at auction for $200.

Lot of two Porthault printed tablecloths, both from the 1950s, one patterned with violets and a green scalloped edge, 86 inches by 67 inches, the second with green vines dotted with orange, and a green scalloped edge, 87 inches by 72 inches, with eight matching napkins. Lot sold at auction for $1,200.

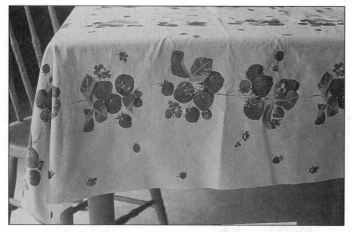

What better for a May or June breakfast table than brilliant red strawberries! Print tablecloths from the 1930s through the 1950s have been rediscovered. Prices for a tablecloth that would seat 4 to 6 range from $25 to $50.

Curious shade of greenish-yellow with border of teal and grey leaves probably dates this tablecloth to the 1930s or 1940s.

Novelty linens

Creativity, wit, and relatively inexpensive fabrics and embroideries were the hallmark of many of the novelty linens of the early twentieth century.

Any and every technique — printing, painting, embroidery, drawnwork, and lace — was used to create these whimsical treats. Most often, these are not technical or artistic masterpieces. Instead, they are worked in very simple techniques, intended as a passing fancy.

Pieces & prices

White organdy tablecloth with grapevine appliqué design. 8 feet 8 inches by 70 inches. Eleven matching napkins. Sold at auction for $275.

White organdy tablecloth with appliqué design in blue depicting grazing deer, flowers, scrolls, and garlands. 9 feet long, 64 inches wide. Twelve matching napkins. Sold at auction for $400.

Round tablecloth for umbrella table, with small center hole. White organdy with white flower appliqué. Diameter 7 feet. Sold at auction for $150.

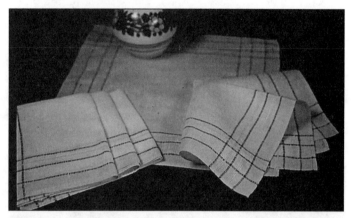

Real linen napkins from the first half of the 20th century offer a cheerful bargain. Striped edges are worked in cheerful butter yellow and bright blue on a natural linen napkin. Set of 6 luncheon size napkins, $20.

Naughty guest towels were the rage in the 1930s and 1940s. This little fingertip towel was offered for $6.

Appliqué flowers accented with embroidery were a novelty in the 1930s. Commercially worked linens were available, and patterns for do-it-yourself embroidery also were offered. In one example, the butterfly was worked in embroidery; in the second, a bit of blue fabric was appliquéd for the wings. $15 for a set of 4 napkins.

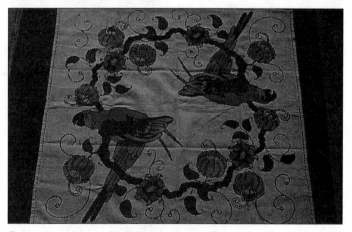

Painted and stenciled linens were offered in the early 20th century as kits to be outlined with a running stitch, usually in black. This bridge-table sized tablecloth sports a pair of brilliant red parrots. Black outline, worked in wool yarn, is deteriorating and would need to be replaced. $15.

Crocheted flower and leaf motifs were appliquéd to this centerpiece to mimic heavy, raised embroidery. Areas behind some of the leaves and flower center were cut out.

Lacy Linens

Crochet

Crochet became popular around the middle to the end of the nineteenth century. It was very popular in Europe, especially Hungary and eastern Europe, and part of the heritage many European immigrants brought with them on their journey through Ellis Island in the early 1900s. Just as a well-stocked linen cupboard was proudly displayed in European peasant cottages, first and second generation American homemakers were expected to make a tablecloth or two, and to provide an assortment of well-trimmed pillowcases for their new homes.

Quality of the thread and tension of the stitching often is the feature that tells the difference between Chinese, Philippine, and other imported crochet tablecloths and late nineteenth and early twentieth century American homemaker's tablecloths.

Most often, domestic homemakers used higher twist, longer staple thread. This gives the work a finer, more crisp look than the import crochet.

Look for more complex designs, especially with small motifs tucked in to fill the spaces between larger circular motifs.

Tablecloth of circular motifs, typical of those popular in the 1930s and 1940s. About 72 inches by 56 inches. $125 to $135.

Pillowcase with large white flowers with purple centers. Lace edge is about 4 inches deep. $15 pair.

Filet crochet bedspread for a child's bed. Variety of unrelated patterns, including a monkey, camel, butterflies and birds, leaping stags and rabbits, and children, gives the bedspread a folk art quality. $225 to $250.

Filet

Filet is a technique of darning a design over a knotted mesh. The origin of the basic technique dates back centuries ago. Although it is time consuming, it is not especially difficult, and has remained a popular craft lace. Because the designs are darned over a square grid, they usually have a quaint angularity and simplicity. It is a lace that can be used and enjoyed.

Small items, including doilies and placemats, with simple geometric or floral designs are relatively plentiful in the antique and flea markets. Designs with figures or animals are more unusual. Large items, such as tablecloths and bedspreads, are less often found. Their simple homespun designs make them very usable and popular.

Tablecloth, probably made in Czechoslovakia in the 1930s. Flowers have been re-embroidered to add dimension. $125 to $150.

Border of bobbin lace, about 4 inches deep, inserted into linen table runner. Small stylized figures give the lace interest and value. $75.

Bobbin lace

For basic characteristics and other information, see Materials section

Pieces & prices

Italian bobbin lace in scrolling Milanese style, and a large central needle lace medallion depicting a pair of lovebirds in a dogwood branch. 100 inches square. Sold at auction for $1,610.

Bobbin lace scrollwork tablecloth interspersed with a variety of birds, including parents feeding their young. 114 inches by 74 inches. Some discoloration. Sold at auction for $1,610.

Black Cluny lace tablecloth, probably 1920s. 74 inches by 68 inches. Sold at auction for $172.

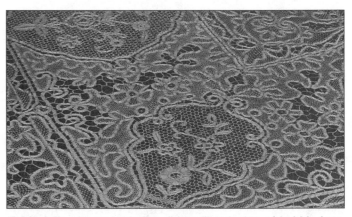

Tablecloth with meandering ribbon-like design of bobbin lace, and floral sprig inserts. Bobbin lace tapes can be distinguished from tape lace (Battenberg) in how the threads weaving the tapes flow smoothly around curves and turns without puckering, gathers, or folds. Like many large pieces of bobbin lace, the background is put in with a needle and thread. 96 inches by 72 inches. $550 to $650.

Four examples from an exceptional set of six 19th century bobbin lace placemats. Floral surroundings are the same for each placemat, but each has a different scene of 18th century courtly couples. Place mat sets like these pose a dilemma when selling them. Because each is so striking, and would display so beautifully, they would probably bring more money if sold separately. In the long run, however, a set of 6 unique but matching place mats tells a fascinating story. Each would sell for $250 to $300. The set of 6 would probably sell for $500 to $600.

Detail of lace place mat. Technique is known as a continuous or straight bobbin lace because the background and design were made at one time. Lace would have been worked in strips about 4 inches wide, and joined with invisible seams. Background mesh is a honeycomb stitch, one of the more complex and difficult to work.

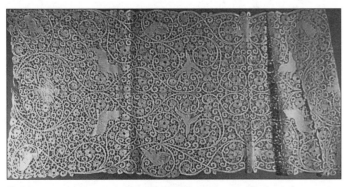

Table runner in a scrolling bobbin lace in a technique known as Cantu. Animals scattered through the lace make it highly desirable. $750 to $800.

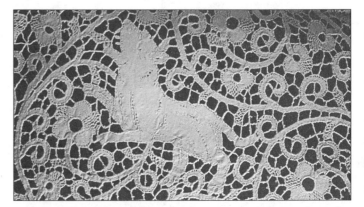

Note subtle rope-like edges along the scrolls. By carrying the threads along the lace in these ropes, the lace-maker can avoid cutting and restarting the weaving. This makes a stronger, more durable lace, and also adds some attractive texture. Animals also are woven of bobbin lace.

Needle Lace

For characteristics and other basic information, see the Materials section.

The most highly collectible forms of needle lace are spectacular large pieces, such as tablecloths, with unusual designs, intricate and unusual decorative stitches, and shading and other special effects. The best quality pieces sell readily for high prices. Ordinary quality, with average quality floral or geometric designs, are not rare enough to sell quickly or for high prices.

Any damage immediately drops the price drastically. Places to send tablecloths and other pieces for repair are rare. Repairs can easily run into several hundred dollars, and only the best pieces warrant such an expense.

Pieces & prices

Early twentieth century needle lace tablecloth, with all-over pattern of urns, flowers, and oval and round medallions. 8 feet 4 inches by 62 inches. Some discoloration. Sold at auction for $150.

Ecru Chinese needle lace tablecloth, 1940s, with bird and floral motifs inset with bands of cream linen. 8 feet by 64 inches. Sold at auction for $150.

Tea cloth, probably 1930s, with floral urn medallions and central round motif. 52 inches square. Minor discoloration and damage. Sold at auction for $172.

Italian needle lace tablecloth, probably 1930s, with flowers, medallions, and male figures in renaissance dress. 116 inches by 66 inches. Some discoloration. Sold at auction for $344.

Tablecloth, probably early 20th century, with design of oriental style flower arrangements. 10 matching napkins. $950.

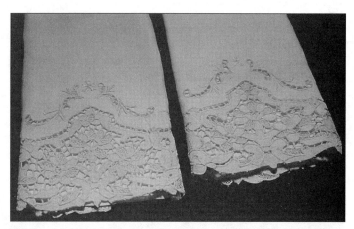

Edging of handmade needle lace is combined with cutwork scrolls and embroidery. Alternating openwork petals and dense clothwork petals are typical of Chinese work. $15 for a pair.

Spectacular, 19th century needle lace tablecloth shown at an antique show. Figural scenes, along with graceful and complex shapes of flowers and foliage, and details of shading and texture add to the value. Thread is fine quality. $3,000 to $5,000. Photo courtesy of Paivi Roberts, West Palm Beach, Florida.

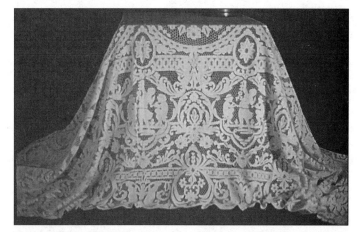

Figures in the design make this tablecloth attractive. A couple years ago, this Chinese needle lace tablecloth would have been slighted because of its comparatively flat stitching, and lack of detail and shading. Thread is short staple, loosely spun, and tends to wear out more quickly. With interest in vintage lace growing, prices even for these lesser-quality, late 19th or early 20th century tablecloths are rising. 108 by 72 inches. $1,200 to $1,500.

Tape laces

Tape lace, often generically called Battenberg lace, was an extremely popular home handcraft from the late nineteenth through the early twentieth century. Because it works up quickly, requires comparatively little training or skill, and makes an attractive product, it remains one of the most commonly produced laces today.

During the decades from about 1960 to 1980, when most lacy linens went out of fashion, Battenberg tape lace remained one of the few that was still recognized and reasonably popular. During the 1980s, it was one of the best selling and highest priced of the home decor laces at flea markets and antique markets. In the 1990s, as more people learned more about other types of lace, and began to develop an eye for quality, technique, and workmanship, the popularity of tape lace — Battenberg — began to wane.

It still makes an extremely attractive presentation, and is one of the best use-and-enjoy laces.

✔ Checklist

Materials

Tape should be properly balanced for the design. Too heavy a tape is clumsy; too thin of a tape is flimsy.

The thread used to weave the tape should be long staple, reasonably high twist. Thread used to join the tapes and make the fancy stitching, likewise, should be high quality. Loosely spun thread shreds, and feels flimsy.

Tape laces made of poor quality materials are not strong enough to support repairs, and is not even worth trying to save.

Design, technique, and workmanship

Designs should be elaborate and interesting. Good designs include recognizable flowers, leaves, grapevine motifs, and graceful scrolls. Poor quality designs are endless loops.

The connecting bars should be attractive and secure. Buttonhole-stitch covered bars, or twisted pairs of threads hold the lace together much better than loops of string.

Background stitches should be attractive and interesting, and well integrated with the overall design.

Condition

Well-designed, carefully stitched pieces may be worth repairing. Loosely worked, shredding examples are not worth the trouble.

Small tablecloth, about 4 feet square, with good design of recognizable leaves inside attractive scrollwork. $150 to $200.

Design of this lace tablecloth, about 4 feet square, is unusually attractive. Background stitches on this tape lace tablecloth are complex enough to add variety and interest without overwhelming the design, and sturdy enough to hold the tapes in position and survive washing and ironing.

Background stitches of carefully twisted threads, secured in the center with tiny wheels, are attractive and structurally secure.

Table runner, about 4 feet long, with cutwork fabric centers. Overall design is initially attractive, but has no movement or grace. Leaf motifs at each end are dense and poorly shaped. Short staple threads make the tapes and background lose it's shape. $50 to $75.

Normandy Work

Normandy work is the name typically given to patchworks assembled from bits and pieces of lace and lacy linens. The origin of this type of work is unknown, but because many of the patchworks include bits and pieces of whitework very similar to that used for nineteenth century French caps and handkerchiefs, it seems likely that the term has some connection to Normandy or whitework from Normandy. These patchworks were popular from the end of the nineteenth century into the first quarter of the twentieth.

✔ Checklist

Design, technique, and workmanship should all be carefully related.

The best and most interesting Normandy work has an overall plan to the patchwork. Look for symmetry, with matching or very similar designs in lace fragments in related places. Pieces in corners and sides, for example, should match.

Laces placed in the overall design should be balanced by weight and style.

Technique and workmanship

Seams should be carefully hand-stitched with no raw edges. This is especially important because there is so much openwork, and because different types of laces are being joined.

Condition

Select examples of Normandy work that are in good condition. Replacing worn, torn, or rotted pieces of lace is expensive. It requires a great deal of lace, and careful handwork to repair.

Because the overall impression of the patchwork is so dazzling, it is especially easy to overlook major flaws. Use some plan or method for looking at the whole piece of lace: look from side to side, corner to corner, looking for symmetry and matching pieces of lace. If there is no symmetry, or pieces don't match anyplace, suspect that it has been repaired, patched on top of patches, or renovated.

Look for deterioration in the lace used to make up the patchwork. If one piece of lace is bad, look for other pieces of the same pattern and type of lace. They probably will be bad as well.

Look on the back for patches of tulle, net, or gauze. These almost always are supporting pieces of lace that are disintegrating.

If the color of the overall piece is very yellowed or stained, look carefully at each patch. If the cloth was repaired while it was dirty, the wrong color patch or thread might have been used. Don't be surprised to find a mix of brown, yellow, and ecru laces and sewing threads in patchworks after they are washed.

Rarity

Examples made with all or mostly handmade lace are the most rare and valuable.

Look for examples that include nineteenth century French whitework cap backs. These are usually round, and about the size of dinner plates. Good-quality handmade French whitework will have minute inserts of handmade needle lace. Look for the nearly microscopic, handmade buttonhole stitches in the needle lace.

Normandy work that combines an imaginative, complex overall design, good-quality handmade laces, and good condition is the most rare.

Pieces & prices

Bedspread worked in embroidered muslin, Valenciennes, and embroidered net. 86 inches by 90 inches. Sold at auction for $287.

Oval centerpiece, pieced of handmade Valenciennes bobbin lace and whitework. Embroidered bird flutters over a full-blown peony, possible it was originally the back of a French cap. Intricate needle lace fillings decorate the flower center. 21 inches by 25 inches. $250-$300.

Tablecloth assembled from both handmade and machine edgings, with large round center medallion assembled from a patchwork, and a striped background of laces. About 72 inches by 56 inches. Sold for about $1,200.

Filet lace with central oval floral medallion, an inner border of leaping and running animals, and a scalloped edge. 120 inches by 82 inches. Some discoloration. Sold at auction for $287.

Corner of a tablecloth assembled from a variety of different laces with no eye to symmetry, balance, or harmony. Odd seams in lace pieces, and lack of balance are a clue that this tablecloth has been repaired.

A close look at the back of the Normandy tablecloth shows the seams were not neatly trimmed and fitted, and the heavy net backing over one section tells us the lace is worn out and shredding. The badly fitted, mismatched pieces could also be an indication the tablecloth was badly repaired over time, with no care given to matching or blending laces.

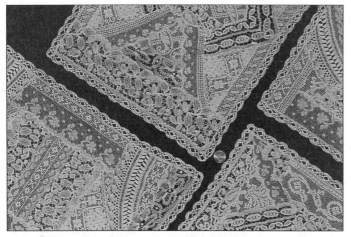

In well-designed and carefully stitched Normandy work, the laces balance each other out. Different laces are selected to accent particular parts of the design. Seams are very neatly hand trimmed and stitched to form precise boundaries between the different laces. Place mats assembled from handmade tape lace, filet, assorted machine laces, and edged with Cluny bobbin lace. Set of 6, 12 inches by 17-1/2 inches. $175 to $225.

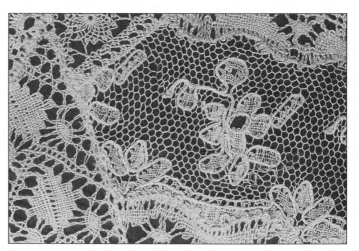

Seams are meticulously matched and stitched in good quality Normandy.

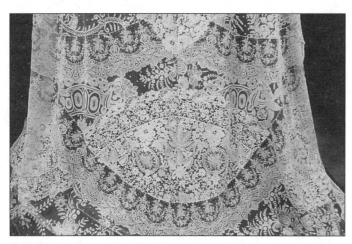

Center section of tablecloth assembled from the finest handmade Duchesse bobbin lace, and Point de Gaze (Rose Point) needle lace. Flounces of Point de Gaze 6 or more inches deep often sell for over $100 a yard. Dozens of yards were used for this cloth. Selling price was not disclosed, but likely was between $4,000 and $6,000. Photo courtesy of Paivi Roberts, West Palm Beach, Florida.

Center line on this table runner a late 19th century needle lace lappet, or headdress streamer. Other laces include fragments of Point de Gaze needle lace, Bucks Point , Valenciennes, and Duchesse bobbin lace; filet and Bebilla (Armenian) knotted lace, whitework embroidery and cutwork, and Battenberg tape lace. 48 inches by 20 inches. $750 to $1,200.

Most sought after and highly valued examples of Normandy work are those that include round French white-on-white embroidery, cutwork, and needle lace motifs about the size of dinner plates. These likely once were French cap backs. Other laces in this example include hand-embroidered machine net laces, handmade Valenciennes, Bucks Point, Lille, and other bobbin lace. A large tablecloth of this quality would sell for $1,500 to $2,500.

Sources

Books

de Bonneville, Francoise; *The Book of Fine Linen*, Flammarion, Paris, 1994

Kurella, E. *Guide to Lace and Linen*, Antique Trader Books, a Division of Landmark Publications, Norfolk, Virginia 1998.

Scofield, E. and Zalamea, P.; *Twentieth Century Linens and Lace*, Schiffer, Atglen, Pennsylvania, 1995

Dealers

California

Jules and Kathe Kliot Lacis
2982 Adeline
Berkeley, CA 94703
Phone 415-843-7178
Extensive line of vintage fashion, linens, and laces. Supplies and books for lacemaking and crafts. Appraisals, repairs, restoration.

Jude Allen
Vintage Collection
356 Main St.
Half Moon Bay, CA 94019
Phone 415-712-0366
Shop; linens, lace, old yardage, fabrics

Paul Freeman
Textile Artifacts
12589 Crenshaw
Hawthorne, CA 90250
Phone 310-676-2424
Fax 310-676-2242
textileguy@aol.com
www.textileguy.com
Shop, web site, shows

Julianna Greenberg
2695 W. Mesa
Fresno, CA 93711
209-436-8633
High quality fashions, linens and laces
Shows and by appointment. Has display in local antique mall; call for information.

Colorado

Sharon Daugherty
The Lace Chest
101 South 25th St.
Colorado Springs, CO 80904
Phone 719-632-1771
Shop; antique linen and lace.

Rebecca Nohe
Quartermoon Market
315 E. Pikes Peak Ave.
Colorado Springs, CO 80903
Phone 719-630-8961
Shop and by appointment. Fine textiles, whites; unusual and high end, quilts, samplers, old buttons.

Connecticut

Debra Bonito Images
32 N. Colony Road
Wallingford, CT 06492-3650
Phone 203-265-7076
Heirloom linens, lace, textiles Early textiles, needlepoint, tapestry, tablecloths, sheets.

Laurie Brady
Stonington Antiques and
Fine Linens
123 Water St.
Stonington, CT 06378
Shop; shows; linens and lace.

Patricia Lea
Orkney & Yost Antique Center
Cutler Street
Stonington, CT 06378
Phone 860-464-0466
Fine linens, lace, and textiles. Tapestries, Victorian draperies. 1950s drapes, Velvets, French Silks.

Patricia Menson
The Linen Merchant
494B Heritage Village
Southbury, CT 06488

Florida

Paivi Roberts
3100 Vincent Road
West Palm Beach, FL 33405
Phone 561-659-3896
Fax 407-835-0079
Fine linens and lace. Shop; antique shows across the country.

Georgia

Reminiscent Rose Antiques
1032 Wildwood Rd.
Atlanta, GA 30306
Phone 404-892-9611
70224.335&compuserve.com
Linens

Illinois

Jan Barishman
Findings of Geneva
307 W. State St.
Geneva, IL 60134
Fine vintage linens and lace; shop and shows in Chicago area.

Sabine Casten
The Lace Collection
558 Monroe
River Forest, IL 60305
Phone 708-366-0756
Vintage linens and clothes. Chicago area shows.

Chris Ebert
Chris' Antiques
5152 Harlem Road
Rockford, IL 61111
Phone 815-654-1610
Quilts, linens, vintage clothing.

Evelyn Forstadt
Swell Stuff
Evanston, IL
Phone 847-475-5716
Wide variety of linens, textiles, Victoriana, laces. Shows and by appointment.

Ellen Germanos
Suburban Chicago, IL
Phone 847-670-4440
Wide range of textiles, linens, vintage clothing. Shows only.

Geneva Antique Market
227 S. Third St.
Geneva, IL 60134
Phone 630-208-1150
Several textile dealers, including vintage textiles, quilts, Victoriana, linens and lace.

Indiana

Dawn Karberg
Blue Mirror
2531 Ticonderoga
Schereville, IN 46394
219-365-3825
Shows; shop in Chicago. Assorted vintage clothing and pre-1950s textiles; Barkcloth fabric, draperies, printed tablecloths.

Kentucky

Cynthia Roeder
Ramblin Rose Antiques
4 Colonel Point Space #82,
Duck Creek Antique Mall (Cincinnati area)
Wilder, KY 41076
Phone 606-441-6254
Linens and lace; vintage hats.

Jeanne Rhea
Victorian Lady
P.O. Box 248
Murray, KY 42071
Phone 502-759-3249
victorianlady@ldd.net
website:
Ldd.net/victorianlady/victorian/html
Linens, lace, textiles, clothing.

J. Parker
The Hound in the Hat Antiques
Rossville, IN 46065
Phone 765-589-3884
Vintage fashion, linens, lots of notions, ribbons, hats. One of three shops in mall devoted to textiles; Also shows and by appointment.

Michelle Stewart-Pruit
Back Through Time Antique Mall
Junction of state roads 26 and 39
9 West main St.
Rossville, IN 46065
Phone 765-379-3299
Vintage fashion, linens, lots of notions, ribbons, hats. One of three shops in mall devoted to textiles; Also shows and by appointment.

Jeanne Rhea
Victorian Lady
P.O. Box 248
Murray, KY 42071
Phone 502-759-3249
victorianlady@ldd.net
website:
Ldd.net/victorianlady/victorian/html
Linens, lace, textiles, clothing

Robert Walker
Just Faboo
107 East Main St.
P.O. Box 3913
Midway, KY 40347
(Lexington area)
Phone 606-846-5606
1780-1920 High quality vintage fashions, paisleys. Large shop, shows, and by appointment.

Louisiana
Victoria Bloom
89 William and Mary
Kenner, LA 70065
Phone 504-469-1847
Linens and lace.

Sherry Kohleri
Erudite Art
605 N. Alexander St.
New Orleans, LA 70119-4511
Phone 504-486-0257,
504-866-7795
Shop: vintage clothing, textiles, linens, and lace

Maine
Marsha Manchester
Milady's Mercantile
21 South Main
Middleboro, ME 02346
Phone 508-946-2121

Shirley Frater
Arsenic and Old Lace
P. O. Box 367
Damariscotta, ME 04543
Phone 207-563-1414
Fine quality linens and lace.

Massachusetts
Lucia Hotton
263 Union
South Weymouth, MA 02190
Phone 781-337-1982
Vintage linens, lace, apparel.

Skinner, Inc.
357 Main Street
Bolton, MA 01740
Phone 978-779-6241
Fax 978-779-5144
Auctioneers. Various auctions, especially Discovery and Decorative Arts auctions include early American textiles, such as samplers, quilts, coverlets, hooked and other rugs, and lots of mixed laces, linens, and textile fragments.

Michigan
Christine Crockett
The Crockett Collection
506 E. Kingsley
Ann Arbor, MI 48104
Phone 313-761-4751
Fine quality linens and lace. Saline (Ann Arbor) show and by appointment.

Donna Hicks
Aldon Antiques
Kalamazoo, MI
Phone 616-388-5375
Linen, lace, white apparel for ladies and children. Shows and by appointment only.

Jean Kenny
901 Ridgewood
Bloomfield Hills, MI 48304
Linens and vintage; Royal Oak Flea Market and by appointment only.

Leslie Saari
Great Lakes Appraisals
201 Iroquois Place
Cadillac, MI 49601-9221
Phone 616-775-6423
Identify and appraise vintage lace and linens.

Missouri
Beverly Donze
Odile's Linen and Lace
34 South Third
St. Genevieve, MO 63670
Phone 314-883-9871
Linens and lace; new and antique Victoriana.

Suzanne Dryer
4101 W. 83rd St.
Kansas City, MO 64114
Phone 816-246-5117
Stall in Mission Road Antique Mall. Lace, trims, ribbons, textiles.

Nebraska
Willa Felzien
1308 Highland Drive
Hastings, NE 68901
Phone 402-463-3620
Linens and lace; quilts; textiles. Shows and by appointment

New Jersey
Joan DeBoer
The Painted Lady
16 Greenwich St.
Belvedere, NJ 07823
Phone 908-475-1985
Shop; linens and lace

New York
Barbara Boyce
Another Time
3164 State Street
Caledonia, NY 11423
boyceTime@aol.com
Phone 716-538-9730
Shop; All kinds of textiles for kitchen, fashion, and the home.

Molly Carroll
329 Berryman Dr.
Amherst, NY 14226
Phone 716-837-5243
Specializing in Irish Lace. New York Pier shows and by appointment.

Jean Ellis
Sussex Antiques
P.O. Box 796
Bedford, NY 10506
Phone 914-241-2919
Victorian Christening gowns, linens and lace; vintage fashion. Shows only and by appointment.

Cherie Everett
Box 344
Carthage, NY 13619
Phone 315-493-4535
Fax 315-493-3832
cwocgret@northnet.org
Wide range of vintage textiles, linens, and lace. Shows and by appointment.

Douglas Hammond
Schmul Meier
Manhattan, NY

Jean Hoffman
207 East 66th St.
New York, NY 10021
Phone 212-535-6930
Bridal veils, paisleys, lace handkerchiefs. Extensive collection of top quality vintage wedding dresses, petit point bags.

David Kincaide
Kincaide and Bragg
130 Water Street
New York, NY 10005
Phone 212-825-1576
oc.davie&aol.com
Lace, quilts, 40s and 50s printed tablecloths/Vintage fabrics.

Mallory and Jeanette Merrill
Red Balloons
10912 Main St.
Clarence, NY
Phone 716-759-8999
Shop with exquisite and rare vintage linens, lace, clothing, lingerie, hats, paisleys, unique Victorian textiles and textile arts.

Florence Merritt
Antiques of Merritt
Rochester, NY
Phone 716-271-0912
Quilts, Coverlets.

Kay Mertens
1788 Everette Place
East Meadow, NY 11554
Phone 516-538-9185
All types of quality textiles, linen, lace.

Maria Niforos
39A Lafayette Ave.
Suffern, NY 10901
Phone 914-369-0830
Shop: high-quality textiles, linens, lace, costume. Also shows.

Audrey Paden
Schoharie, NY
Phone 518-295-7220
Textiles, by appointment.

Melanie Rahiser
Docuswatch
990 Sixth Avenue 6L
New York, NY 10018
Phone 212-695-8877
Fax 212-695-8969
Fragments of vintage textiles for designer's inspiration.

Rosse, Betty
Gallerie Enchantment
Hammondsport, NY
Phone 607-569-2809
Shop: vintage clothing, hats, etc.

Susan Simon
New York, NY
Phone 212-663-5318
Shows and by appointment. Very high quality European textiles, late nineteenth early twentieth century. Pillows, silk shawls, bedspreads, table linens.

Stan Slavin
PM Vintage
New York, NY
Phone 212-752-8451
Shows and by appointment. Late Victorian to 1920. Shawls, heavy draperies and brocades.

Ann Solicito
6 Village Green
Bardonia, NY 10954
Linens, lace. Shows only.

Patricia and Richard Dudley
8 Montcalm St.
Glens Falls, NY 12801
www.dudleyanddudley.com
Shows and by appointment. Also appraisals and consulting. Nineteenth century and earlier American and Anglo needlework, hooked rugs, textiles of all kind of kinds, blankets, rugs.

Jana Starr
Jana Starr Antiques
236 East 80th St.
New York, NY 10021
Phone 212-861-8256
Shop. Vintage white dresses, lots of old lace and textiles.

The Fassnachts
American Samplers
Box 795
Canandaigua, NY
14424
Phone 716-229-4199
American Samplers. Shows and by appointment

Sid Warshafsky
240 Overlook
Woodstock, NY 12499
Designer clothes; lace, linens. By appointment

Beehive Antiques
Route 21
North Cohocton, NY
Phone 716-534-5770
Shop. Vintage clothing.

Cora Ginsburg
19 East 74th St. 3rd Floor
New York, NY 10021
Shop. Specializes in seventeenth and eighteenth century fabrics, tapestries, lace, linens.

Heritage Antiques
42 W. Main St.
Angelica, NY 14709
Phone 716-466-3712
Vintage clothing.

Marie Auermuller
Fine linens
P.O. Box 07936
East Hanover, NY 07930
By appointment.

Metropolitan Antiques
110 West 19th Street
New York, NY
Phone 212-463-0200
Call for information on shows and auctions of vintage fashion, textiles, textile and lace sample books, and other related materials.

Chris Dreissen
Shop: 3256 State Route 30
Esperance, NY 12066
http:www.hickoryhillquilts.com
518-875-6133
Antique quilts, tops, blocks, vintage fabrics, reproduction fabric sewing notions. Restoration, appraisals.

Cather and Dembrosky
43 East 10th St.
New York, NY 10003
Phone 212-353-1244
Shop: specializing in Arts and Crafts antiques, including textiles. Also does Asheville Arts and Crafts show.

Rabbit Goody
Thistle Hill Weavers
101 Chestnut Ridge Road
Cherry Valley, NY 13320
(near Cooperstown)
518-284-2729
rabbitg@albany.net
www.albany.net/~rabbitg
www.quilthistory.com/thistlehill
Resource on coverlets, quilts, weaving, and vintage fabrics. Specialist in identification of hand-produced textiles, and textiles from the transition period of from home to factory technology, circa 1750 to 1850. Early block, roller cylinder and copperplate prints. Custom textile mill producing reproductions of antique silk, linsey-woolsey, textiles for museums, reenactors, decorators.

Cheryl Anne VanDenburg
Pieces of the Past Antiques
Cuddebacks Antique Center
Canandaigua, NY
Phone 716-396-3224
*Shows, exhibits at antique mall.
Quilts, and antique textiles.*

MUSEUMS

New York
Brooklyn Museum of Art
200 Eastern Parkway
Brooklyn, NY 11238
Phone 718-638-0005
*Patricia Mears, textiles specialist,
Ext. 251.*

Metropolitan Museum of Art
New York, NY

North Carolina
Elizabeth Bright
Elizabeth Bright Antiques
26 Williams Circle
Lexington, NC 27292
Phone 910-249-2448
*Linens and lace; vintage textiles
and Victoriana. Shows and mail
order.*

Ramona Spain
Of Cabbages and Kings
111 West Main
Aberdeen, NC 28315
Phone 910-944-1110
*Shop; linens and lace; vintage
clothing; quilts.*

Ohio
Cynthia Barta
2568 Kendall Road
Shaker Heights, OH 44120-1141
Phone 216-281-1959
*Shows and by appointment. 1940s
to 1970s men's and women's cloth-
ing and accessories featured at
Suite Lorain antique mall, 7105
Lorain Avenue, Cleveland, OH.*

Linda Bowman
Legacy
12502 Larchmere Boulevard
Cleveland, OH 44102
Phone 216-229-0578
*Shows and by appointment. High
style vintage clothing from 1920
through 1960.*

Libby Gower
618 Superior Ave.
Dayton, OH 45407-2303
Phone 937-223-4615
*Shows and by appointment. Art
Deco and Vintage clothes and tex-
tiles.*

Linda Ketterling
Toledo, OH
Phone 419-536-5531
*Antique linens and lace. Shows
and by appointment.*

Tim & Barb Martien
1229 Bell St.
Chagrin Falls, OH 44022
Phone 440-338-3666
*Samplers. Shows and by appoint-
ment.*

Betty Parker
Pieces of the Past
159 Franklin
Doylestown, OH 44230
Phone 330-658-6161
*Quilts; linens and lace. Shows and
by appointment*

MarionSteinbrunner
14747 Sisson Road
Chardon, OH 44024
*Linens, lace, and textiles. Shop
and Atlantic City shows.*

Shirley and Jim Wolf
Stitches in Time
61 Truax
Plymouth, OH 44865
Phone 419-687-2061
wolf@stitchesintime.com
*Shop, shows, and by appointment.
Wide range of vintage clothes,
bridal, hats, etc. from nineteenth
century on.*

Mary R. Yarton
Whitehouse, OH 43571
Phone 419-875-5310
*Samplers and other American
antiques. By appointment.*

Reflections of the Past
P. O. Box 40361
Bay Village, OH 44140
Phone 440-835-6924
*Website only. Vintage clothing, tex-
tiles, linens, lace.*

MUSEUMS:
Kent State University Museum
Kent, OH
330-672-3450
*On the campus of Kent State Uni-
versity. Exhibits of vintage fashion,
textiles, and related always on display.*

Cleveland Museum of Art
1150 East Blvd.
Cleveland, OH 44160-1797
Louise Mackie, curator of textiles
Christine Starkman, assistant cura-
tor of textiles
Phone 216-421-7340

Oklahoma
The International Linen Registry
4107 S. Yale Avenue #247
Tulsa, OK 74135
Phone 918-622-5223
1-800-581-5223
*Lace and linens always on display.
Classes in lacemaking. Appraisals
and identification.*

Oregon
Norma Bernady
Vintage Whites
320 Court St. NE
Salem, OR 97301
Phone 503-587-8998
Shop: vintage linens and antiques.

Pennsylvania
Helen Lake Smith
Meadville, PA
Phone 814-333-9267
*Shows and by appointment only.
High-end linens and laces.*

Katy Kane, Inc.
34 W. Ferry St.
New Hope, PA 18393
Phone 215-862-5873
Antique clothing and fine linens

Natasha's
Natasha Green
551 Beaver St.
Sewickley, PA 15143
Phone 412-741-9484
*Shop, specializing in old linens,
laces, and fine vintage fashions.
Also shows and by appointment.*

Pat Edleman
1945 Meadow Lane
Wyomissing, PA 19610
Phone 610-796-0320
*Shows and by appointment. Vin-
tage lace and linens.*

Tennessee
Laura Muller
7200 Stamford Cove
Germantown, TN 38138
Phone 901-754-4222
Linens and lace.

Ann Williams
P. O. Box 743
Brentwood, TN 37024
Phone 615-373-4725
Linens and lace, handkerchiefs.

Vermont
Karen Augusta
31 Gage
N. Westminster, VT 05101
Phone 802-463-4958;
800-OLD LACE
Designer vintage, fine linens and lace. Shows and by appointment.

Virginia
Sally O'Brien
P.O. Box 29534
Richmond, VA 23242
Phone 804-364-3488
Fine nineteenth century English linens, lace, and accessories. Lectures and programs on linens and lace.

Ann Kovalchick
P.O. Box 608
Front Royal, VA
Antique lace, vintage textiles. By appointment.

Gretchen Noyes
P.O. Box 948
Alexandria, VA 22313
Phone 703-920-0348
Appraisals of antique needlework and textiles, including quilts, samplers, embroidery, hooked rugs, linens, and lace.

Washington
Nancy Evans
Legacy of Lace
220 South First
Kent, WA 98032
Phone 206-852-0052
Linens and lace, appraisals, repair and conservation.

Maureen Matich
M.A.M.s Vintage Linens
35 Main St.
Edmonds, WA 98020
Phone 206-771-5310
Shop; shows: linens and lace.

West Virginia
Dixie Elmore
Rt. 1, Box 211
Washington, WV 26181
Phone 304-863-5460
Vintage clothing, hats, clothing 1800-1945. Linens, lingerie, assorted trims. Shows, and by appointment.

Wisconsin
Joe Vonnie Anderson
and Jenne Aton
Vintage Vamps
489 Broadway St.
Berlin, WI 54923
Phone: 920-295-6959 (Joe) and 920-361-2893 (Jenne).
By appointment quilts, bed linens, quality linens and laces, kitchen tablecloths and towels, vintage clothes.

Tracey Jones
Retrofit, Pilgrim Antique Mall
W156 N 11500 Pilgrim Road
Germantown, WI 53022
Phone 414-774-6041(Home)
Shop 414-250-0260
Men's and women's vintage clothing, soft goods, textiles. Stalls in Germantown and Grafton malls. Shows and by appointment.

Pat O'Brien
Flapper Alley
1518 N. Farwell
Milwaukee, WI 53202
Phone 414-276-6252
Shop, mail order, and by appointment. Nineteenth century vintage fashion, linens and lace.

Idlewild Antiques
5121 Glen Road
McFarland, WI 53558
Phone 608-838-8410
Wide range of high-end vintage and textiles. Shows and by appointment.

Wyoming
Celia Howarth
P.O. Box 4616
Jackson, WY 83001
Phone 208-787-2181
English and French textiles. Shows and by appointment.

Europe

Italy
E. Kerer
Palazzo Miari
(Behind St. Marks Church)
Calle Canonica 4328 A
Venice, Italy
Phone 52.35.485

Spain
Concha B. Roig
Enmedio, N 103 Atico
12001
Castellon, Spain
Phone 964-21.51.75
Specialists in mantillas, and vintage lace.

Pepita Sanchez
Beatriz Castello
Alfonso XII, 63
Detras Clinica del Pilar
08006, Barcelona, Spain
Phone 201.46.89
Vintage clothing and lace.

El Nino Seise
Piazza de la Pescaderia 4
41004, Seville, Spain
Phone 95-4561916
Antique laces and vintage clothing.

London
Phillips International Auctioneers
101 New Bond Street
London, W1Y OAS
Phone 44-171-629-6602
(textile department)
New York phone for catalogs
and sale information
212-570-4830.
Regular sales of textiles, about 6 per year, include European band, spot, and European and American needlework samplers from the seventeenth through the nineteenth centuries.

Pillows

No sofa is complete without a few throw pillows. Most of these either came from the store with the furniture, or were made up from upholstery fabric.

For centuries, the pillow also has been used as an ideal place to show off needlework skills. It is a manageable size, a neat square, rectangular, round, or oval shape ideally suited to either a picture or an abstract design, and best of all, everybody needs a few. A homemaker with a creative passion can stitch away on neat projects that can be finished in a relatively short time. They can either deck their own home with these treasures, or pass them along as gifts to friends.

Embroidery and needlepoint have been popular techniques. The most interesting and collectible are the original designs worked in the needleworker's own choice of colors and stitches. In the nineteenth century, when the home hand-craft movement really started to get big, merchants found a large market for preprinted designs on fabric, and for complete kits with a printed design, a supply of thread, and an instruction booklet. Kits, unless they were individualized by the stitcher, tend to be predictable and boring.

A pillow also is the perfect place to throw a spot of color to brighten up a room, or to soften a harsh line. It is also a great place to use small fragments of interesting textiles that are just too good to throw away. A decorator's atelier has always been an ideal place to find wonderful fragments of centuries-old tapestries, cut velvets, brocades, needleworks, rugs, and embroideries.

Pillows are probably the most common fate of many of the world's most unique and interesting textiles. Before putting scissors to that fabric you just found, ask, "Is this something that likely will never be duplicated?"

✔ Checklist

What is the most likely source of the fabric on this pillow? Does the shape and border suggest the needlework was specifically designed to be a pillow, or was another fabric cut up?

Pieces & prices

Pair of Victorian needlepoint pillows, each with delicately shaded oval floral design on a black velvet background, edged with greed tassel fringe. Sold at auction for $345.

Pair of raspberry cut velvet pillows with champagne flowers and fringe. Sold at auction for $402.

Pair of nineteenth century Jacquard tapestry pillows in woven leaf pattern, with twisted cord fringe. Sold at auction for $1495.

Original artwork, such as these pillows stitched from children's crayon drawings, make delightful decorator items, and always are one-of-a kind.
Needlepoint pillow made in the 1970s by the author. The clown design was taken from a childhood crayon drawing by Mary Fryxell.
Needlepoint pillow made in the 1970s by the author. Fish design was taken from a childhood crayon drawing by Elizabeth Poder Michael.

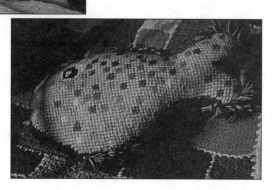

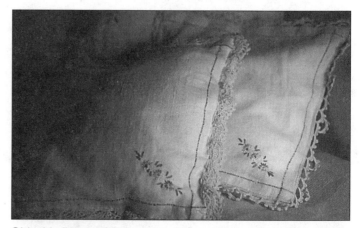

Old table linens often are recycled as pillow covers. These linen napkins, trimmed with embroidery and edged with crochet just needed a backing to become pillows. Colorful embroidered napkins often sell for $3 to $5 each.

A

B

C

D

Arts & Crafts era pillows, dating from the early 20th century, are gaining in popularity along with trends toward Arts & Crafts decorating. Prices range from $45 to more than $100, depending on condition, and quality of the design, stitching and shading of the embroidery. Background material is most often a natural linen.

A - Design in shades of blues and golds. Graceful design, and quality of the stitching make this a high quality pillow. Photo courtesy of Arts and Crafts Period Textiles, Oakland, California

B - Tulip-shaped elements are worked in various shades of gold. Checkerberry motifs are worked in blue and red. Graceful design, and quality of the stitching make this a high quality pillow. Photo courtesy of Arts and Crafts Period Textiles, Oakland, California

C. Satin stitches on these motifs are nicely shaded in burnt orange, and golds, the foliage in shades of pale green. Motifs are outlined in black. Satin stitches are worked wide apart, giving it a loose quality that will wear out quickly with use.

D. American Indian motifs sometimes were adapted for Arts and Crafts kits. This design is worked in golds, oranges, and golds, outlined in black on an average quality cotton fabric. A stiff, and less desirable design. Pillow is edged in stiff machine trim.

Pot Holders

Generations of pre-boomers grew up weaving pot holders out of loops of cotton jersey. For decades, clever, imaginative, and colorful pot holders have been away for homemakers to express creativity, make token gifts, and supply church bazaars and school fund-raisers.

Great creativity is expressed in simple weaving, crochet, sewing, quilting, and embroidery. Only rare examples can be dated with any precision. Although certain styles and motifs hit high points of popularity, once a clever design was introduced, it was endlessly copied generation after generation. Synthetic yarns can provide a "not earlier than" date, but dating more specifically is impossible.

Often, pot holders were shaped to match up with a wooden, painted holder. Half-rounds or triangles hanging on a hook, for example, often were the skirt for a painted half-doll.

Although novelty pot holders are not highly collectible now, and may never be, they do offer a relatively inexpensive way to add a spot of color and whimsy to a kitchen.

Somewhere about the 1930s or 1940s, the crocheted flower basket with two or three little round pot holders inside hit the pop chart. Almost always, the color choice is white or natural white for the basket, with a bright red rose with kelly green leaves as the accent. The little round pot holders usually are too small to be particularly useful, except to add a cheery note hanging on the wall. Price about $15 for a set.

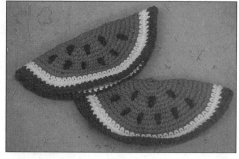

Just a little leftover yarn in red, white and green, and in about half an hour a homemaker with a crochet hook can create a slice of watermelon. A plate-sized crocheted round is folded over, seeds are embroidered on in black yarn. The supply of these is endless, and they rarely sell for more than $5.

Crocheted pot holders were created in endless round, hexagonal, and square patterns, in variegated, and assorted bright colors. Look for attractive colors, lots of dimension and extra layers for texture. All sell for between $5 and $10 today.

Flaunting imagination, cleverness, and creativity seems to be the objective in designing many crocheted pot holders. The little hanging ring at the top, the absence of a neck hole, and the general flatness of this bright green and white "doll dress" betrays it as a pot holder.

Quilts

The term "quilt" refers to a very broad range of bedcovers. The idea is very simple: layers of fabric are joined together to provide warmth and comfort.

It's not too hard to figure out how to identify the basic parts of a quilt: the tops, the stuffing, and the backing. Finally, the edge has to be finished off in some form — either with a binding, such as a bias-cut strip of fabric, or some sort of border and hem.

Then the fun begins. Each of the basic parts can be worked and or embellished in many ways.

There are a couple of basic ways the layers can be joined. They may be stitched together with long running lines of stitching. This is the form generally called quilting. These lines of running stitches may be arranged in an infinite number of patterns, from straight lines to fancy tracings of flowers, shells, feathers, or other patterns.

Layers may be joined by running yarns or strings through the layers at intervals, and tying them together. This is known as tufting.

The top can consist of a solid sheet of fabric, known as a whole-cloth quilt, or it can be assembled from cut pieces. Again, these two possibilities have infinite variations. The whole cloth can be one plain color, or it can be a print, stripe, plaid, or other decorated fabric.

The cut pieces that make up the assembled top can be taken from new yard goods, or leftovers and recycled materials, artfully arranged in any classic way, or a mixed jumble of assorted pieces to form a crazy quilt. Many times, a quilt is pieced from novelty fabrics: old dress labels, ribbons, handkerchiefs, scarves, bookmarks, neckties, or other bits of fabric.

Either the solid fabric, or the pieced top can then be embellished in any of dozens of ways. Cut pieces can be stitched to the pieced or solid top as an appliqué, and the top can be painted, stenciled, or embroidered.

The embroidery can be flowers, animals, figures, or other designs, or it can be names, mottoes, snatches of poetry, or a diary to form a personalized quilt symbolizing friendship, mourning, a wedding, or a birth.

The joy of quilts is that no two are alike, and the technique, colors, shapes, materials, and embellishments are governed only by the wit, imagination and skill of the maker, and whatever materials she or he could lay their hands on. Friendship quilts may be pieced, appliquéd, solid, embroidered or painted. Crazy quilts can be made of luxurious fabrics carefully edged with elaborate embroidery stitches, or cotton feedsacks looped together in lopsided stitches.

✔ Checklist

Top design

Consider the design from an artistic standpoint — is it balanced, colorful, flowing, graceful, pleasing.

Consider the design from a storyteller's standpoint. What does the quilt tell us about who made it, when it was made, why it was made. What does it tell us about the times when it was made?

Look for signatures, dates, mottoes, bits of poetry embroidered into the quilt.

In seventeenth and eighteenth century quilts, a large central motif, such as the Tree of Life, a large bouquet or basket of flowers, or some variation of scrollwork and flowers was popular.

In the nineteenth century, the central motif was much less popular. Overall designs, especially blocks and other pieceworks, were much more popular.

Quilting pattern

How imaginative, elegant and witty is the pattern of stitching used to quilt or join the layers of fabric?

How much thought went into choosing the pattern of stitching?

Does the pattern of quilting somehow relate to the design of the top? Does it consist of flowing curves that echo the motifs? Is the stitching in a pattern — feathers, curves, shells, flowers — totally unrelated to the design of the piecework or appliqué?

Materials

What fibers — cotton, silk, wool, linen, synthetics — were used to make the fabrics on the top, borders, and bottom?

What kinds of fabrics were used – prints, solid colors, painted fabrics, resist or batik dyed? Were any luxury fabrics like velvets, satins or brocades, used in the quilt?

What patterns are used in any prints used? Small overall design, printed characters, figures, animals, plaids, stripes.

Look for novelties, especially in crazy quilts. Woven silk ribbons, pictures, printed cigarette silks, bookmarks, old silk neckties, etc.

What is the batting material? Cotton, with or without cotton seeds still in; wool batting, or a woven fabric of some sort: all are possibilities.

Technique

How is the top put together? Does it consist of a solid piece of fabric, or is it appliqué, or pieced?

If it is an appliqué, does it consist of a single cut piece, or many smaller bits?

How are the top and bottom joined? Is the quilt tufted (held together with little ties of yarn) or quilted (stitched at intervals in decorative patterns)?

Is the top put together by hand or machine?

Is the quilting hand or machine?

Look for additional embellishments, especially embroidery. Crewel, or embroidery with wool yarns, was typically used on eighteenth century palampore and broderie perse quilts. Embroidery with silk and cotton yarns and threads was very popular in the nineteenth century.

Workmanship

How many stitches are there per inch?

How close are the rows of stitching?

How even are the stitches?

How straight are the lines of stitching, and how graceful and smooth are the curves?

Is the quilting handmade or machine?

Embroidery should be neat, precise, and stitches should be very even. Look for a variety of imaginative stitches, especially in crazy quilts.

Condition

Look at each fabric carefully. Some dyes were notoriously unstable, and cause areas of a fabric to deteriorate. If you notice holes, look for a pattern. All the black dots in a print, the green leaves in a floral, the yellow dots in flower centers may have dropped out.

Are all the components, top, appliqués or designs, quilting, borders, and bottom original?

Look at the stitching of all components — quilting, seams in piecework, stitching attaching the background fabric and any appliqués. Is it sound, or coming apart?

Look for stains and discoloration. Some stains, especially blood and rust, eat away the fabric. There is no way to get them out. Accept them as part of the history of a quilt, and decide if you can live with them.

Is the fabric torn, or worn out? Tears in an otherwise solid fabric sometimes can be mended. Worn out fabrics won't support mending, and need to be replaced or supported.

What is the batting? If it is wool, check for moth damage.

Evaluating an old quilt

The value of an old quilt often goes beyond the sum of all its features. Look at it to discover its soul. Why was it made? Who made it? When and where was it made?

Was it made all at once, or over the course of several years by many people? Often, a quilt top is assembled into a finished quilt decades after it was first started, and the different fabrics and stitching will reflect the work of many individuals and different time periods.

How much human personality is worked into choosing the design, the materials, and the stitching patterns? What kind of thought does it reflect? Whimsy, cleverness, artistry, imagination, plodding determination? Perhaps a harried homemaker that was trying to put just a bit of creativity in her life while dealing with children, a leaking roof, a failing crop, or a cheating husband?

Quilt techniques

Trapunto

Trapunto is a raised effect achieved by inserting stuffing, usually cotton, into certain areas outlined by stitching. Some of the earliest quilts, dating back to seventeenth century India, are whole-cloth (not pieced) covers with intricate figural designs puffy with stuffing. Because of the great amount of time involved in going back to carefully insert stuffing only in certain design areas, these often are highly valued by those who know quilting.

Trapunto may appear in pieced, patchwork, or solid quilts.

Pieces & prices

Pieced and appliquéd cotton star and rose quilt, mid nineteenth century. Three rows of three large radiating stars pieced in green and red on a white ground. Red roses centered in intervening squares and diamonds. Sold at auction for $1,035.

Cotton quilt, nineteenth century, white on white, worked in quilted stars and circles. 109 inches by 111 inches. Sold at auction for $862.

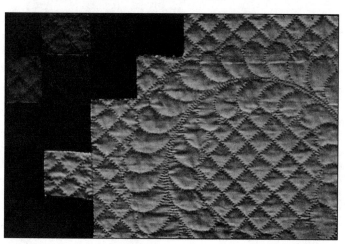

High relief in a quilt suggests additional stuffing was added just in the design areas. A look at the back is necessary to confirm that it is trapunto — tiny holes will appear where filling was stuffed in. Photo courtesy of the University of Nebraska Lincoln International Quilt Study Center.

Early fabric quilts

We take colored and printed fabrics for granted today. In the seventeenth and eighteenth century, before chemical dyes, printing machines, and other technology came along, finishing of fabrics was a mysterious and elaborate process. Among those who understand the difficulty and complexity of the processes, very old fabrics, such as the seventeenth and eighteenth century chintzes, calicos, calamancos, and palampores, are especially valued today.

Calamanco was a fine, glossy fabric popular in the eighteenth century. It is an extremely fine version of linsey-woolsey, a linen and wool blend. It was given a high shine by rubbing it with stone, and/or glazing it with egg white. Quilts made from solid pieces of calamanco are some of the earliest known, and are highly prized by collectors.

India perfected the art of printing fabrics with colorful, indelible patterns long before Europeans. In the seventeenth and eighteenth centuries, beautifully printed fabrics from India were imported to Europe.

In addition to the mystery of dyeing, printing was labor-intensive, involving multiple applications of hand-placed printing block, application and removal of waxes for resist printing, and touches of hand painting.

Palampore is a region of India noted for fabulous printed fabrics in the seventeenth and eighteenth centuries. Solid fabrics with exotic colorful printed designs and minimal stitching are among the most prized and treasured among quilt collectors. The fabrics also were printed with motifs, such as flower baskets, bouquets, and other motifs that easily could be cut out and used as appliqués. These wonderful fabrics were imported to Europe by the East India Company. By the end of the 1700s, good quality print fabrics were made in the American Colonies as well.

Quilts from all these old fabrics are some of the most rare, and most valued.

Palampore print quilt, circa 1750-1770. Large central design, often known as the Tree of Life, was a popular 18th century motif. Quilt is from the James Collection, University of Nebraska, International Quilt Study Center.

Piecework quilts

The seventeenth and eighteenth century print fabrics were extremely expensive, and often individual motifs, such as flower baskets or bouquets, were cut out of the whole cloth and applied to a larger solid color fabric to form a patterned quilt. This technique was known as broderie perse. By the end of the eighteenth century, printed and decorated fabrics were much more available and economical, and this practice was no longer needed.

Pieced quilts, however, were just beginning to come into their own as a popular form. By the middle of the nineteenth century, hundreds of traditional designs, usually based on geometric shapes, as well as the irrational collections of odd shapes known as crazy quilts, were known and used. They may be patchworks, formed by sewing together bits and pieces of fabric, or appliqués, formed by applying cut bits of fabric to another. It is not uncommon to find combinations of both techniques in the same quilt.

Appliqué

One common type of piecework is appliqué. The design in appliqué quilts consists of cut fabrics arranged in a decorative pattern and applied (stitched) to another fabric.

Hawaiian quilts are a unique variation of the appliqué. They are not pieced. The design is done in one cutting on a solid piece of cloth in eight-fold and triangular shapes. This symmetrical cut pattern is stitched onto a bed sheet or other large, sometimes seamed cloth. Designs of authentic old Hawaiian quilts were taken from nature, and were inspired by papaya, fig, breadfruit leaves, pineapples, lily, hibiscus, rose, pearl oyster shells, and the lei. The carrier pigeon, honeycreeper, and other native birds also served as inspiration for designs.

The stitching followed the outline of the design, and radiated out in concentric lines, like ripples on the water, to fill the entire backing.

Quilting was introduced to Hawaii in the early 1800s by missionaries, and the traditional Hawaiian appliqué style appeared in the mid 1800s.

Pieces & prices

Flower bouquets. Early twentieth century. 72 inches by 82 inches. Excellent condition. Offered for $675.

Whig rose in red and green on white background. Early twentieth century. 66 inches by 84 inches. Very good condition. Offered for $585.

Urns of pink and red flowers, green leaves. Early twentieth century. 66 inches by 84 inches. Needs mending. Offered for $265.

Hawaiian appliqué quilt in bright red on cream background. Stitched rows of quilting radiate like ripples around the appliqué. This quilt is part of the James Collection, University of Nebraska, International Quilt Study Center.

Appliqué of floral motifs cut from Palampore prints, a technique sometimes known as Broderie Perse. This quilt with a large lone star motif dates to about 1830. This quilt is part of the James Collection, University of Nebraska, International Quilt Study Center.

Broderie Perse quilt, consisting of floral motifs cut from Indian Palampore prints, and swags and scallops of red calico. This quilt is part of the James Collection, University of Nebraska, International Quilt Study Center.

Patchwork quilts

It is impossible to name or to count all the possible patterns that can be formed by cutting and stitching bits of fabric. Patchworks, whether formed from bits of fabric salvaged from old clothes, from the rag bag, or cut from new pieces of yardage, from leftover ribbons, labels, bookmarks, or other fabrics, are one of the most common forms of quilt found in America's attics, closets, and bedrooms.

The value of the quilt depends on the originality and workmanship of the patchwork design, the age, and the unique quality of the fabrics in the patchwork.

Pieces & prices

"Trip around the world" piecework of tiny squares in pastel and deeper shades. Early twentieth century. 86 inches by 96 inches, Excellent condition. Offered for $675.

Small checkerboards of red and white, and blue and white alternate with off-white blocks made from old, washed-out salt and sugar sacks. Speculation was that the quilt top was made for the centennial in 1876, but this is unlikely, as all the sacks were not available that early.

Crazy Quilts

Crazy is the term applied to any quilt made of irregularly shaped pieces. These may be arranged in no particular order, or have just a semblance of a plan, such as squares of irregular pieces arranged in rows like a windowpane.

The best of the crazies are not crazy at all, but clearly reflect a thoughtful but whimsical mind. Look for unusual materials, fancy and elaborate stitches neatly worked along the seams between the pieces, and most of all, look for the personality of the quiltmaker to show through.

Pieces & prices

Victorian satin, cotton and velvet crazy quilt, late nineteenth century. Worked in assorted colors with irregular patches, some faded and some embroidered with flowers, animals, shells, and figures, all within a velvet and lace border. 69 inches by 58 inches. Sold at auction for $345.

Pieced wool and velvet crazy quilt, late nineteenth century. Worked in assorted colors, centering irregular patches, some embroidered with flowers, moons, stars and leaves. 62 inches x 56 inches. Sold at auction for $431.

Pieced satin, silk and velveteen embroidered crazy quilt, twentieth century. Worked in angular pieces in varied colors interspersed with applied flower heads and stars. 84 inches x 70 inches. Sold at auction for $230.

Pieced wool satin and velvet crazy quilt, dated 1898. Worked in assorted colors, centering irregular patches, some embroidered with initials and inscribed, "Bless Our Home, My Happy Home, Farewell Summer 1896." 62 inches x 78 inches. Sold at auction for $230.

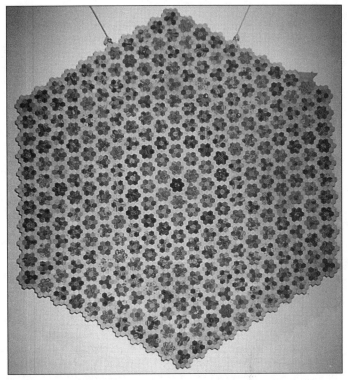

19th century hexagonal quilt, assembled from 4,390 hexagons formed over paper templates. The background is white, with assorted cotton prints with yellows, reds, and blues dominant. Photo courtesy of Maury Bynum, Textile Conservators, Chicago, Illinois.

Crazy quilt, attributed to a quiltmaker in Mount Clemens, Michigan, in 1884. Quilt is made from silks, velvets, and an assortment fabrics, and richly decorated with embroidery and novelty woven and embellished fabrics, with a wide border of cut velvet. This quilt is part of the James Collection, University of Nebraska, International Quilt Study Center.

Pieced silk, satin, wool and cotton crazy quilt, Pennsylvania, late nineteenth-early twentieth century. Each block worked in a varied colors with angular pieces sewn with varied stitching within a wide printed cotton border. 68 inches x 70 inches. Sold at auction for $489.

Pieced silk satin, velvet and wool crazy quilt, dated 1895. Worked in angular blocks in various medium to dark colors. Design includes a central quartered fan embroidered with peacocks, flowerheads, leaves and stars. 69 inches x 70 inches. Sold at auction for $489.

Silk crazy quilt, circa 1880. Worked in assorted colors. Design of circular and radiating fans, central floral and foliate sprigs within a banded border, each corner embroidered with a daisy sprig. 69 inches x 54 inches. From the Margaret Cavigga collection, illustrated on the cover of the 1992 Hallmark calendar. Sold at auction for $12,650.

Combination quilts

Most quilts refuse to fit neatly into any category. Instead, they consist of both piecing and appliqué, and are embellished with embroidery. The pieced, appliquéd and embroidered quilts, in any pattern including crazies, become album, sampler, or friendship quilts when they are worked by several people, and imbued with a family, parish, congregation, or friendship group history.

Album and friendship is a catch-all term for quilts made by several people, usually as a gift for someone. Variations on this theme are endless. Album quilts tell the story of an event, or a whole lifetime, or the history of a family.

The value depends on the importance and significance of the signatures and the story the quilt has to tell. More and more collectors are using the newly available resources, especially the Internet, to research the history of album and friendship quilts, tracking down the community, the family, or the congregation that contributed to these registries of human life. It is perhaps telling that at the recent Butterfield and Butterfield auction of the Cavigga quilt collection, album and friendship quilts with real human drama and history sold for more than twentieth century celebrity signature quilts.

Pieces & prices

Blocks of blues and beiges alternating with off-white. Nineteenth century. 87 inches x 92 inches. Sold at auction for $575.

Floral blocks, each signed in ink by a family member within red bars on an off-white quilted background. Nineteenth century. Sold at auction for $1,300.

Pieced and appliquéd minister's quilt, early twentieth century. Rows of embroidered names surrounded by a square patched band border. Made for Reverend and Mrs. Curtis Ringness in Tampa, Florida. Sold at auction for $402.

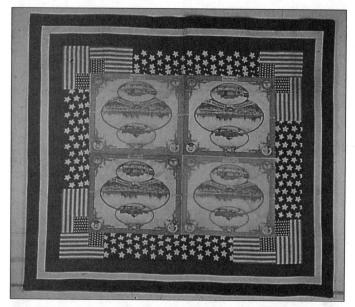

American centennial quilt, circa 1876. Pieced with printed reserves of various centennial exhibition halls. Flag, star, and stripe borders in red, white, blue, and black on white ground. Some staining. 74-1/2 inches by 83 inches. Sold at auction for $747. Photo courtesy of Skinner, Inc., Bolton, Massachusetts.

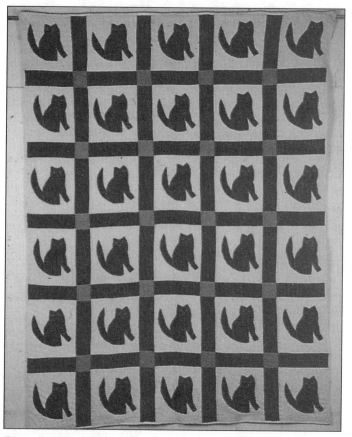

Pieced and appliquéd quilt, circa 1930, with blue seated cats in white background with red strips and green corners. 63 inches by 84-1/2 inches. Sold at auction for $1,265. Photo courtesy of Skinner, Inc., Bolton, Massachusetts.

Civil War signature quilt, circa 1865. One side worked in a repeating star and block pattern in red. Off-white, and medium blue, embroidered with names of soldiers and regiments, and other names; the reverse worked in a feather star variant in similar colors, with triangles and squares, embroidered with names and initials. Sold at auction for $4,887. Photo courtesy of Butterfield and Butterfield, San Francisco, California.

Mourning quilt, probably from southern Indiana. Dated 1913, the quilt is made of somber tones of deep wine red, greys, blues, browns, and black. Embroidered mottoes include, "Glory be to God," stitched above the church, "In God We Trust," "Jesus Our Lord Who Died for Us," "Peace be to you," "God is Love," (stitched along seam above the stars), and, "I am earth"(stitched alongside the church.). 73 inches by 90 inches. Photo courtesy of Textile Conservators, Chicago, Illinois. Offered for $5,000.

Sampler quilt, 19th century, with 30 different pieced and appliquéd blocks arranged in rows, separated by a blue, leaf-print background. 90 inches by 75 inches. Sold at auction for $575. Photo courtesy of Butterfield and Butterfield, San Francisco, California.

Novelty pieced quilts

Embroidered and
"Penny Square" quilts

Penny squares were small designs marketed in the late nineteenth and early twentieth century intended to fit neatly into blocks. Subjects covered anything from flowers and flower baskets, nursery rhymes, animals, birds, fruit, and figures. Embroidering these designs in red thread on white fabric was the rage for a long time. This work is sometimes called "turkey work," harking back to the days when the red dyes came from Turkey. Or they are simply called redwork.

Designs could be selected at a shop, where the chosen patterns would be "pounced" onto off-white muslin with colored powder. Later, they were sold or offered in pattern books as iron-on transfers, or sold as pre-printed cloth squares.

Silk flag quilt, early 20th century, assembled from printed cigarette silks. Printed flags from around the world form the center, some with figures holding flags in the air, all within a banded edged border. 51 inches by 52 inches. Sold at auction for $2,300. Photo courtesy of Butterfield and Butterfield, San Francisco, California.

Pieced panel assembled from woven cigarette silks with emblems of universities. It is an important distinction that the emblems are woven into the cigarette silks. Often, they are merely printed. Photo courtesy of Textile Conservators, Chicago, Illinois. Offered for $600.

Small doll bed-sized crazy quilt made from wide silk handpainted neckties of the 1940s.

Amish Quilts

Simplicity, solid color fabrics in bold colors, and basic geometric designs are characteristics associated with nineteenth century Amish and Mennonite quilts. A large central square, or diamond, and a deep border are typical. A large, eight-pointed central star, known as the star of Bethlehem or blazing star, was also popular. These patchwork designs were, in the nineteenth century, distinctively different than other styles of quilt being worked at that time. Different Amish and Mennonite communities abided by different rules. The Lancaster, Pennsylvania Amish were more strict, for example, than those in Indiana, and their designs were often simpler.

While the piecework or patchwork designs might have been more spare than other quilt styles, the stitching of the actual quilting was often extremely fine, closely worked, and stitched in elaborate designs.

By the twentieth century, the Amish made many types of quilts out of many types of materials, including natural and synthetic fabrics, and solid and print materials in dark and bright colors. Once the quilt has left the hands of the maker and gone off into the world, it is nearly impossible to tell whether or not it was made by the Amish.

Even if a quilt is identified as Amish, it still should pass the same tests of quality as any other quilt. The design, technique, workmanship, and condition should be what determines the value, not the origin.

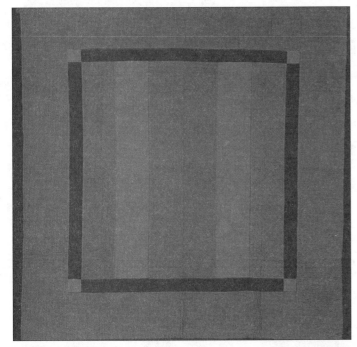

Amish pieced cotton "Bar" design, 20th century. Worked in reds, teal blue, purple and black on a quilted teal blue ground. 81 inches by 84 inches. Sold at auction for $1,035. Photo courtesy of Butterfield and Butterfield, San Francisco, California.

Early 20th century pieced and appliquéd Amish quilt of light green bow ties on black background. Minor imperfections. 71-1/2 inches by 82-1/2 inches. Sold at auction for $863. Photo courtesy of Skinner, Inc., Bolton, Massachusetts.

Assorted floral squares, embroidered in bright pink, purple with bright kelly green leaves. Squares typically sell for $1 to $5 each. This set of 20, enough for a small quilt, would sell for $30 to $45.

Yo-Yo quilts are one of the easiest quilts to make. Stitching is run around the edge of a fabric circle, and pulled tight to form a yo-yo-like round. These gathered rounds are stitched together to form quilts, mats, pillow-covers, and other novelties. These pineapple-textured quilts can range in quality from awful, when the edges are left raw, to very fine if colors are carefully selected. The edges carefully turned in, and the rounds carefully stitched together.

Sources

California
San Jose Museum of Quilts
and Textiles
110 Paseo de San Antonia
San Jose, CA
408-971-0323
Jane Przybyz, Executive Director

Herb Wallerstein
Calico Antiques
611 N. Alta Vista Drive
Beverly Hills, CA 90210
Phone 310-273-4192
Fax 310-273-1921
Fine quality pre 1930 quilts.

Indiana
Auctions:
Swartzentruber auctions
805 N. VanBuren
P.O. Box 331
Shipshewana, Indiana 46565
219-768-4621
Quilts, from antiques to the latest made, from all over the U.S. Shipshewana is Amish country in Indiana, and this auctions typically includes many Amish-made.

Kentucky
Museum of American Quilt Society
215 Jefferson
Paducah, KY 42002
Phone 502-442-8856
Permanent collection of quilts. 60 to 70 quilts from permanent collection always on display. Changing exhibits vary from contemporary to antique quilts. Publish newsletter for members.

Nebraska
International Quilt Study Center
Carolyn Ducey
Phone 402-472-6301
Cducey@unl.edu
The University of Nebraska
HE 234
Lincoln, NE 68583-0838
9 a.m. to 12 p.m. open to public Monday, Tuesday, Wednesday. Comprehensive collection that represents antique and contemporary quilts. Permanent collection contains about 950 quilts; some almost always will be displayed on campus. Also quilt related classes for non-traditional students

Quilt Restoration Society
P.O. Box 19542
Omaha, NE 68119
QuiltHF@aol.com
http://www.quiltheritage.com
800-599-0094
A network for sharing information about quilt restoration techniques, products, and tools. Newsletter serves to share and teach methods to extend practical life of textiles. Society develops and sponsors touring exhibits, and encompasses

the Quilt Rescue Squad, a group of volunteers who work to rescue quilts, quilt tops, and blocks. Restored quilts are kept as teaching quilts, or sold at a charity auction to raise money for QHS Scholarship Fund.

Dealers:
Nancy Kirk
The Kirk Collection
1513 Military Avenue
Omaha, NE 68111-3924
800-398-2542
402-551-0386
fax 402-551-0971
Kirk Coll@aol.com
KirkCollection@msn.ccon
http://www.auntie.com/kirk
Extensive collection of vintage quilts, fabrics, and supplies for repair and restoration.

New York
Rabbit Goody
Thistle Hill Weavers
101 Chestnut Ridge Road
Cherry Valley, NY 13320
(near Cooperstown)
518-284-2729
rabbitg@albany.net
www.albany.net/~rabbitg
www.quilthistory.com/thistlehill
Resource on coverlets, quilts, weaving, and vintage fabrics. Specialist in identification of hand-produced textiles, and textiles from the transition period from home to factory technology, circa 1750 to 1850. Early block, roller cylinder and copperplate prints. Custom textile mill producing reproductions of antique silk, linsey-woolsey, textiles for museums, re-enactors, decorators.

Chris Dreissen
Shop: 3256 State Route 30
Esperance, NY 12066
http:www.hickoryhillquilts.com
518-875-6133
Antique quilts, tops, blocks, vintage fabrics, reproduction fabric sewing notions, restoration, appraisals.

Thomas Woodard
Woodard & Greenstein
506 East 74th St.
New York, NY
Phone 11209
212-988-2906
Gallery specializing in hooked rugs, quilts, coverlets

Texas
Vintage Quilt and Textile Society
vqts1@airmail.net
2401 Blue Cypress
Richardson, TX 75082
972-783-4149
Lisa Erlandson, newsletter editor
erland@cooke.net
An organization devoted to the studies of vintage quilts, textiles, and related subjects. Goal is to share knowledge about quilt history and to perpetuate the art of quiltmaking in a cooperative manner.

texas_quilt.co@airmail.net

Virginia
Gretchen Noyes
P.O. Box 948
Alexandria, VA 22313
Phone 703-920-0348
Appraisals of quilts and other needlework.

Washington
Ann Bodle Nash
Prof. Appraiser for quilted textiles
annbow@c10.net
840 Halloran Rd.
Bow, WA 98232
Canadian Quilt Study Group
www.geocities.com/~cqsg/
Encourages study of contemporary and vintage quilts.

Books
There are hundreds of books on quilts, and a comprehensive directory is impossible. Here are just a couple that generally are considered classics by the quilters.

Brackman, B. *Clues in the Calico*

Brackman, Barbara, *1001 Pieced Quilt Patterns*

Brackman, B. *Encyclopedia of Appliqué*

Brackman, B. *Encyclopedia of Pieced Quilts*

Trestain, E. *Dating Fabrics*

Zegart, Shelly, *American Quilt Collections.* A guide to public and private quilt collections in the United States.

Quilter's Travel Companion, quilt shops, fabrics shops, and antique quilt dealers listed by state

Additional information, lists of books, and resources in available on the Internet:

Hickoryhillsquilts.com

quiltguilds.com

QRS@albany.net

ghl@cuenet.com

American Flags

The snap of colors in the wind stirs passion like nothing else. Decades after they first flew, flags and banners still have power, invoking memories of parades, battles, and down-home picnics in the park.

Even long after the admission of new states made the number of stars obsolete, old flags still can be flown. When old American flags and banners show up in your attic, it is not illegal, immoral, or tacky to try to find a home where they can be appreciated. Collectors are especially interested in very early flags, flags with unusual arrangements of stars and bars, and flags with unusual numbers of stars. Sometimes they were only current for a year or so before the addition of more states to the Union resulted in more stars.

✔ Checklist

The number of stars, which was dictated by the number of united states, is a key factor that influences the value of a flag. The events that occurred while that flag was flying (who was president, what wars were fought, etc.) all bear in how important and interesting a flag is.

Human drama and the ability to stir passions and memories gives flags value. The more specific, the better. Flags known to have been carried in at Gettysburg, for example, have much more importance than generic Civil War era national flags.

Merely flying over the Capitol does not give American flags value. It has become a nearly mechanized ritual to hoist flags for a few seconds on a special, obscure flag pole, bring them down and hoist another. These make lovely mementos for Americans visiting the Capitol, or interested in a flag flying on the day a special law went into effect, but there are far too many of them to make them valuable.

Design

The number of stars alone does not determine the value. Prior to 1912, the arrangement of the stars, the number of points in each star, and many other details were left up to the individual. The arrangement, and the number of points on the stars makes a great deal of difference.

Materials

Original eighteenth century flags usually were made of linen, wool or silk. Flags made of natural materials are more valuable than those made of synthetics. Experts also use the type and twist of the thread to authenticate important old flags.

Technique and workmanship

Technique and workmanship in flags and banners are valued differently than other needlework. They are clues used to authenticate the age and origins of a specific flag or banner. Homemade flag-making efforts of a child in the nineteenth century, for example, would be valued as folk art. Perfect, machine-stitched examples are more common and less interesting.

Key Dates in American Flag Design

1777 — First Flag Act. Flag was to have 13 white stars in a blue field; 13 stripes. Stars could have any number of points, and be arranged in any fashion, stripes could be any combination of red, white, and blue.

1794 — Flag was to have 15 stars and 15 stripes, recognizing the admission of Vermont and Kentucky.

1818 — Although several new states were admitted between 1794 and 1818, no new stars or stripes were added. This act fixed the number of stripes at 13, one for each original state, alternating red and white, and allowed for one star to be added for each new state, on the Fourth of July following the date of admission. No restrictions were set on the arrangement of stars, or the proportion of the flag.

1912 — Proportions of the flag established at hoist (width) of one unit and fly (length) of 1.9 units. Set arrangement of stars in six horizontal rows of eight. One point of each star should be upward.

1959 — Following the admission of Alaska, the arrangement of stars was set at seven rows of seven.

1960 — The admission of Hawaii set the design at today's current arrangement of 50 stars.

Technique and workmanship provide the main clues for dating flags. Sewing machines, for example, were not available until after the mid nineteenth century. Any machine-stitched thirteen-star flags must be later imitations, made for the centennial, bicentennial, or some other occasion.

Hand stitched seams, and stars stitched on by hand are more attractive to collectors than machine-stitched.

Type and placement of grommets are additional clues to help place and date flags, but are not always conclusive. Metal grommets may have been taken out and the holes repaired with hand stitching. They also may have been added later to old flags. Whether or not a flag has a heading, and how it was attached may help authenticate old flags.

Condition

Few blanket statements can be made about the effect condition will have on a flag. A few battle scars on a flag known to have been carried in the French and Indian War will probably add to the value. For the more common flags, condition becomes important. Forty-eight and fifty-star flags, especially printed or machine-stitched of synthetic fabrics, are so common they should probably be gracefully retired and destroyed when worn out.

Rarity

Rarity almost always is the sum of the other factors. Rarity alone, however, does not make a flag valuable. Flags that people can relate to because of a moment in history or life-shaping event typically will bring higher prices than rare flags that have no ties to human events.

Some of the most rare and collectable American flags are those that were overprinted with political candidates and slogans, or nineteenth century advertising. By the end of the nineteenth century, it was considered a desecration of the flag to use it for advertising or as a decoration.

Thirteen-star flags are some of the most common. Many were produced for the centennial in 1876, and even more in 1976. Obviously the later flags will have far less value than the originals, but each, if they are nicely stitched and attractive, may, over the decades, acquire more value as mementos of their respective events.

Printed election political flag with 26 stars promoting Clay and Frelinghuysen in 1844 presidential election. Likeness of the candidate, in addition to the campaign slogan, makes flag especially valuable. Size about 26 by 17 inches. Flags printed with political candidates later became not only unfashionable, but considered a desecration of the American flag. Value estimated as in excess of $2,000. Photo courtesy of Mark Sutton.

Grand Army of the Republic (G.A.R.) flag, with 38 stars around the image of a G.A.R. medal. Used for veterans of the Civil War who met at reunions for many years. Fly length about 22 inches. 38 stars would suggest flag was used at one of the reunions between 1876 and 1889. Value estimated at $125 to $150. Photo courtesy of Mark Sutton.

Pieces & prices

48-star flag, about 3 ft. by 5 ft., fair condition, $35.

33-star flag, arranged in two concentric rings with large center star. Political flag, Douglas and Johnson. 13-1/2 inches by 21 inches. Some damage to top stripes. Offered for $5,250.

31-star flag, arranged with four corner stars, large center star, shield shape. Political flag, "For President, John Bell for Vice President, Edward Everett. The Union and the Constitution." 8 inches by 12 inches, excellent condition. Framed. Offered for $2,500.

Political campaign flag, "for president, John Bell, for vice president, Edward Everett, The Union and the Constitution." 8 inches by 12 inches, framed. $2,500.

Political campaign flag, Douglas and Johnson. Printed muslin, 13-1/2 inches by 21 inches. Some fading, and missing pieces from top stripe. $5,250.

Portrait of Theodore Roosevelt surrounded by four naval commanders and sixteen ships printed on a silk flag. 23 inches by 18 inches. Framed. $2,500.

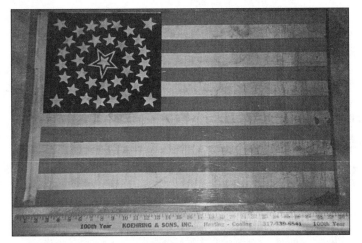

Printed flag with 35 stars arranged as a double medallion with a haloed center star and four corner stars. Fly about 28 inches. May be a centennial reproduction dating from 1876. Highly desirable to collectors because of unusual star configuration, and the fact that 35 stars were current during the Civil War with West Virginia's admission to the Union on June 20, 1863. Value estimated at $150 to $250. Photo courtesy of Mark Sutton.

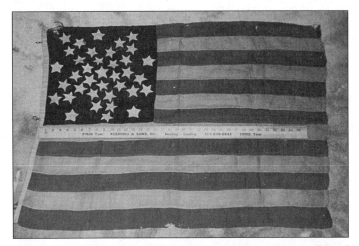

Hand-sewn 38-star flag with stars arranged as a "camouflaged great star." Great star is enclosed in a circle of stars. Hand sewing adds to value. Yardstick in center of flag suggests the fly is about 38 inches. Value estimated at between $200 and $250. Photo courtesy of Mark Sutton.

Sources

Books

There are almost no books currently in print to help identify and evaluate old American flags. Some out-of-print books often are available in local libraries:

Cooper, Grace Rogers; *Thirteen Star Flags*, A Key to Identification, Smithsonian Institution Press,1973, Washington, D.C.

Mastai, Boleslaw, *The Stars and The Stripes: The American Flag as Art and as History*, Knopf, 1973,New York

Collectors and Dealers

Mark Sutton
2035 St. Andrews Circle
Carmel, IN 46032
317-844-5648

Robert Banks
Stars and Stripes
18901 Gold Mine Court
Brookville, MD 20833-2711
301-774-7850

Rex Stark
P.O. Box 1029
Gardner, MA 01440
978-630-3237
Fax 978-630-2388
Publishes catalogs of Americana which often include flags.

Number of Stars	Dates Official	States admitted	Presidents and history notes
13 Stars	First Flag Act (1777)	Original thirteen	Washington
15 Stars	1795	Vermont, Kentucky	Washington, Adams, Jefferson, Madison, Monroe (This was the "Star Spangled Banner" flying during the war of 1812, and the writing of the national anthem.)
20 Stars	1818	Tennessee, Ohio, Louisiana, Indiana, Mississippi	Monroe
21 Stars	1819	Illinois	Monroe
23 Stars	1820	Alabama, Maine	Monroe
24 Stars	1822	Missouri	Monroe, Quincy Adams, Jackson
25 Stars	1836	Arkansas	Jackson, Van Buren
26 Stars	1837	Michigan	Van Buren, Harrison, Tyler, Polk
27 Stars	1845	Florida	Polk
28 Stars	1846	Texas	Polk
29 Stars	1847	Iowa	Polk
30 Stars	1848	Wisconsin	Polk, Taylor, Fillmore
31 Stars	1851	California	Fillmore, Pierce, Buchanan
32 Stars	1858	Minnesota	Buchanan
33 Stars	1859	Oregon	Buchanan, Lincoln
34 Stars	1861	Kansas	Lincoln (Civil War flag)
35 Stars	1863	West Virginia	Lincoln, Johnson
36 Stars	1865	Nevada	Johnson
37 Stars	1867	Nebraska	Johnson, Grant, Hayes
38 Stars	1877	Colorado	Hayes, Garfield, Arthur, Cleveland, Harrison
43 Stars	1890	North Dakota, South Dakota, Montana, Washington, Idaho	Harrison
44 Stars	1891	Wyoming	Harrison, Cleveland
45 Stars	1896	Utah	Cleveland, McKinley, T.Roosevelt
46 Stars	1908	Oklahoma	T. Roosevelt, Taft
48 Stars	1912	New Mexico, Arizona	Taft, Wilson, Harding, Coolidge, Hoover, F.D. Roosevelt, Truman (The flag of World Wars I and II)
49 Stars	1959	Alaska	Eisenhower
50 Stars	1960	Hawaii	Eisenhower

Embroidered Pictures

Embroidering pictures in silk was a popular pastime in the late eighteenth and early nineteenth century. Painted pictures were embellished with silk thread embroidery, usually in satin stitch, long and short stitches and split stitches.

Although they are approximately the same vintage as samplers, they have not attracted the following of samplers. They are found less often, especially in the United States.

The name of the embroiderer rarely appears in the work, and rarely is known. They are small, usually less than ten inches across, and very subtle. Most of them were done in England, and occasionally in America.

Their beauty is very subtle, and requires a close look to appreciate it.

✔ Checklist

Materials

Look for good quality silk in both the base fabric and in the embroidery threads. Materials should be durable, and appropriately chosen for the piece.

Design

Classical scenes, characters from myths, legends, and poetry were popular in the early nineteenth century. Look for originality in the subject matter, complexity of the design, movement and shading of colors. The technique and workmanship should be taken in to account to enhance the design.

Technique and workmanship

Early nineteenth century embroideries typically were worked in a few basic stitches, especially satin stitch, long and short stitch, and split satin stitch.

Look for occasional use of couched metallic threads, especially as accents.

Quality of the detail in the pictures should very delicate and fine. Look especially for embroidered faces and hands. More often, because of the great difficulty in working these exquisitely enough in thread, they were instead painted or drawn in.

How the threads were laid in determines how they reflect the light, and how the color is perceived. This also affects the texture. Notice in any embroidered picture whether this was consciously taken into account, and deliberately worked to enhance the picture.

Condition

Old silk was prone to deterioration and shattering. This cannot be repaired. Look for fading and running in the colors. Look for missing stitches, catches and snags in the threads, and fraying.

Foxing is a brown staining of the materials. A little is inevitable in very old fabrics, but pieces with major staining are a problem.

Rarity

Silk embroidered pictures are neither extremely rare nor common. Each auction at Phillips in London offers at least one or two, and they occasionally are offered at Skinner's auctions in Bolton, Massachusetts.

Pictures become far more valuable when they have a known history, when information is embroidered into the picture, or when it's accompanied with letters and documentation. When the story of the embroiderer and family are known, they become far more interesting.

Pieces & prices

Silk needlework memorial, New England, early nineteenth century. Depicts a young girl at three neoclassical urn-form memorials. Attached note reads, "This embroidered memorial was done by Elmina Clarinda Walker Greene, my great grandfather's sister and daughter of Sally Gates Walker and a half sister of Relief Smith Jackson, Elmina was born 1805 and died 1836." Some foxing and minor staining. 17-5/8 inches by 21 inches. Sold at auction for $5,175.

Silk needlework picture, America, early nineteenth century. "Edgar & Mathilda" with watercolor and sequin highlights. Identified and signed on eglomisé mat "Sally Aldrich." Minor paint losses to mat, minor fading of needlework. 16 inch round. Sold at auction for $977.50.

Silk embroidered picture, early nineteenth century, of a romantic couple in Elizabeth an dress seated on a bench in an ornamental garden, worked in silk long and short stitch on painted silk. Oval, 9.25 inches by 12.5 inches, glazed and framed in eglomisé beaded and gilded frame. Sold at auction for about $615.

Silk embroidered picture of a young lady wearing a wide brimmed hat picking a rose. Worked in long and short stitch and chenille on ivory satin. Features and hands are drawn. Oval picture, 8.5 inches by 6.1 inches, in rectangular eglomisé beaded and gilded gesso frame. Sold at auction for about $220.

Silk embroidered mourning picture, signed Penelope Howland while at Mary Balch's School, Providence, Rhode Island 1802. Sold at auction for $14,950.

English silk embroidered picture, of a young woman wearing a cream silk dress and hat, her bodice and sash trimmed with crimson, scattering flowers on Werter's tomb. Worked in long and short stitch on painted ivory silk, a small chenille tree to one side. Oval picture, 9-1/2 inches by 7.7 inches, in rectangular verre eglomisé frame. Sold at auction for about $289.

Sources

Embroiderers Guild of America (E.G.A.)
335 W. Broadway
Suite 100
Louisville, KY 40202-2105
Phone: 502-389-6956
Fax: 302-584-7900
EGAHQ@aol.com
www.egausa.org
Association of contemporary embroiderers, has a small display of comtemporary and historic embroideries at their headquarters. Their newsletter also sometimes includes articles on historic techniques.

Amy Finkel
M. Finkel and Daughter
936 Pine Street
Philadelphia, PA 19107
Phone: 215-627-7797
Fax: 215-627-8199
Gallery and shows. Samplers, embroideries, needlework. Well-researched and documented pieces.

Skinner, Inc.
357 Main Street
Bolton, MA 01740
Phone: 978-779-6241
Fax: 978-779-5144
Auctioneers. Various auctions, especially Discovery and Decorative Arts auctions include early American and some English embroidered pictures.

Phillips International Auctioneers
101 New Bond Street
London, W1Y OAS
Phone: 44-171-629-6602 (textile department)
New York phone for catalogs and sales information: 212-570-4830. Regular sales of textiles, about 6 per year, include English and American silk embroidered pictures.

Fabrics

Ever since the late nineteenth century, when the sewing machine inventors succeeded in getting a sewing machine into nearly every home in the United States, and made a good effort at getting them into every home in the world, no self-respecting homemaker did not have a drawer, a box, or a closet full of yard goods she hadn't yet had a chance to sew into something. Any economy-minded person who could wield a needle saw yard goods everywhere. An old curtain panel was just yard goods with a hem. An old coverlet or paisley shawl were yard goods — period. Feed sacks were just yard goods stitched up on one or two sides, usually in a chain stitch that zipped right out. The world is blanketed with old textiles just waiting to be recycled. (See also Feed Sacks)

There is both opportunity and danger in this view of the world. Certainly, good fabrics should not be wasted. Some, however, are too wonderful to be chopped up. A few decades ago, we would have divided this section neatly into two categories: collector's fabrics and usable old fabrics.

Older and wiser, we now see the problem with this view. Who is to decide which are which, especially when they all are dirt cheap and dumped in an auction box?

We might also have said collector's fabrics are those that can no longer be duplicated. Give enough time to study a process, and enough patience to learn labor and skill-intensive methods, nearly anything can be duplicated. Workshops in Venice, Italy, for example, are reproducing centuries-old cut brocaded silk velvets. The cost, however, is well into the thousands of dollars per yard.

We are thus dividing this section into culturally significant textiles, designer textiles, and utility textiles. Checklists suggest a way to see the cultural significance in old textiles, then let your conscience, not your purse, determine whether or not they should be cut up and recycled as pillows, skirts or quilts. Hopefully, more and more people will make an effort to find an appreciative home when it is appropriate.

Culturally significant textiles

Textiles that represent some special human achievement or event in human history have cultural significance.

The achievement might be a special skill or technique. It might be a first: a unique dye process, a special hand weave. When looking at any old textile, check the threads, the fibers, the weave and the embellishment. Think about each aspect — the design, technique (how hard is the trick), workmanship (how well was the trick done), and rarity.

Ethnic textiles, including Indonesian, African, South American, Indian, and others, often use unique weaving, dyeing and decorating techniques. These are highly collectible and popular for decorating, especially when the represent great skills, imagination, and techniques not likely to be easily reproduced.

Textiles have to be hundreds and hundreds of years old before age alone gives them great significance. Pre-Columbian textiles, for example, usually are valued for the technique and workmanship in addition to their great age.

Designer textiles

"By design" implies careful thought, and that's what we mean by "designer textile." These are fabrics that reflect some thoughtful human effort put into the pattern, the color selection, the fiber selection, and the weave. Because of the extra effort that went into planning and making these fabrics, they often were more expensive when they were new.

Unless the name of the designer, the novelty of a first use of a design style, or a special technique a designer developed for this textile represents a cultural "first" or historic event, these should be used and enjoyed.

There is, of course, a fine line that determines whether designer fabrics should be used, enjoyed, and appreciated. Special embroideries and decorations often were worked just in the areas needed when the garment was made up. Dress lengths of fine fabrics sometimes are found with exquisitely hand-embroidered areas that can be used for a bodice, neckline, cuffs, dress front, or hemline. These can represent significant bargains to those who can sew themselves, or who have access to dressmakers. They also serve as envoys, showing what superb craftsmanship people are capable of producing by hand. Discovering these represents the best chance these will have for being appreciated.

Utility textiles

Textiles that involved no particular skill, or no special fiber, weave, or embellishment should be used and enjoyed. Bushels and boxes of fine-quality pure cotton flannels, woolens, and silks turn up regularly in garage and estate sales. Often, fabrics have better colors, higher thread counts and more absorbent and comfortable fibers than anything found in today's stores, and they often sell for a pittance. Use them and enjoy them.

Fabrics produced pre-synthetic are beginning to attract a following among home sewers, decorators, and quilters. It is still possible to shop garage sales for bargain cottons, but prices at vintage clothing and textile shows have risen. The attraction to authentic 30s, 40s, and 50s replicas is because of their better quality in fiber and thread count

Remember: recycling works both ways. Curtains, valences, tablecloths, and napkins are just a big piece of fabric with finished edges. Anyone who is willing to turn a hem, or do a bit of cutting and sewing can have better quality pillow covers, table cloths, curtains, valences, skirts and nightgowns than are offered in even the better department stores at far higher prices.

✔ Checklist

Fibers

Special grades of natural fibers qualify as luxury fibers. Cashmere, pashmina, camel's hair and alpaca are types of wool that are so much lighter, softer, and silkier than any other wools that they usually are easily identified. Some silks, too, are more interesting and fine than others.

Cotton and linen rarely are considered luxury fibers, but some grades of long staple cottons and extremely fine linens produce fabrics that are unusually satiny, soft and supple.

Weaves

Complex patterns and textures in woven fabrics produced before the invention of the jacquard mechanism and before mechanized and powered looms represented an incredible investment in human skill, patience, and achievement. Humans can produce single unique pieces.

The amount of time and effort required to set up a machine for a textile run usually means huge amounts of the same thing must be produced.

Embellishments

Fabrics that were imaginatively decorated, embellished with techniques that required exceptional cleverness, skill, and workmanship are collectible. This includes some painting, printing, and embroidery techniques.

Techniques and designs that are unique to a time period and fabrics that are key examples of these special techniques are collectible.

Condition

Check vintage fabrics for natural problems:

Wools are often attacked by moths. Holding a fabric up to the light can show the tiny holes and weak spots that indicate moth damage.

Vintage silks often were weighted with chemicals to add body. Over time, these chemicals destroy the fibers. Old silks become brittle and literally shatter with age.

When buying garage sale fabrics to use in sewing, take a close look for dirt. It probably will be necessary to lay out patterns differently, because the dirt simply will not come out of the fold, even after a couple of good machine washings.

Pieces & prices

Genoese velvet panel, late 17th century. Large floral bouquet and scrollwork pattern of cut and uncut velvet in shades of green, peach, and deep red voided to cream background. From the estate of Mrs. Alys Litchfield. Two joined panels. 8 feet 3 inches by 41 inches. Fragile condition. Sold at auction for $1,840.

English silk brocade, circa 1730, designed with a bouquet of flowers, scattered sprigs and meandering ribbons. Four matching pieces of different lengths: 51 inches by 20 inches, 45 inches by 20 inches, 31 inches by 20 inches, and 31 inches by 20 inches. Sold at auction for about $820.

Length of Art Moderne plush furnishing fabric, circa 1940. Woven with stylized bamboo leaves on a grid, in shaded of slate blue, tan, and cream. 17 yards 10 inches by 4 feet 7 inches. Sold at auction for $402.

Sources

The Kirk Collection
Nancy Kirk
Shop: 1513 Military Avenue
Omaha, NE 68111-3924
Phone 800-398-2542
Fax 402-551-0971
Kirk Coll@aol.com
www.auntie.com/kirk
Buys and sells vintage fabrics. Shop, mail order, and via Internet.

Chris Dreissen
Shop: 3256 State Route 30
Esperance, NY 12066
518-875-6133
Oldquilt@albany.net
http:www.hickoryhillquilts.com
Buys and sells vintage fabrics. Shop, mail order, and via Internet.

Lavinia Tackberry
Eye on Design
Hinsdale, IL
Phone 630-986-5228
Wide variety of ethnic textiles, with particularly strong African collections.

Textile artifacts
12589 Crenshaw
Hawthorne, CA 90250
Phone 310-576-2424
textileguy@aol.com
www.textileguy.com

Silk brocade panel French, mid 18th century. Sold at auction for $750. Photo courtesy of William Doyle Galleries, New York.

Detail from curtain panel, circa 1800, of French Toile de Jouy cotton ground printed in red with Le Meunier, Son Fils et Ane, designed by Jean-Baptiste Huet. 2.6 yards by 1.3 yards. Some damage and wear. Sold at auction for about $325. Photo courtesy of Phillips Auction in London.

Assorted bolts of bark cloth, a nubby cotton weave popular in the 1950s for drapes and slip covers. Print colors often were shades of green, brown, and orange on a neutral background. Prices, spurred by a reprise of popularity of 50s fashions in decorating, currently are very high. These are decorator's, not collector's, fabrics. Prices can go up to $25 per yard.

Detail from length of Toile de Juoy, cotton printed in red with Le Quartre Elements. 2.9 yards by 1 yard. Sold at auction for about $275. Photo courtesy of Phillips Auction in London.

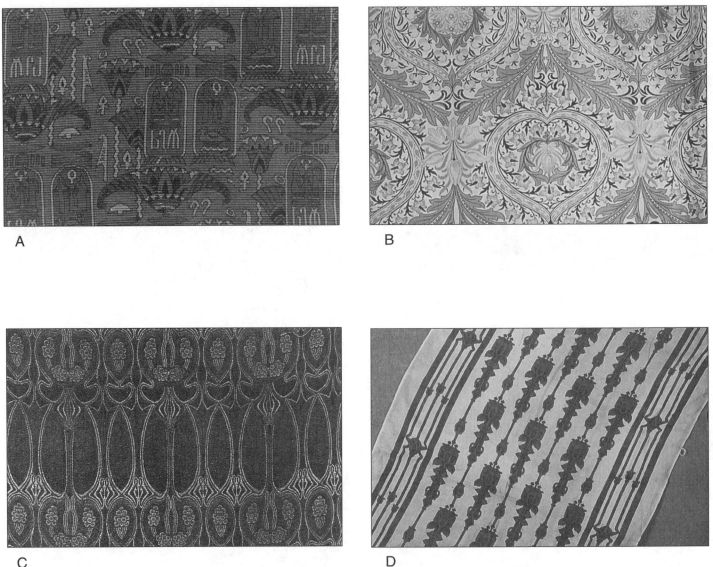

A

B

C

D

(A) Panel of printed rayon, circa 1900, printed in Egyptian revival style with cartouche and stylized lotus. Ground is brown with red, blue, purple, cream and black print. Square panel, 2 yards on a side. Photo courtesy of Textile Artifacts, Hawthorne, California.

(B) Design of geo-floral repeats of bulbs and ovals printed in brown tones. French double-weave cotton, circa 1910. 102 inches by 42 inches. Photo courtesy of Textile Artifacts, Hawthorne, California.

(C) Block printed cotton panel, marked Morris & Company, 4219 Oxford Street, London, in a design by Henry Pearl, circa 1904. Width 36 inches. From the collection of Louisa and Bob Lauver. Photo courtesy of Textile Artifacts, Hawthorne, California.

(D) Sheer cotton panel roller printed with stylized rosettes repeating in a grid pattern. Width 36 inches. Photo courtesy of Textile Artifacts, Hawthorne, California.

Assorted printed cottons from the mid 19th century. These are culturally significant fabrics, representing early dyes and printing techniques. They are highly prized for restoration of old quilts and other restorative and historic purposes. Prices can range from $25 per yard to well over $100 per yard. Photos courtesy of the Kirk Collection, Omaha, Nebraska.

Fine cotton dress length of fabric, probably made in India, embellished with embroidery for the bodice, sleeves, and skirt. Style suggests it was done early in the 20th century. Embroidery on these dress lengths often is extraordinary. They are attractive for use in bridal or other couture uses.

African Kuba cloth, woven of grass fibers in narrow bands and stitched together and embellished with simple embroidery. These ethnic cloths traditionally have a brown background, and are embroidered in black or black and white. From the ethnic textiles collection of Eye On Design, Hinsdale, Illinois.

Feed Sacks

Feed sacks replay American history like no other antique. Early in the 1800s, Whitney's gin made cotton economical enough for sacks to replace barrels, boxes, and tins. Early sacks carrying grain to the mills were stamped with the farmer's name.

Sack manufacturers in the 1840s were among the first to take advantage of the new sewing machines. Most often, bags were sewn with a double-thread lock stitch that could be easily unraveled. Occasionally, thrifty homemakers even saved this cotton twine, and used it to crochet doilies, dresser scarves, or place mats.

By the end of the nineteenth century, cotton sacks had almost entirely replaced barrels. Odd weights stamped on the bags — 196 lbs., 98 lbs., 49 or 48 lbs., still corresponded to barrel, half barrel, and quarter barrel weights well into the twentieth century. It was not until 1943 that the War Products Board standardized sack sizes to 100, 50, 25, 10, 5 and 2 pounds.

From the beginning, cloth bags were recycled. Thousands of bags filled with flour, sugar, or grain were shipped to Belgium during World War I. Each bag was carefully recycled as clothing, pillows, or other useful objects. Hundreds were beautifully embroidered, and returned to the United States as thank-you gifts or as fundraising projects.

Early in the twentieth century, bags were made in off-white, browns, and a few other colors. Thrifty homemakers recognized the value of the fabrics in the bag. From the 1920s up until the 1950s, the more than two dozen mills producing textile bags competed to choose the fabrics most enticing to the American homemaker. Cheerful, color prints were introduced to make even prettier dresses, pillow covers, aprons, bonnets, curtains, place mats, underwear, pajamas, and handbags.

Pattern manufacturers offered patterns designed to use one or more bags. Many farmers went off to the feed mill with swatches of prints to match so mama could finish a project. Failing that, unfilled new bags could be ordered from the National Cotton Council to get the right number of bags for a pattern. The National Cotton Council also held sewing contests to promote use of the bags.

Three types of cotton fabric were used in sacks. High-count, premium quality cotton was used for flour, sugar, and salt to keep them from sifting out in shipment and handling. These were equivalent in quality to cotton sheets. Print cottons had slightly lower thread counts. These were the most typical of the fancy prints promoted for use for dresses, blouses, and bonnets. The lowest grade, a low-thread count, off-white cotton, was called osnaberg. This grade was used for feeds, grains, and seeds. These often were reused as feed sacks.

Many different methods were used to label the bags. Band labels were put around the middle and stitched into the side seams. These could be dissolved in the wash, or removed when the seams were unraveled. Paper labels were spot-pasted in the center of the bag with an easily dissolved paste, and removed in the wash.

Washable inks almost always were used when labels were printed directly on the bag, and instructions for washing out the labels were provided.

By 1948, double, triple, and quadruple-walled paper sacks had taken over the majority of the shipping-sack business.

As late as 1950s, however, the National Cotton Council and the Textile Manufacturers Association were actively promoting feed sacks in sewing contests and other promotions. Cotton Bag Loan Wardrobes were loaned to women's groups for fashion shows, and the Cotton Bag Sewing Contest offered prizes of electric appliances and trips to Hollywood for the best ideas for use of the bags.

Interest is growing for textile bags as collectibles. Printed feedsacks are highly prized by quiltmakers to make new quilts, to finish partially worked quilts, and to repair and restore old quilts. Bags with quaint printed labels are collected for their own sake, perhaps to be framed and displayed as artifacts of bygone days. These collectors seek historically interesting bags as well as interesting labels. In competition with the collectors are the sewers, who seek them out to be reused for anything from vests, jackets, flags and banners. Sewers are particularly interested in colorful, attractive graphics. Those who reuse the labeled bags have to keep in mind that the labels often were not indelible, but were intended to wash off so the clean bag could be reused.

Some additional categories of collectible bags:

- Bags printed with patterns for stuffed toys, such as rag dolls.
- Bags printed with quilt blocks and embroidery patterns.
- "Convertible" bags, such as bags with stitched-on ties, designed to open up into a ready-to-use apron.

Garage sales, flea markets and antique malls are excellent sources for finding feedsacks of all kinds.

✔ Checklist

Designs

Earliest bags dating to the nineteenth century were simply printed with the farmer's name.

Designs for feed and grain labeled bags are those with great down-home drawings of farmyards, animals, flowers and those with good color.

Designs for all-over-print bags intended to be reused in dresses, shirts, and other household uses were essentially the same as those used in any prints currently fashionable. Most can be approximately dated by the designs and colors.

1930s: Small prints in butter yellow, pastels, pink and pale green.

1940s: Large-scale graphics in bright colors, especially cherry red, kelly green, bubblegum pink and teal blue.

1950s: Intense colors, especially the trademark olive green along with tans, browns, and aquas, deep blues, dark pinks.

Because the same prints were used for yard goods as well as feed sacks, it is sometimes impossible to know if a fragment ever was a feed sack.

Condition

Clear, sharp, cleanly printed labels are the most sought after. Dirty or stained labeled bags pose a problem. Because many of the labels were supposed to wash off so the plain fabric bag could be reused, washing the stained bag will seriously damage the graphics.

Bags in original condition with stitching up the side are more valuable as collectibles than cut bags.

Pirate pictured in red and black on this feedsack would make it attractive to recyclers for a vest or jacket. 100 pound weight suggests it dated to the 1940s or later. $15.

Detailed picture of small boy printed in gold, brown, and black on this Ceresota flour bag makes this a highly collectible bag. Distributed by Northwestern Consolidated Milling Company, bag made by Bemis of Minneapolis. Weight is 96 pounds, or a half-barrel size. Bag probably dates to about 1891. Label still is used today. $40. Photo courtesy of Ronald Bennett.

Rose flour sack. Fifty pound weight marking suggests it dates to the 1940s or later, after sacks were converted from barrel weights. Red roses make bag attractive. Mint condition $20.

Fresh-from-the-oven biscuits on this flour sack are printed in gold, yellow and brown. Mint condition, probably never used. Dates to the 1940s or later. $15.

Linen homespun bag dating to 1853, probably a 3 bushel size, with original drawstring top. Early grain sacks were labeled with the name of the farmer, so grain could be tracked at the mills. This bag is labeled John Stager. Part of private collection of Ronald Bennett, not for sale.

Pieces & prices

100 pound sack of chicken feed with black hen and chicks, red lettering. "Homemade feeds Manufactured by Frutchey Bean Co. Saginaw Cass City Greenleaf Deford Millington St. Charles Pinconning Clifford Kingston Mayville Fostoria. $35.

100 pounds Meco Poultry Mashes Mason Elevator Co, Mason Mich. Blue and red lettering, barn, hen, rooster, and chicks. Some stains. $12.

100 pounds Hughes Special Medium Water Softener salt packed for Dobos and Hughes, Lansing, MI. Stained and faded. $3.

Rare and unusual feedsacks, like this print of frolicking children, should be kept as collectibles and not cut up and recycled. Part of private collection of Ronald Bennett, not for sale.

Sources

Book

Cook, Anna Lue, Textile Bags, Identification and Value Guide; Books Americana, 1990. Out of Print, Available from Anna Lue Cook, Box 2326, Florence, AL, 35630

Dealers

The Kirk Collection
1513 Military Avenue
Omaha, NE 68111-3924
800-398-2542
402-551-0386
Fax 402-551-0971
Kirk Coll@aol.com
KirkCollection@msn.ccon
http://www.auntie.com/kirk

The Feedsack Club
Jane Stapel, Editor
25 Starr Avenue, Apt. #16
Pittsburgh, PA 15202
412-766-3996
baglady111@aol.com
Publishes newsletter
Information on all aspects of feedsacks, with strong emphasis on materials for quilting.

Ronald Bennett
1870 Strong Road
Victor, NY 14564-9134

Hickory Hill Quilts
P.O. Box 273
Esperance, NY 12066
Phone 518-875-6133
Fax 518-875-9141
http://www.hickoryhillquilts.com/feedsacks.htm

Details of assorted feedsack prints from the 1930s to the 1950s.

Handkerchiefs

In the 1940s, the Marshall Field's department store in Chicago, Illinois, provided a choice of thousands of handkerchiefs from eight-hundred drawers in a main floor department devoted exclusively to handkerchiefs. Within a few years, Kleenex paper tissues nearly eliminated the "for blow" handkerchiefs, but "for show" handkerchiefs have begun to make a comeback. They are extremely popular for weddings and gifts, and fine white handkerchiefs recently were featured in the *New York Times* fashion section as a fashionable, gentile way for a gentleman to deal with a sweaty brow on a hot, muggy summer day.

The exact origin of handkerchiefs has not been known for centuries, but it would not be surprising if the person who invented the first loom used a scrap of newly made cloth to wipe his brow. One of the first references to such a cloth was by Catullus in 87-57 B.C. He called the cloth "sudarium," a derivation of the Latin word for "sweat." For as long as cloth was a luxury, handkerchiefs have been a symbol of wealth and power, often depicted in statuary and mosaics from the turn of B.C. to A.D. By the third century A.D., the working class was using cloth squares for cleaning and wiping.

By the 1500s, clear distinctions in language were made for functional and decorative handkerchiefs. In the 1500s, the term "sudarioli" was used for the functional cloths, "fazzoletti" for the decorative. About that time, the fashion seems to have spread from Italy to France, where the French, "mouchoir," is traced to Latin.

Little evidence remains of any non-square handkerchiefs, but tradition has it that Louis XIV fixed the shape in 1685. Extraordinarily beautiful lace and embroidered handkerchiefs survive from the eighteenth century. The functional, colorful "snuffing cloths" of that era, used to protect extravagant clothing from tobacco stains, mercifully have disappeared.

Dating handkerchiefs with any accuracy is difficult. Unless dates, crests, or designs are worked into the handkerchief itself, or other solid documentation is available, the best that can usually be done is to place a handkerchief within a half century.

The most expensive and extravagant handkerchiefs are the lace, drawnwork, cutwork, and embroidered handkerchiefs. Printed, painted, and other decorative handkerchiefs, however, also can be highly collectible.

✔ Checklist

There are a few basic parts of any handkerchief that provide clues to the quality and the age. First of all, look to see whether the edge is plain or decorated. The hem is also a clue. Look to see whether it's rolled, handstitched, embellished with drawnwork, or plain. Notice if the corners are turned, especially in lace handkerchiefs. Finally, the shape of the center cloth area can provide dating information. Notice each of these when looking at materials, design, and embellishments.

Materials

Fine quality natural fibers were used in the best vintage handkerchiefs. Cotton fabrics that were so fine they were translucent were typical of eighteenth and early nineteenth century handkerchiefs. Pure linen handkerchiefs were common well into the twentieth century.

Silk is not as successful a fabric for handkerchiefs because it did not stand up to washing and using as well as cotton and linen.

In the mid twentieth century, translucent synthetics were used for some decorative handkerchiefs. These were not suitable for use as handkerchiefs, because of the plastic-like quality of the fabric. Whether they will ever regain favor as a decorative handkerchief is questionable.

Design

The most interesting handkerchiefs are those where care has been taken to create a design that takes the most advantage of the size and shape of the fabric. The design should be complex enough that new details are revealed each time it is viewed.

The trademarks of any good design, namely balance, harmony, flow and complexity, also apply here.

When the subject matter depicts a specific historical event, the importance of the event often determines the value.

Size as a guide to dating

Handkerchiefs of the Louis XIV era of the late seventeenth and early eighteenth century, were immensely large, often on the order of twenty-four square inches.

By the first quarter of the eighteenth century during the reign of Louis XV, the size usually was more on the order of eighteen inches. These often were elaborately embroidered squares with an inch or two of handmade lace stitched to the edges, and gathered to go around the corners.

Toward the end of the eighteenth century, around the time of the French Revolution, they varied from about eighteen to twenty-four inches.

Some records suggest that during the eighteenth century, the English exchanged tiny, three to four-inch square handkerchiefs as love tokens.

In the mid nineteenth century, mid-sized handkerchiefs, about eighteen inches square, were popular. The best of these had shaped cloth with lace and embroidery edges. Lace designs usually were shaped to flow around the corners without gathering.

In about 1900, very small square handkerchiefs were in vogue. Sizes ranged from eight to twelve inches.In the early twentieth century, until about 1940, linen squares about twelve inches square typically were edged with a little homemade crochet or tatting worked directly onto the hem.

Technique and workmanship

Many different processes were used to produce handkerchiefs: drawnwork, cutwork, embroidery, lacemaking and printing to name a few. Complex, difficult-to-work stitches add more value. It remains important, however, that the technique enhance the design.

One feature common to all is the hem or edge treatment. Hemstitches typically include a row or more of drawnwork. Hand-rolled edges are typical of colorful print handkerchiefs. Cheap twentieth century print handkerchiefs are merely edged with machine overcast or zigzag stitches.

Condition

Linen is not elastic, and tends to crack when stretched over folds. Even mint condition handkerchiefs, never taken out of the box, can be cracked.

Many handkerchiefs were ironed into folds each time they were washed. Over the years, this places extreme stress on the fibers where they were stretched around the fold. Eventually the folds crack.

Drawnwork in extremely fine fabric eventually shreds. Look carefully at all exposed threads in drawnwork for evidence of shredding and tearing.

Labels left on handkerchiefs leave a residue of glue on the fibers. Unless the handkerchief was used and washed, this glue eventually will permanently stain or eat away at the fibers. Be especially watchful with antique handkerchiefs that have never been taken out of the box. Expect the area under the label to be damaged.

Stains on vintage handkerchiefs can be impossible to identify. Oils from perfume, blood, rust from pins — all can leave permanent stains. Because the fabric almost always is unusually fine, expect any stains to have damaged the fibers enough to create holes.

Because the fabric on handkerchiefs is so fine, it often is impossible to repair any tears or worn spots. Finding a needle fine enough to stitch the fabric without causing further damage is difficult. Decide before you buy if you can live with the damage.

Fine lace handkerchiefs with damaged centers but good quality lace may be repaired by replacing the fabric. Notice how the lace was attached to the fabric. Crochet edges usually were crocheted directly on the fabric, and cannot reasonably be taken off to use on another fabric. Simple crochet edges can be worked on a handkerchief in about a quarter of an hour, and are not worth saving.

Personality and provenance

Commemorative handkerchiefs printed or embroidered to celebrate a special event may be collectible. The event, however, must be important, and the design and workmanship on the handkerchief must be exceptional for it to have great value.

Unless a family is prominent, unusual, or notorious, their handkerchiefs will be of value only to the immediate family. Document your own family's heirlooms carefully, putting notes of special events and copies of wedding photographs, etc., in with the handkerchief to ensure that future generations will appreciate the family history and mementos.

Rarity

A combination of complex, unusual design, workmanship based on a technique that requires exceptional skill and training, and craftsmanship's precision, usually add up to rarity, although the item should still be in good condition.

Plain linen handkerchiefs

Plain handkerchiefs are very popular among lacemakers, who are always looking for good quality linen handkerchiefs to stitch their handmade lace edgings to. The quality of the linen, and the condition determine its value. Expect to pay up to $10 for a fine plain, pure-white linen handkerchief with a fine hemstitched edge.

Lace handkerchiefs

There are several categories of lace handkerchiefs:

Lacy whitework, in which the fine cloth itself has been turned into lace by withdrawing and deflecting threads, cutting eyelets and silhouetting designs, and inserting needle lace into cut holes. Fine white-on-white embroideries on nearly translucent cloth frequently are open enough to qualify as lace.

Cloth handkerchiefs, perhaps also embroidered and decorated, to which an edging of lace has been added.

Crochet typically is worked directly on the edge of the handkerchief, and cannot be removed without cutting the handkerchief or unraveling the crochet edge. The wider, the better with crochet, and the more complex designs are more difficult to work, more rare, and more valuable. Handkerchiefs with simple scallop edges sell for about $5, more complex edges for $10 to $15.

Mid 19th century handkerchief with deep border of handmade Brussels lace appliquéd onto machine net. Handkerchief is 17-1/2 inches square; lace is 7 inches deep at the corner. Net has several small holes; fabric center has some small tears. Offered at $250.

True lace handkerchiefs, in which the lace is designed like a fabric sculpture specifically for the handkerchief. The finest are almost entirely of lace, with only a few inches of cloth in the center.

With machine lace handkerchiefs, the chemical lace forms a particularly crisp, sharp-edged lace that makes great corner motifs for handkerchiefs. The process, also known as schiffli lace, dates back to the late 1880s and is still popular today.

The schiffli machines also embroidered net. These usually are not as bold and sharp as the chemical lace. They do make attractive pocket trims, but are very flimsy, and must be in perfect condition to be attractive.

Tatting is typically worked as a narrow edging, and hand sewn onto the edge of the handkerchief. Tatted edges usually are crisper, more sharply defined, and hold their shape better than crochet. Also they do not require as much fuss when washing and ironing. Handkerchiefs with quarter-inch edgings sell for $10 to $15, those with wider edgings for up to $20.

Corner motif in this early 20th century handkerchief is chemical lace. Mint condition vintage handkerchiefs, about 10 inches square, with attractive corner motifs sell for $20 to $30. Early 20th century handkerchief at right, about 10 inches square, has edge of machine-embroidered net. Sells for about $3 to $5.

Embroidered handkerchiefs

Anybody can — and in many cases did — pick up a needle and thread and decorate a piece of fabric to create a handkerchief. Embroidered handkerchiefs range from confections fit for a queen and made by professional artisans who had studied for years to little homemade amusements made for the pleasure of their owner.

They are always worth a second look, whether it's to admire their artistry or chuckle over the whimsical human spirit they display. The finest can be reserved for a special bride to carry, or can be framed and displayed. A dozen or two of the little homespun whimsies can be gathered together and shown off in a clear glass apothecary jar, and taken out to admire on a cold rainy day or whenever your spirit needs a lift.

Commercially produced embroidered handkerchiefs sometimes were hand-embroidered, and sometimes machine embroidered. Often, it is possible to tell only by looking at the rigid, repetitive jogging of the machine on the back side of the embroidery. With brightly colored, twentieth century floral embroidered handkerchiefs, the marketplace makes almost no distinction between handmade and machine. Both sell for only a dollar or two at most.

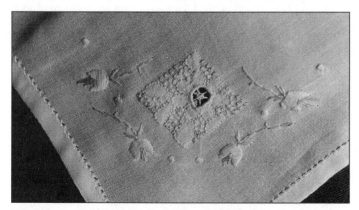

Tiny Treasures: Some of the most endearing little handkerchiefs have very small, almost secret little embroideries meant only for the pleasure of the owner. Today they are almost always overlooked in the marketplace, and are simply tossed into a shoe box at a garage sale. It takes time and a sharp eye to notice the detail that makes these thoughtful little embroideries so special. Microscopic French knots in purple and yellow provide a background for the shadow-stitched petals of the central flower. A tiny web of needle lace sets off the flower center. Rosebuds are worked in a rich yellow silk floss with purple centers. All this for just 50 cents!

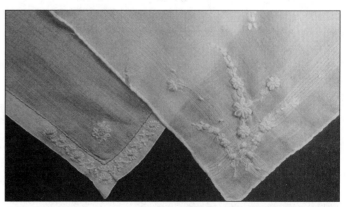

Raised rope stitches and French knots create flowers that float above the translucent muslin fabric. Smaller sprigs decorate the other three corners. Offered at a garage sale, this tiny treasure was offered in a shoe box full of printed handkerchief priced 5 for a dollar. A hand-stitched chain of white daisies with gold centers decorates the hemline of this little handkerchief. Offered for 25 cents at an antique mall.

Whitework handkerchiefs

Whitework is generic term for white embroidery, drawnwork, and lace on fine white fabric. Some of the best known types are Swiss Appenzell, French and Moravian. Most underrated, however, are good quality late nineteenth and early twentieth century Chinese. Embroidery was their forte, and when the Europeans sought to exploit Chinese labor for export, the Chinese excelled at embroidery.

The best of the whitework handkerchiefs have extremely tiny stitching and needle lace inserts. The fine work is so subtle, it is visible only with magnification. Very few people understand the quality and complexity of the work, and the fine detail is often overlooked. These often sell for far less than what sophisticated workmanship of this kind deserves, and it represents one of the best bargains in antique textiles.

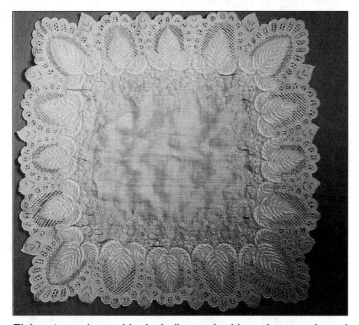

Elaborate workmanship, including embroidery, drawnwork, and needle lace stitching within the cutwork, and scalloping on the outside edge of this 19th century handkerchief make it attractive to a connoisseur. Numerous cracks in the fine cotton fabric and repairs to the drawnwork held the price down to $75.

Monogrammed handkerchiefs

Monogrammed handkerchiefs currently are very popular as gifts associated with weddings — for brides to give to bridesmaids, as presents for mothers-in-law, as the "something old, borrowed, or blue" for the bride to carry.

Many lace and linens dealers make a point of carrying a large stock of monogrammed handkerchiefs. Even though prices are rising, it will still be awhile before prices actually

Whitework checklist

The white-on-white work is so subtle that it does not get the attention it deserves, and these are especially great bargains.

- Look especially for elaborate embroidery so dense it completely covers the fabric.
- Little cutwork holes often are filled with microscopic, buttonhole-stitched and needlewoven lace inserts.

Look carefully for damage:

- Because the fabric on handkerchiefs is so fine, and the embroidery so heavy and dense, the embroidery often breaks away from the fabric.
- Drawnwork often is repaired. Look for reinforcing threads in the drawnwork, or a backing of fine net to support damaged fabric.

Look for uncut, unfinished handkerchiefs:

- Look for handkerchiefs still "in the fabric." Handkerchiefs typically have no hem. The edge is covered with minute buttonhole stitches. The handkerchiefs apparently were sometimes sold without being cut out of the fabric.

Elaborate bouquets of hand embroidered flowers, and a hem decorated with cutwork and needle lace inserts make this a wonder of handwork. Offered for a bargain price of about $125.

reflect the value of the time and care invested in the embroidery.

Nineteenth century monograms most often were tiny and intricate with lots of scrollwork and were intertwined with flowers and trailing vines. Twentieth century monograms were much larger, and less intricate.

Joined rings and monograms suggest this was a wedding handkerchief. Size about 18 inches square. Trail of tiny leaves is embroidered over the fold of the inch-deep hem. Fabric is translucent cotton. Condition is excellent. Any price below $75 is a great bargain.

Stork motif suggests this exquisitely embroidered and monogrammed 19th century handkerchief was meant to commemorate the birth of a baby. About 14 inches square. Offered for $65.

Printed handkerchiefs

Handkerchiefs were printed, primarily in England and in the United States, since about the first part of the nineteenth century. Printing on small textiles for handkerchiefs is thought to be an offshoot of the engraving trade. It was logical for book printers and engravers to add a profitable sideline by adapting their printing plates to print small textiles suitable for handkerchiefs. Some plates were adapted from engravings originally used for printing books, newspapers, and other publications, and others were designed specifically for handkerchiefs.

Several different designs often were printed on a length of cloth to make the job more economical. Stores bought lengths containing several designs. When a customer selected the one they wanted, it was cut from the bolt and hemmed.

Any subject was fair game for printing handkerchiefs. Nursery rhymes, scenes, and text and schoolwork, including multiplication tables for children, were printed on handkerchiefs. Handkerchiefs also were printed with maps, especially during wartime, when it was easier to carry a small textile than a fragile paper.

These techniques are only of interest in the earliest nineteenth century handkerchiefs. Engraved and copper plate printing makes handkerchiefs collectible. By the time printing became commonplace, and handkerchiefs were printed literally by the mile in the late nineteenth and early twentieth century, the design becomes more important.

Hot Cross Buns is the design in this small handkerchief from the 1930s. Approximately 9 inches square. Price about $10 to $15. Photo courtesy of J.J. Murphy.

Printed handkerchief depicting a series of winter scenes, probably circa 1830-1850. This most likely would have been printed as a series with the other seasons. Scenes included on this handkerchief include a farmer, a hunter, children playing a game of blind man's bluff, and clumsy skaters falling on the ice. The central motif is an early depiction of a Christmas scene, with the wording, "Tis fair, at Christmas time, you know, to kiss beneath the mistletoe." On the right, beside the Christmas scene, is a large plum pudding. Price $275 to $350. Photo courtesy of J. J. Murphy.

Children's handkerchiefs often came in boxed sets, ideal for gift-giving. This mid 20th century set would sell for $20 to $35. Photo courtesy of J.J. Murphy.

Commemorative handkerchiefs

The handkerchief is a natural souvenir. It is small, and provides a neat, contained surface for decoration. It can be designed as a cheap souvenir or extravagant memento.

Any technique — printing, drawnwork, embroidery or lace — can and has been used to decorate handkerchiefs as souvenirs of special events. The value depends on the importance of the event, the complexity of the design, and the difficulty and complexity of the technique and workmanship.

Probably because they are the easiest to understand, verify, and display, handkerchiefs commemorating American history have by far the highest values.

The event commemorated by this whitework handkerchief is not known. The prominence of South America on the globe suggests it might have been the Pan American Exposition of 1901. The technique includes fine quality embroidery and drawnwork, and the workmanship is exquisite. Photo courtesy of Pat Earnshaw.

Souvenirs for travelers typically have limited value. This pre-pipeline Alaska handkerchief was offered for $5.

19th century machine-embroidered silk handkerchief could be celebrating the U.S. centennial. It is not apparent why the embroidery is facing the center of the handkerchief. It may have been intended to wear in a pocket, or it may be a mistake. These handkerchiefs are relatively common, and must be in mint condition to bring even $5.

Pieces & prices

Bright blue silk kerchief with color portrait of Buffalo Bill in the center, black and white border with Indian motifs. Circa 1895-1910. 28 inches square. Price $775.

Red, white and blue printed handkerchief, "Remember the Maine." Price $65.

Multi-color printed Dewey political handkerchief. 11 inches square. Price $125.

Civil War child's handkerchief, printed "Battle in Missouri -- Rescue of Col. Smith's Command at Monroe Missouri by Gov. Wood of Illinois. Five lines of printing give details of battle. Printed in royal blue on white cotton. Price $700.

Reagan-Bush victory kerchief, with portraits under flying eagle, surrounded by stars. Two-tone blue rayon. $50.

Sources

Books

Murphy, J.J.; *Children's Handkerchiefs,* Schiffer, 1998.

Dealers

Rex Stark
P.O. Box 1029
Gardner, MA 01440
Phone 978-630-3237
Fax 978-630-2388
Catalogs of Americana collectibles, including textiles.

J.J. Murphy
920 Emerald St.
Madison, WI 53715-1614
Phone 608-257-3855
Fax 608-257-3730
jjmurphy@facstaff.wisc.edu
Collector, seeking rare nineteenth century printed children's handkerchiefs and bandannas. Author of Children's Handkerchiefs.

Jan Barishman
Findings of Geneva
307 W. State St.
Geneva, IL 60134
Fine vintage linens and lace; shop and shows in Chicago area. Always has a fine collection of good quality lace and embroidered handkerchiefs, and a good assortment of monograms.

Military Embroideries

Military embroideries were a phenomenon in the years roughly between 1900 and 1930, and their history remains very largely unknown. Hand-embroidered in colorful silks in the Orient, they were offered as souvenirs to American and other servicemen. Open vignettes in the midst of colorful satin stitch embroidery personalized the embroidery with painted battle scenes, ships, pictures of servicemen, or dates and places.

They have many features that give them the potential to be hot collectibles: designs are colorful and stirring, with soaring eagles, rampant horses, and glorious flags. The materials are beautifully colored silks, and the workman-ship and technique, mostly satin stitch, are superb. They sometimes are embellished with gold and silver threads.

Finally, they have importance and congeniality. Emblazoned with patriotic slogans like "Virtue, Liberty and Independence," or "In Remembrance of my cruise, China, Japan, and Philippine Islands," and with symbols of America's expansionist past, they display easily and impressively.

The day quickly will pass when the few known collectors are able to pick these little-known treasures up cheaply from people who don't recognize either the beautiful handwork, or the cultural significance.

Pieces & prices

Eagle silk embroidery, China, nineteenth century depicting a spread eagle clutching arrows and laurel atop an American shield and flags with banner "E Pluribus Unum," silver bullion highlights, very minor staining, 19-3/4 by 22-3/4 inches, framed. Sold at auction for $920.

Framed Oriental silk embroidery, with a picture of George Washington surrounded by a shield, American flags, cannon, and motto "Eluribus. Unum" on a brown silk background. Sold at auction for $125.

Sources

Howard Averbach
1919 Delaware Avenue
Pittsburgh, PA 15218
412-441-6904

Stan Clark
915 Fairview Avenue
Gettysburg, PA 17325
Phone 717-337-1728
Fax 717-337-0581

Ship suggests this impressive embroidery of flags, eagle and dragon was meant as a souvenir for a Navy man. Center vignette is not filled. Size about 24 inches high. Photo courtesy of Howard S. Averbach.

Painting of the battle of Manila adds drama to already impressive embroidery of soaring eagle and flags. Size about 51 inches by 38 inches. Photo courtesy of Howard S. Averbach.

Regalia

The dictionary offers many definitions of regalia: the emblems and symbols of royalty, the distinguishing symbols of a rank, office, order, or society, and finally, magnificent attire or finery.

In theory, the trappings of the officers of lodges, fraternities and sororities, and other secret societies are supposed to be quietly retired to the lodge headquarters or to museums, or else destroyed. In truth, it's not uncommon for them to surface in flea markets, antique shops, and occasional garage sales. A generation or two passes, and the origins of "that funny bathrobe" are lost. Some carry labels, identifying the lodge and the office. More often, all identification has been removed.

Antique shops and vintage clothing dealers near college campuses occasionally have them, as do dealers in towns near where they were made. Early regalia, especially nineteenth century, is the most collectible. Materials usually are opulent and heavy, including velvet, satins, brocades, heavy bullion (metallic embroidery threads) and beading. Later twentieth century regalia included many synthetic materials and machine embroidery. Kalamazoo Regalia, a division of Ihling Brothers in Kalamazoo, Michigan, made regalia until the late 1980s.

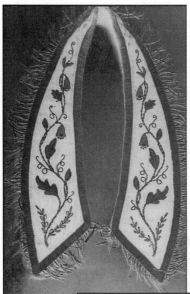

Collar for fraternal robe. Markings indicating specific office and association have been removed. Fabric is maroon velvet with silver satin trim, and embroidery of heavy silver bullion. Rich embroidery and heavy metallic thread make it attractive. Offered at Chicago vintage clothing show for $125.

Maroon velvet robe with gold braid offered in a Tempe, Arizona, antique shop near the Arizona State University campus. Price tag was $45.

Sources

Museum of our National Heritage
John D. Hamilton, Curator
P.O. Box 519
Lexington, MA 02173
718-861-6559
Collection of Masonic and other fraternal costumes and history.

Pieces & prices

Ostrich-feather decorated hat labeled "Knights of Colombus" or "Knights of Pythias." $60

Shriner's beaded and rhinestone-decorated felt fez, Tripoli temple. $35.

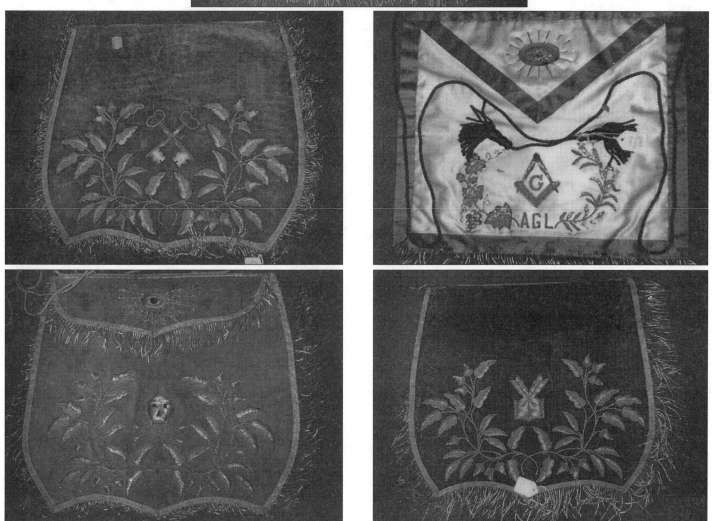

Set of five 19th century fraternal aprons, all with silver bullion embroidery and fringe, scrolling flower and leaf designs, and symbols such as Masonic compass and square, all-seeing eyes, crossed swords, crossed keys, skull and crossbones, and open book with crossed quills. Materials include velvet and silk, one with painted highlights. Some tears, fading, and staining. Sizes approximately 14 inches by 15 inches. Set of 5 aprons sold at auction for $230. Photos courtesy of Skinner Inc., Bolton, Massachusetts.

Samplers

The earliest samplers, dating to the centuries before pattern books were readily available, were a record in cloth of various fancy needlework stitches. Needleworkers used them as a reminder of possible decorative stitches to use in various projects, and of how they were done. These include long, narrow band samplers, which were unrolled to reveal an assortment of drawnwork, cutwork, needlework and embroidery stitches. Spot samplers were pieces of cloth dotted with little vignettes of flower sprigs, perhaps butterflies and little birds, and other spots of decorative stitches.

Those most often found are late eighteenth and nineteenth century schoolgirl samplers. These usually included cross-stitched alphabets, sets of numbers, various bits of poetry or biblical verses, and little figures, flowers, animals, and other decorations. Schoolgirl samplers from early America have become extremely popular as records of the social evolution of the education system, of women's place in society, and as highly personal glimpses into life in other times. This form came to America from Europe.

By the middle of the nineteenth century, pattern books and needlework instruction sheets were readily available in America through Godey's, Munsey's, Harper's Bazaar, Ladies Home Journal, and other fashion and needlework publications. Except as practice pieces, a homemade reference of individual needlework samples was no longer needed. The form, however, had become an integral part of society, a symbol of home, hearth, and feminine accomplishment. The popularity of the sampler survived well into the twentieth century. Instead of surviving as an art or folk-art form, with each individual needleworker choosing and arranging their own motifs, emblems, mottoes, bits of poetry, floral and decorative borders, the sampler evolved into a simple craft, mindlessly stitched over printed patterns.

Samplers, especially those of English and Dutch origin, often appear in the textile auctions in London. Prices for fine quality American schoolgirl samplers reached new highs at the 1997 Sotheby's auction of Joan Stephens' sampler collection. Although these occasional auction surprises are not reliable indicators of everyday prices, they do show that extraordinary needlework that has all the most sought after traits — unusual, charming design, excellent and varied stitches, and early, interesting provenance — can bring very substantial prices.

Checklist

Materials

Base fabric

Weave and fiber content should be appropriate to the time. Seventeenth and eighteenth century samplers were worked on plain-weave linen, wool, or sometimes silk. Twentieth century samplers almost always are worked on plain-weave cotton fabric.

Embroidery and needlework threads

Fiber content, color, and twist should be appropriate for the time. Loosely twisted or untwisted multi-strand silk floss was typical for many of the earlier samplers. Crinkly thread, called chenille, was popular in certain schools in the eighteenth century.

Mercerized thread did not appear until the nineteenth century. The appearance of mercerized cotton thread suggests that repairs have been made, it's a late sampler, or a forgery.

Twentieth century samplers are usually worked in DMC cotton floss or perle cotton.

Design

The choice of motifs, shape of the letters, and choice of border design all are clues to the age and origin of a sampler.

In schoolgirl samplers, the top third to half usually was devoted to the alphabet, while the center, or center bottom, was usually a picture, motto, poem, or biblical verse.

Different schools chose different border styles.

Notice if the sampler is symmetrical, a mirror-image, or asymmetrical.

Look for motifs with enough detail and careful stitching to give figures and animals personality and vitality. The more imaginative, detailed, and unusual the design, the more valuable and interesting the sampler.

Technique and workmanship

Early band and spot samplers served both as practice pieces and as a reference for choosing stitches in future projects in times when printed pattern books were not readily available. Look for a wide range of exquisitely worked complex stitches.

Cross-stitch was the most popular stitch for most lettering in schoolgirl samplers.

In a fully worked sampler, the background is entirely covered with stitching, typically a tent stitch as in needlepoint. These are very time consuming and very rare.

Condition

Mint condition always is highly prized, but should be suspect in seventeenth and eighteenth century samplers.

In addition to quality and value, the condition helps determine age and authenticity. The type and distribution of dirt and staining can also be clues to the authenticity. Look for a balance in dirt and wear in the base fabric and in the brightness or fading in the stitching.

Samplers generally are delightful to display. Great care, however, must be taken to protect the sampler from fading because of bright light, and from deterioration that results from moisture and rot. Framing samplers without providing for air circulation, and hanging them in sunlight or other bright light invites disaster.

Be wary of old samplers in frames backed with paper or cardboard. The acidity of the paper or cardboard, especially combined with moisture trapped behind a frame, very likely will have damaged the sampler beyond repair.

Importance and congeniality

The popularity of samplers comes primarily because they are charming glimpses of life in earlier times. The more clues a sampler provides to that life, the more important and attractive they become.

If you are able to identify a particular maker, a particular teacher, or a particular school it will add to the value of the sampler. If the maker was a member of a prominent family, the value also generally grows.

Samplers are one of the most congenial of all textiles because they offer a glimpse into history and the everyday life of known individuals in specific cities. This is a key element that has made samplers more and more popular as collectibles.

Rarity

Rarity in samplers generally is a combination of all the features: good design, known maker or school, excellent workmanship, and good condition.

Certain schools are better known, and more respected than others. Consult good textbooks on samplers for list of known schools and teachers.

Band and Spot samplers

Pieces & prices

Needlework sampler, stitched "Haverhill August 29 Betsey Gage Plummer Burn AD 1782 this wrought in the 14 year of her age…." Alphabets in the top half, the bottom section included grapevines and stylized trees. The border is double, an inner simple border and outer border of twining flowers. 19 inches high. Sold at auction for $10,925.

Fully worked, symmetrical sampler. Stitched "Sarah Blank 1834." Probably Chester County, Pennsylvania. Classic baskets, fat birds, flowers, geometric stars worked in silk floss, background solidly tent stitched in burgundy wool. 19 inches by 17 inches. Glazed and framed in beveled cherry frame with maple bead. Offered for sale for $9,800.

Needlework sampler by Mary Cook Saltonstall at age 9 in 1790. The Saltonstall family lived in Haverhill, on the northern edge of Massachusetts. Designs includes alphabet and mottoes, tent-stitch fruit tree, grassy hills, and saw tooth borders worked in silk on linen. Glazed with walnut frame. 13.25 inches by 10 inches. Offered for $4,800.

Family record in a needlework sampler by Mary Young, Cape May County, New Jersey, circa 1812. Inscriptions include birth date of father Stephen, a farmer and shipbuilder, and mother Elizabeth Evans Young. House depicted is two chimney Federal style, with an oversized bird on the roof, and windows with open and closed shutters. Glazed and mounted in striped maple frame with ebony bead. 19.25 inches by 17 inches. Offered for $7,200.

Alphabet sampler, with two different stylized trees at bottom sides. Stylized flower-like tree suggests New England origin. Worked in silk on linen. 4.25 inches by 7.5 inches. Offered for $925.

Highlights of 1997 Sotheby's sale of Stephens samplers:

Sampler stitched by Elisabeth Greiger in Philadelphia in 1797, sold at auction for $31,050.

Sampler depicting a lady and gentleman wearing black top hats, stitched "Hannah Nimblett her work aged 12 years." Attributed to the Marblehead, Massachusetts, school kept by Mrs. Martha Barber and her daughter. Sold at auction for $28,750.

Lettered sampler with alphabets, and motto, stitched " Wilmington Boarding School Martha Newbold 1818." Featured in Girlhood Embroidery by Betty Ring. Sold at auctionm for $8,050

Sampler of stylized motifs, birds, animals, and a large central building, with verse. Stitched by Anna Braddock at age 12 in 1826 while at the Westtown School in Burlington County, New Jersey. Sampler by Anna's sister Jemima is in the Philadelphia Museum of Art. Sold at auction for $145,500.

Several examples of band and spot samplers. Photo courtesy of Phillips Auction, London.

Clockwise, from top right: English linen sampler, with 11 bands of cutwork, needle lace, and needleweaving, circa 1650s. Design is of stylized geometric shapes and flowers. About 20 inches by 4 inches. Sold at auction for about $3,800.

English linen sampler, drawnwork, needle lace, and needleweaving. Sold at auction with another similar for $1,280.

Spot samplers, circa 1620 - 1630, with wild rose, variegated pink and yellow tulip, blue and purple pansy with yellow face highlights, red and white strawberries in blue ground, two small butterflies, caterpillar, and floral and geometric embroidery stitches embellished with purled and plaited sliver threads, raised knot detail. Linen base fabric. 10 inches by 9 inches. Sold at auction for about $11,200.

Spot sampler, circa 1620 to 1630, with small grouping of tulip, carnation, pea flowers, cherries, and lilies with tiny spider inside a simple border. Two small butterflies and two caterpillars at the outside edge of the linen panel. About 10 inches by 6 inches. Sold at auction for about $3,250.

English band sampler, circa 1650s, worked in colored silks on linen. One panel of honeysuckle and roses in an arcade, roses in an arcade, narrow rows of tiny birds, one figure holding a flower between two stylized rose plants. Worked in a variety of stitches including raised and padded details. Initials "H.B." and other small motifs. 16-1/2 inches by 6-1/2 inches. Sold at auction for about $12,800.

Linen drawnwork and needlework sampler, English, circa 1650s. Top consists of complex, stylized embroidered plants with acorns, pansies, roses, and other flowers in colored silks. Bottom of sampler has 6 bands of cutwork and geometric needle lace and needle weaving, including an "s" motif, a lily, and other flowers. One unfinished section is still on original parchment. About 15 inches by 6.6 inches. Sold at auction for about $9,600.

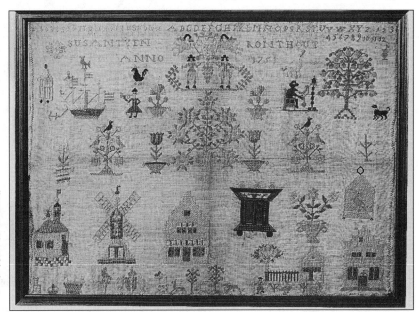

Mid 18th century Dutch sampler. Narrow band of alphabet letters at top, with a variety of motifs worked in cross stitch on linen by "Susantyen Ronthout, Anno 1751." Motifs include the Spies from Canaan, Joshua and Caleb, a spinning ape, a Dutch dresser, a windmill, a gabled house with a child looking out, a ship at anchor, various small people, animals, and plants. 14.4 inches by 19 inches. Sold at auction for about $935. Photo courtesy of Phillips Auction, London.

American sampler, either Massachusetts or New Hampshire, stitches "Mary Stillman sampler wrought in the year 1811 in her 14th year." Alphabets, verses and motifs embroidered and stitched on dark linsey-woolsey background. Border of trailing flowering vine. Some fading and minor fiber wear. Framed. 12-1/2 inches by 15-1/2 inches. Sold at auction for $2,185. Photo courtesy of Skinner, Inc., Bolton, Massachusetts.

Unfinished needlework sampler, "Lucy Deweys sampler wrought in the eleventh year of her age, 1794." Upper panel has flowering vine with bow, lower panel is potted flowering plant flanked by foliate design. Border of flowering vines. 15-1/2 inches by 17 inches. Some fading. Sold at auction for $2,070. Photo courtesy of Skinner, Inc., Bolton, Massachusetts.

American sampler, probably Pennsylvania, stitched "Lydia Ritter, aged 11 years." Panel of pious verses surrounded by flower sprays, and urns with flowers. Border in a flowering vine. 20.2 inches by 24.8 inches. Framed. Sold at auction for $1,265. Photo courtesy of Skinner, Inc., Bolton, Massachusetts.

Needlework sampler, stitched "Paulina F. Freeman, aged 9 years August 31 1820." Upper panel has alphabets and pious verse, lower panel has swags of flowers tied with ribbon. Border is geometric floral. Framed. Fading, some minor scattered staining. 16-1/2 inches by 17 inches. Sold at auction for $1,495. Photo courtesy of Skinner, Inc., Bolton, Massachusetts.

Needlework sampler, stitched, "Cornelia Donaldson aged 9 years New York July 6th 1822." Upper panel has alphabets; lower panel has a pious verse and flowering vines. Border is geometric. Fading, minor stains and holes. 17.2 inches by 13.6 inches. Framed. Sold at auction for $1,495. Photo courtesy of Skinner, Inc., Bolton, Massachusetts.

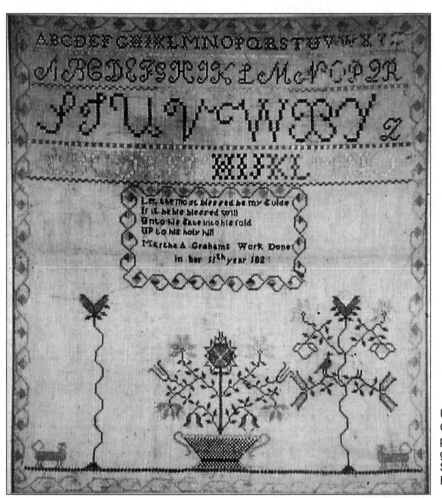

Unfinished needlework sampler, "Martha A. Grahams Work Done in her 11th year, 182.." Upper panel of flowering plants and animals, border of geometric floral. Fading, minor losses, and staining. Sold at auction for $805. Photo courtesy of Skinner, Inc., Bolton, Massachusetts.

Sampler, stitched "Fanny Anderson Aged 11 Years March 15 1833." Wool ground-embroidered mainly in cross-stitch with brown, green, cream and blue silks and wools. Design includes house, bowls of fruit, birds, vases and flowers, and Adam and Eve. 16 inches by 13 inches. Glazed and framed in birds eye maple frame. Photo courtesy of Phillips Auction, London.

Cross stitch sampler designed and made in the 1940s in the Rochester, New York, area by a Lithuanian emigrant. Motifs reflect ethnic heritage of the maker. Background is plain weave cotton khaki. Heavy silky thread, probably rayon, in bright primary colors. Thread is two-ply and highly twisted, giving the stitching a high relief, and making the cross stitch look like Smyrna stitch. Offered for $150.

Needlework sampler, stitched, "Wrought by Fanny M. Eager 1828." Upper panel has genealogical information and alphabets; lower panel has pious verse, flowering plants and basket of fruit. Border is geometric floral. Fading, minor staining. Framed. Sold at auction for $575. Photo courtesy of Skinner, Inc., Bolton, Massachusetts.

Sources

Dealers

Amy Finkel
M. Finkel and Daughter
936 Pine Street
Philadelphia, PA 19107
Phone 215-627-7797
Fax 215-627-8199
Gallery and shows. Exceptionally high quality samplers, usually well researched and documented.

Fourscore and More Antiques
Box 611
Boonton, NJ 07005
Phone 201-335-2284
English and American samplers, coverlets. By appointment only.

The Fassnachts
American Samplers
Box 795
Canandaigua, NY 14424
Phone 716-229-4199
American Samplers. Shows and by appointment

Tim & Barb Martien
1229 Bell St.
Chagrin Falls, OH 44022
Phone 440-338-3666
Samplers. Shows and by appointment

Mary R. Yarton
Whitehouse, OH 43571
Phone 419-875-5310
Samplers and other American antiques. By appointment.

The Scarlet Letter
Box 397
Sullivan, WI 53178
Phone 414-593-8470
Fax 414-593-2417
Antique samplers and kits.

Daughters of the American Revolution Museum
1776 D Avenue
Washington, D.C.
202-686-1776
Extensive collection of samplers; available for study by appointment.

Heritage Center Museum
13 W. King Street
Lancaster, PA 17602
Phone 717-299-6440
Moravian and Amish, needleworks, samplers, hooked rugs, decorative towels, quilts, coverlets. Exhibits are constantly changing. Call for appointment to study textiles in any specific area

Books

Bolton, E. and Coe, E. J., *American Samplers*, The Pyne Press, Princeton, New Jersey, 1973. An extensive listing of American samplers compiled by the Massachusetts Society of Colonial Dames.

Herr, Patricia, *The Ornamental Branches Needlework and Arts from the Lititz Moravian Girls' School*. Available from the publishers, Heritage Center Museum, Lancaster, PA

Virginia Samplers: Young Ladies and Their Needle Wisdom; catalog of 1998 exhibit at Colonial Williamsburg's DeWitt Wallace Gallery.

Ring, Betty, *Girlhood Embroidery*

Auctioneers

Phillips International Auctioneers
101 New Bond Street
London, W1Y OAS
Phone 44-171-629-6602
(textile department)
New York phone for catalogs and sale information 212-570-4830
Regular sales of textiles, about 6 per year, include European band, spot, and European and American needlework samplers from the seventeenth through the nineteenth centuries.

Skinner, Inc.
357 Main Street
Bolton, MA 01740
Phone 978-779-6241
Fax 978-779-5144
Discovery and Decorative Arts auctions frequently include early American samplers.

Horst Auctioneers
50 Durlach Road
Ephrata, PA 17522
Phone 717-738-3080
Fax 717-738-2132
Located in Amish country in Pennsylvania, Horst Auctions frequently include samplers and other textiles.

Threads and Yarns

Every garage sale yields a few spools of thread, a bag or two of yarn or crochet thread, and perhaps some embroidery floss. When are these valuable and interesting, and when should they just be pitched out? First of all, don't expect to sell your old yarns and threads for any significant amount of money. The effort it takes to clean and reuse old threads is too great — and there is a risk that the thread may have deteriorated.

Really old threads and yarns are of interest to those who repair and restore vintage textiles. Finding just the right weight and color of old thread to complete a project, or repair a lost section is key to quality repair work. The expression "they just don't make it like they used to!" really is true. The fibers, twists, and chemical dyes are really different, and cannot be duplicated. The most valuable are fine old silk and metallic embroidery threads, and good quality woolen yarns that are at least a century old.

Again, these rarely are worth any significant money, but those who do restoration work appreciate and value them.

Synthetic threads and yarns made since the middle of the twentieth century, and ordinary knitting and crocheting yarn are of no interest to textile professionals. Most of all, they don't have time to take calls from everybody with a bag of twenty-year-old cotton thread. These may be greatly appreciated by local churches and charities that use them for knitting and crocheting projects.

Selling and buying old threads and yarns

It is not easy to find the unique individuals who would like to purchase old threads and yarns. Depending on the materials, it might appeal to weavers, rug hookers, embroiderers, and those who do restoration work. The Internet auctions do offer good visibility to a wide audience. If the one person who wants your products does not see the ad, it is possible that someone in a chat group will spread the word to a wider audience.

One of the best-known Internet auction sites is www.Ebay.com. They offer a special subdivision for antique textiles.

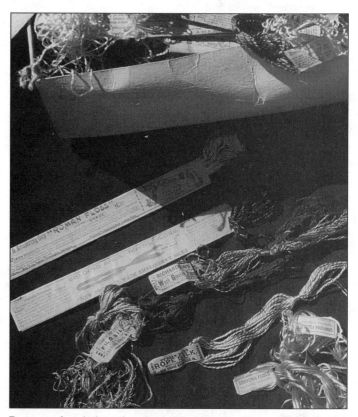

Dozens of varieties of embroidery threads were available at the turn of the century, each in a slightly different weight, twist, or ply. Single skeins of pure silk thread typically sell for about $1. Rayon thread, called artificial silk, sells for about the same price as silk.

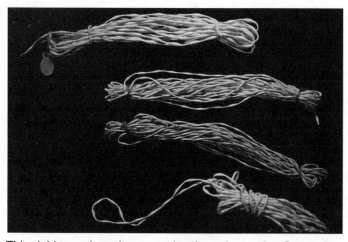

This slubby cord was known variously as rice cord or Coronation cord when it was a popular craft material at the turn of the century. The cord was couched to fabric to imitate heavy raised embroidery, or incorporated into crochet work to form craft laces.

Salesman's sample box, filled with an assortment of artificial and real silk threads, and a few skeins of fine metallic threads. Sold for $35.

Sources

Maury Bynum
Textile Conservators
Chicago, IL
Phone: 312-329-0097
maurybynum@textileconservators.com
www.textileconservators.com
Has one of the most extensive inventories of old threads and yarns for repair work.

Embroiderer's Guild of America (E.G.A.)
335 West Broadway, Suite 100
Louisville, KY 40202
Phone 502-589-6956
The E.G.A. can help provide names and addresses of local chapters and lacemakers who might be able to use old silk and metallic threads.

International Old Lacemaker's, Inc.
P.O. Box 554
Flanders, NJ 07836
Can help provide names and addresses of local chapters and lacemakers who might be able to use extremely fine old lacemakers threads. Don't bother them with old spools of sewing thread.

The Lace Museum
552 S. Murphy
Sunnyvale, CA
Does keep some old threads and lacemaker's supplies on hand. Might be interested in fine old lacemaker's threads. Don't bother them with old spools of sewing thread.

Paul Freeman
Textile Artifacts
12589 Crenshaw
Hawthorne, CA 90250
Phone 310-676-2424
Fax 310-676-2242
textileguy@aol.com
www.textileguy.com
Shop, website, shows

Has a large collection of unfinished projects from many eras. Purchases only the most unusual and rare kits and unfinished projects; sells almost anything imaginable.

Unfinished Projects

For the first twenty or thirty years, unfinished projects hang around giving us guilty feelings. The next generation is faced with the difficult choice: keep it, finish it, give it away, throw it away, or try to sell it. (See also Samplers, Quilts).

Wait a few hundred years, and the unfinished projects in your closet will be highly sought after — maybe. Great age does not necessarily give an unfinished project any great value. Very few, however, really deserve to be arbitrarily thrown away. Nearly everything is interesting to someone, someplace. Finding that someone, however, is what takes time and effort.

There are several ways unfinished projects are of interest:
- As items that just need a little more work to become finished, useful objects.
- As discovery examples to determine how unusual techniques were done.
- As teaching tools to explain the steps involved in different projects.
- As items to be displayed for their charm, and simple beauty.
- As historic objects, to show crafts of other times and places.

✔ Checklist

What is it, and what was it intended to be? If you have an unfinished project, look around to see if the materials needed to complete it, the original pattern, and the original instructions are still available. The more pieces there are to the puzzle, the more valuable it is.

Design

Good designs always are a primary concern. Anything with a bad design probably is not worth completing. Good designs that have simply gone out of fashion, however, may come back again, or may be worthwhile as collectibles.

Materials

What are the fibers? How good is the ground material? Natural materials — linen, cotton, silk, wool — almost always are more interesting and valuable. You must also ask yourself if there is enough material available for the project to be completed.

Technique and workmanship

Projects like embroidery, needle lace, tape lace, or other crafts that remain attached to their patterns or directions may be possible to complete, and make more interesting demonstration pieces.

Projects like knitting and crochet that are not attached to patterns may be more difficult to complete, and without instructions, less interesting for demonstrations.

Partially assembled garments are interesting when the materials are unusual or distinctive, the pattern or if the silhouette is unique or representative of a special fashion period.

The more unusual the technique, the more interesting the unfinished project. Laces that remain attached to their original patterns are more interesting. Needle lace projects, with the unfinished lace still attached to the pattern, are extremely interesting. Tape lace is far more common,

Bobbin lace has a different relationship to the pattern and the working pillow.

Embroideries that do not require a great many complex stitches may be easy enough to complete.

Rarity

Unfinished needle lace projects are quite unusual and always of interest.

Tape lace, also known as Battenberg, is relatively common. If the design is good, and enough tape and thread is available to finish the project, it sometimes is worth completing. Other examples are of interest as teaching samples.

Embroidery and needlepoint kits are relatively common. They may not often appear in the market, but many homes have several lurking in the closets.

Unfinished quilts, quilt blocks, and quilt tops are fairly common. The value depends on the age and curiosity of the fabrics.

Condition

Kits and original projects often may be worth completing if the colors have not faded. Check both sides of the fabric, the top and the bottom, for any color changes. If the surface colors no longer match the color of the threads supplied with the kit, it may be difficult or impossible to complete.

Even unfinished projects get dirty, and often, perspiration from the craftswoman's hands will have discolored and possible deteriorated the threads. This might not be a problem for very old projects that are only going to be used for demonstrations and teaching. But, it might mean that an unfinished project is not worth completing for use.

Extremely old and unusual unfinished projects may have considerable value regardless of whether or not they're in poor condition.

Summary

If an unfinished project fails in three or more of the above categories, it probably is not worth finishing, and is not worth selling. Individual pieces of the project — fabric, threads, yarns, tapes, laces — may be worth keeping, using for another project, or selling.

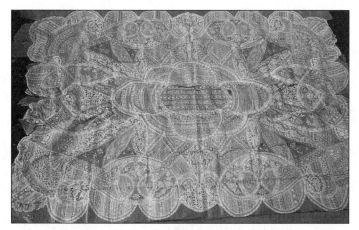

Unfinished tablecloth of Normandy work, a patchwork of vintage lace. The most difficult aspect of this work is developing and laying out a good overall design that incorporates and shows off available antique lace. The most expensive aspect is coming up with enough antique lace to complete the patchwork.

An unfinished tablecloth about 70 inches by 100 inches, if the layout is good, and enough lace comes with the unfinished project, can easily be worth $500 to $700. Because really good examples of Normandy work are not common, and they would be very expensive to make from scratch, nearly complete examples like this one should not be cut up for scrap, but should be completed.

Tape lace pattern printed on pink chintz. These patterns have become collectible. Patterns for large centerpieces or tablecloths might sell for up to $40 or $50 if they have complex, graceful designs.

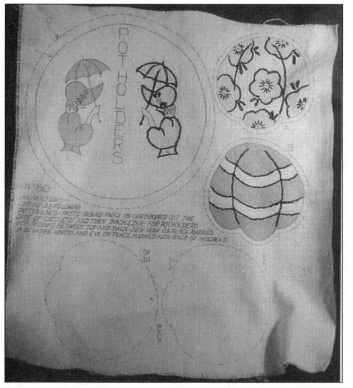

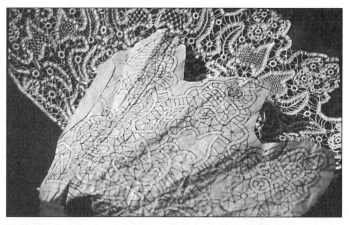

Unfinished tape lace collar project from the early 20th century was not found with enough tape to complete the collar according to the original design. There was, however, enough to fashion a suitable matching corner, and make a wearable collar. The collar, when complete, was worth approximately $150.

Unfinished printed pot holder, probably dating to the 1950s. Until pot holders become novelty collectibles, this will have minimal value. If it had been printed on a feedsack, tying in with another collectible interest, it would have far more value.

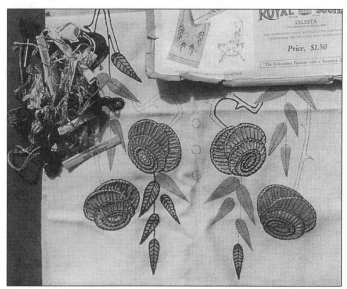

Unfinished kit for a turn-of-the-century Arts & Crafts table runner or dresser scarf. Design features bright blue and red stylized roses, outlined in black, with leaves outlined in black. Thread is included with this kit, presumably enough to finish the project, and the part already completed has not significantly faded. The project could be completed if it fit current décor. Priced under $30, it would be worth buying to complete.

Bright pink, painted stylized geraniums and shaded green leaves on this centerpiece were expected to be outlined in satin stitch in deeper shades of the same colors. Stitching would not be difficult; if thread were available, it would make an attractive centerpiece. At about $25, it would worth buying to complete.

Giving unfinished projects up for adoption

Before throwing away unfinished projects, try contacting a local chapter of the Embroiderer's Guild, sewing club, or lacemaking group. A good way to find these is through local businesses: yarn shops, embroidery shops, craft shops, or sewing and fabric shops.

Many churches can also use unused skeins of yarns for knitting and crocheting projects for charity.

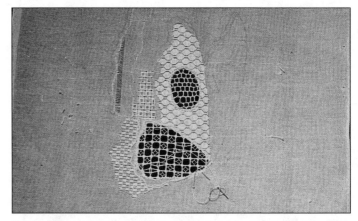

Started as project in a drawnwork class in Arizona in the late 1970s, this butterfly remains half finished. Because it was never finished, washed, and blocked, it has become discolored from perspiration. It is very useful as a demonstration piece in teaching lace and embroidery identification, and will probably stay happily unfinished.

Selling unfinished projects

It is not easy to find the unique individuals who would like to purchase old unfinished projects. The Internet auctions do offer visibility to a wide audience. If the one person who wants your project does not see the ad, it is possible that someone in a chat group will spread the word to a wider audience.

www.Ebay.com is one of the best-known Internet auctions, and offers a special subdivision for antique textiles. Other auctions can be found be searching the Net.

Unfinished quilt project identified as a bicentennial kit offered by Better Homes and Gardens magazine. The unfinished project has already passed through several hands in the nearly 30 years since the bicentennial, and it is still only partially complete. The fabric is part polyester, which makes it a little less desirable today.

A close look gives a good clue why the project was never finished. Although the pieces were precisely die-cut by machine, the initial star blocks were assembled carelessly using a sewing machine. They do not form neat squares. To complete the project as it was originally designed would require a lot of dismantling and restitching. An alternative would be to completely redesign the quilt. Stitching in the names of all those who had a hand in making it and turning it into a friendship quilt would make it very attractive for the tricentennial or some other patriotic event.

Sources

Maury Bynum
Textile Conservators
Chicago, IL
Phone: 312-329-0097
www.textileconservators.com
maurybynum@textileconservators.com
Has extensive collection of yarns and threads for tapestry and textile repair.

Quilt Rescue Squad
P.O. Box 19452
Omaha, NE 68119
Phone 800-599-0094
In addition to rescuing damaged quilts, which are auctioned to raise money for the Quilt Heritage Foundation Scholarship fund, the foundation accepts unfinished quilt tops, blocks, and fabric.

Embroiderer's Guild of America (E.G.A.)
335 West Broadway, Suite 100
Louisville, KY 40202
Phone 502-589-6956
The E.G.A. can help provide names and addresses of local chapters and lacemakers who might be able to use old unfinished projects in teaching, or usable old materials in projects.

International Old Lacers, Inc.
P.O. Box 554
Flanders, NJ 07836
Can help provide names and addresses of local chapters and lacemakers who might be able to use old unfinished lace projects in teaching, or usable old materials in projects.

The Lace Museum
552 S. Murphy
Sunnyvale, CA
Accepts rolls and skeins of unused tapes for tape lace, and unfinished laces in progress. Materials may be sold to raise funds for the museum, or may be used in repairing other damaged but valuable pieces. Unfinished projects also are used as teaching tools to explain old techniques.

Paul Freeman
Textile Artifacts
12589 Crenshaw
Hawthorne, CA 90250
Phone 310-676-2424
Fax 310-676-2242
textileguy@aol.com
www.textileguy.com
Shop, web site, shows
Has a large collection of unfinished projects from many eras. Purchases only the most unusual and rare kits and unfinished projects; sells almost anything imaginable.

Woven Silk Pictures Including Stevengraphs

The idea of weaving pictures in silk seems to have originated in Lyons, France — the home of some of the most beautiful of the figured and fancy silk fabrics. One of the earliest known is a silk portrait of Jacquard, inventor of the mechanism used to weave fancy designs in fabrics. It was produced by the firm, Carquillat, and introduced in 1840. Carquillat and Potton, Rambaud & Co., also of Lyons, France, both were awarded prizes at the 1851 Exhibition in London for woven silk portraits.

French woven silk pictures, resembling fine black and white etchings, were quickly eclipsed by English pictures produced in brilliant colors. The colorful silk pictures by Thomas Stevens, called Stevengraphs, are by far the best-known, and today are the most collectible.

Thomas Stevens' silk weaving company in Coventry, England, was producing fancy silk ribbons in the mid nineteenth century when disaster struck. Tariffs on imported ribbons were removed, and the English market was flooded with cheaper, high-quality French and other European ribbons. Fashions also were changing. Ribbons on bonnets were going out of style, while feathers and other trims were coming in.

To save his company, Thomas Stevens began producing colorful little silk weavings for greeting cards, calendars, sashes, and badges. In the 1860s, he began developing a whole new market area, selling to booksellers and stationery stores instead of to the drapery and fashion trade. By 1879, he began mounting little pictures in cardboard frames, adding informational labels, and selling them ready to be framed as pictures.

Stevens' firm produced hundreds of designs in dozens of series. Categories included portraits of historical figures, royalty, and politicians; religious pictures; assorted pictures of exhibitions, castles, buildings, and architecture and engineering; endless sports scenes including fox hunting, horse racing, coursing, boxing, bicycle racing, bullfighting, and rowing, trains, fire engines, coaches. Not all the Stevens ribbons were woven in their Coventry factory. Looms were reasonably portable, and often were set up at exhibitions where small pictures or bookmarks were woven and sold at the exhibition.

Each picture was mounted on cardboard, matted, and labeled. Collectors are very particular that the picture be in its original mat with all labels complete. It was not uncommon for more than one version of each picture to be produced. The scene of Lady Godiva's ride, for example, includes a Peeping Tom in a cottage window in one version, not in another. Stevengraphs were marketed worldwide, and consequently similar pictures will show up with different labels in different languages.

Another major weaver of silk pictures was Neyret Freres of France. Neyret Freres is best known for exquisite silk interpretations of whimsical paintings in black, white and shades of gray, with occasional accents of color. In the late 1990s, the firm began producing additional copies of a few of the original designs, using stocks of original silk thread. Prices for pictures range from about $35 for postcard size to about $150 for larger pictures.

The Chinese silk weavers in Hangchow, known for export souvenir pictures in the 1930s, began weaving a series of "saints" of Communism in the late twentieth century. These "saints" include Mao, Lenin, and other figures.

Because of the great number of designs produced, the great number of manufacturers, the excruciating detail in the silk pictures, and the great number of tiny details that greatly affect the price and value, it is well worth joining the Stevengraph Collectors' Association for information.

Note: Reference numbers in captions and Pieces & Prices are those used in the book *Stevengraphs* by Sprake and Darby.

✔ **Checklist**

Materials
- Pure silk threads were used in the early, best weavings.
- A wide range of brilliant colors make the most popular, most attractive designs.

Design
- Look for exquisite detail in the pictures: attractive faces with pleasant or charming expressions; details like buttons and fine patterns designed into clothing.
- Colors should be bright; many colors should be worked into the pattern.

Condition
- Make sure the woven picture is complete, and includes both selvages (edges) and top and bottom margins, which usually include the title of the picture, designer, manufacturer, and sometimes the weaver.
- Colors should be bright and unfaded. Look on both sides, if possible, to see what the original, unfaded colors look like.
- Stevengraphs should include the entire original mat and labels. Absence of the mat and labels drastically reduces the price of Stevengraphs.

Neyret Freres' picture known as "La Pavanne" was produced in several sizes. Postcard and a mid-sized picture are shown here. Picture is woven in black, white, and shades of gray. Dress of central figure is woven in different colors in the two versions.

#145, Columbus Leaving Spain, one of the designs produced by Stevens to be produced at the World's Colombian Exhibition in Chicago in 1898. (Note: photo shown is an example of Stevengraph #145, not the specific one that sold at auction.) $400.

#134, Niagara Falls. (Note: photo shown is an example of Stevengraph #134, not the specific one that sold at auction. $1500.)

Neyret Freres' picture known as "La Villageoise." Scene is woven in black, white, and shades of gray. Minute detail includes village in the window, pots and jugs atop the fireplace mantle, detail of flickering fire in the fireplace, and figures in the background.

Detail of "La Villageoise" shows exquisite detail of faces.

#146, Landing of Columbus, one of the designs produced by Stevens to be produced at the World's Colombian Exhibition in Chicago in 1898. (Note: photo shown is an example of Stevengraph #146, not the specific one that sold at auction.)$400.

#150, The Lady Godiva Procession. $200.

#182, HMS Majestic $875

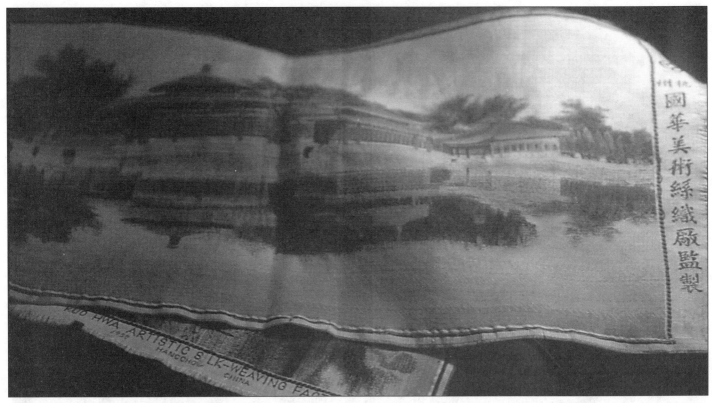

Chinese woven silk picture of a building reflected in a pond, woven in pastel blue, with dark green trees, golden brown roof, pink hazy background. Size about 14 inches long, about 6 inches high. Labeled, "Kuo Hwa Artistic Silk Weaving Factory, Hangchow, China." Offered for $25.

Two scenes of San Francisco in silk weavings. One is labeled, "Tu Chin Sheng Mfg. Hangchow." The other is very similar, and is presumed to be by the same manufacturer. Both are labeled, "Distributed by China Products Company, Shanghai, China."

Detail from aerial view of San Francisco and the Bay, labeled, "Copyrighted 1935 W. Blondel."

Pieces & prices

Neyret Freres weavings still available from the manufacturer, produced from original silk threads:

#125, La Lecon de Billard, a scene by Alonzo Perez of an eighteenth century billiard game with two intense billiards players and a flirting couple in the background. 15.7 inches by 7 inches. $55.

#122, La Lecon D'Escrime, a scene by Alonzo Perez of an eighteenth century fencing lesson, with a fencing master at the left, two women fencing, and four women at the background right. 15.7 inches by 7 inches. $55.

#210, Confidence, from a painting by Walliam with a little Dutch boy and girl telling secrets, a windmill in the background. 13 inches by 7 inches. $55.

Stevengraphs sold at auction in 1998 (Numbers cited are those used in Sprake's Stevengraph book.) Stevengraphs sold at auction were in the original gray mats, marked "woven in silk by Thomas Stevens (Coventry) Ltd.," and were accompanied by a bill of sale from the company dated July 23, 1934.

Bookmarks

A slip of colorful ribbon makes an excellent book mark, and it should come as no surprise that weavers of ribbons, labels, and other narrow lengths of cloth all produced commemorative and decorative bookmarks to round out their product line, and increase sales.

Stevengraphs are probably the best documented, but U.S. firms from the late nineteenth through the early twentieth century participated in this market. Patterson, New Jersey, was the location of several weaving companies producing ribbons and woven labels. These included Warner Woven Label Co., Inc., William Wicke Ribbon Company, E. Ianson & Son,

Collectors take note: silk was the preferred material through the beginning of the twentieth century, but synthetics quickly replaced the expensive silk toward the middle of the twentieth century.

Pieces & prices

Stevengraph, A Birthday Token, 5 inches by 1-1/4 inches; red rose with blue and green leaves, sold at auction for $25.

Stevengraph, Centennial 1776-1876, Philadelphia USA, 7 inches by 1-9/16 inches, sold at auction for $150.

Stevengraph, General George Washington, 8-3/4 inches by 2-1/9 inch sold at auction for $300.

Stevengraph, Queen of An Empire on Which the Sun Never Sets, 8-1/4 inches by 2-1/2 inches, sold at auction for $185.

Stevengraph, May Christmas Bring Thee Joy, 5-3/8 inches by 3/4 inch, sold at auction for $15.

Stevengraph, Wishing You Many Happy Returns of the Day, 5-3/8 inches by 3/8 inch, sold at auction for $50.

Sources

Museum in Pattterson, New Jersey has a comprehensive collection of woven silk bookmarks.

Collectors Club

Stevengraph Collectors Association
David Brown, President
2103-2829 Arbutus Road
Victoria, B.C. V8N 5X5
Canada
604-477-9896
Publishes a newsletter, which includes information on all types of woven silk pictures, bookmarks, calendars, and related silk weavings. Members are active and communicative, and readily exchange information on sales, auctions, prices, new findings, etc.

Books

Both are out of print, but often available through libraries.

Godden, G.; *Stevengraphs and other Victorian Silk Pictures*, Barrie & Jenkins, London, 1971.

Sprake and Darby; *Stevengraphs*. Fletcher and Son, Norwich, England, 1968. Sprake's numbering system is that most often used to refer to woven silks.

(Out of print) Coysh, A.W. *Collecting Bookmarkers*, Drake Publishers, N.Y. 1974

Auctions

Jerry Tubaugh
1702 8th Avenue
Bell Plaine, Iowa 52208
Phone 319-444-2413
Has held auctions of woven silk pictures, and is likely to have more.

Mark Cottrill
The Moat House
Lyme Hall
Lymm, Cheshire, England WA130AJ
Phone 01925-754097
Knowledgeable about the woven silks scene, including sales and auctions, especially in England and Continental Europe.

Manufacturers

This is by no means a comprehensive list. Additional manufacturers undoubtedly will turn up.

France

Carquillat, Candy & Company, Lyons, France. First manufacturer known to make a woven silk portrait, exhibited in London's 1851 Exhibition.
Neyret Freres
Potton, Rambaud & Co., Lyons

England

Thomas Stevens, Coventry and London
R.X. Cox
Welch & Lenton, Coventry. Designers as well as manufacturers. Their designs were also manufactured by other firms.
J. & J. Cash, Coventry
W.H. Grant & Co., Coventry
Brockelhurst and Whiston, Macclesfield

Germany

H.M. Krieger
Rudolff and Knuffmann
United States:
Anderson Bros., Patterson, New Jersey
Wm. Wicke Ribbon Company, Patterson, New Jersey
Best and Company
Warner Woven Ribbon Company,
Switzerland:
Adolph Grieder & Cie., Zurich

China

Tu Chin Sheng Mfg., Hangchow (Distributed in the United States in the 1930s by China Products Co., Shanghai)
Kuo Hwa Artistic Silk-weaving Factory, Hangchow

Milestones Introduction

Is it handmade or machine, how old is it, and how much is it worth? These are the questions everybody asks about their old dress, embroidered or lace pillow sham or handkerchief, wedding lace, tablecloth, drawstring bag, or any other old textile artifact.

Many factors besides age and whether an item is handmade or machine-made contribute to the value, and we have discussed that in another chapter. Very often the question of handmade versus machine is not so simple to answer, either. Consider a fashionable, circa-1900s dress. The fabric almost certainly would have been woven on power-driven looms, and most likely sewn on a machine. The machine, however, would have been a foot-powered treadle machine, and more than likely, the dress would have been draped, cut, and basted by hand for the individual customer. The elaborate trimmings might include machine-woven ribbons, elaborately gathered, ruched, tucked, and bowed into confections what would shame a wedding cake, then further embellished with handmade and machine embroideries. The laces decorating the dress might be newly handmade, newly machine-made, or machine-made but outlined and embellished with hand embroidery. The decorations also very likely could include handmade motifs of lace and embroidery rescued from decade or century-old flounces, and hand-stitched onto a fresh, machine-made net.

Evolution rather than revolution would be a better label for the industrial upheaval that started in the late eighteenth century and consumed the nineteenth. One step at a time the weaving process gradually evolved from a hand process that required several workers to produce a single length of cloth, to power-driven monsters watched over by a single worker. The revolution or evolution also looks different depending on whether you are standing in the eighteenth century looking forward, or in the twentieth looking backward.

The invention of the Jacquard mechanism is a good example. Today, we generally consider the quaint cotton and wool coverlets to be the handmade products of individual artisans. They are treasured because we can connect a specific cozy product to specific people. Book after book lists the weavers active in each state by name, and by personality. We can imagine Matthew Rattray or Sarah La Tourette in Indiana getting up early in the morning, stringing hand-spun, hand-dyed warp threads, then spending the day rhythmically shuttling and beating the filler threads. We cannot imagine the exhausting, painful work of the draw-boys that lost their jobs when Jacquard's mechanism swept the industry. The fact that punched cards rather than young humans controlled the motion of each individual warp thread does not lessen the "handmade" quality of these handwoven coverlets in our eyes.

The invention of handmade nets around 1800 is another milestone that forever changed the nature of fashion and the lacemaking industry. The word "nets" was put in the plural form on purpose. Dozens of varieties were invented within a decade. Each fought for market share, and many lost. They disappeared, along with the machines that made them.

Wonderful laces could be produced comparatively quickly by sewing motifs on to these varied machine nets. Even middle class brides could expect to have a beautifully decorated net veil, and middle class housewives could drape a beautifully decorated veil over a bonnet. Looking backward from today, these are marvelous hand-stitched laces. Looking forward from the eighteenth century, they were pale imitations of what had been. Some welcomed these impostors, eager to wear and enjoy what had been restricted to royalty, to be thoroughly modern and wear the latest fashion produced on the machines that were forever changing the world. Others sneered at them and said they were not "real" laces.

Fast-forward to today. Every moderately sized town in America has a shop that holds heirloom sewing classes. Each person in the class has their own high-power computer-directed machines, one for sewing, one for serging. There is no hand-sewing done in the room. Compare the unique vests, quilts, dresses, and pillows they make to store-bought, assembly-line products offered in every shopping mall across the country, and they are unique, whimsical, and certainly one-of-a kind. How will generations in the next millennium view these homemade creations? Has homemade become the new handmade?

The table of milestones on the following pages gives us insight into the evolution of textile production. Its intent is more to put things into perspective, rather than to offer a definitive chart for dating artifacts. Automation happened step by step, and many steps are involved in the production of each dress, tablecloth, drapery set, Santa Claus costume, compact-cover, handkerchief and handkerchief bag. Many more are involved in remodeling each, and making handkerchiefs into patchwork quilts, or wedding gowns into Christening dresses.

Many steps were involved in the mechanization of each weaving, sewing, spinning, and knitting process. Many of these inventions were introduced at nearly the same time, and many were quickly swept aside by newer-better-faster inventions.

So many kinds of sewing machines were introduced in such a short period of time that even the patent office could not sort out who invented what. Rather than fight endless legal battles, the industry compromised and split shares of the markets and royalties. Within a few decades, sewing machines completely covered the globe.

Browse through the chart of milestones to get a feel for the complexity and rapid change of the textile industry. Use it as a guideline for some tentative dating. A woven coverlet bearing the date "1847," but woven in brightly colored synthetic yarns must be a reproduction. Before the 1860s, only natural dyes were available, and although beautiful colors were produced, they were limited in range. Rayon, originally known as "artificial silk" was the first synthetic fiber, and that was introduced at the end of the nineteenth century. Others were not widely available until well into the twentieth.

Likewise, be suspect of any cotton lace purported to be made in the early eighteenth century. Before the cotton gin was invented at the end of that century, linen was far more common. It's much more likely that any early peasant laces would have been made of linen thread.

The table of milestones provides perspective on how old some textiles are, and show that these beautiful textiles are astonishing human achievements. Fabulous brocades, cut velvets, tapestries, and embroideries were made centuries before machines. The amazing amount of ingenuity, skill, and plain hard work that went into these is largely unrecognized and unappreciated in the marketplace.

Eyebrows raise when tapestries bring tens of thousands of dollars at auction, or early printed chintzes sell for over two to three-hundred dollars a yard. This still leaves plenty of room for prices to go even higher, if in fact they are to truly reflect the human achievement in skill, technique, workmanship and artistic beauty.

Year	Fibers	Spinning	Fabric Making	Finishing	Sewing
B.C.	Cotton used by ancient cultures in China, Egypt, India, Mexico, Peru.				
Circa 1000	Evidence of flax being used to make linen textiles.				
2640 B.C.	Silk production beginning in China.				
1300s		Spinning wheel introduced to Europe from India.			
1530s			First mentions of handknitted stockings.		
1589			Stocking frame knitting machine invented, producing plain knit.		
1609	Jamestown Colony imports sheep-raising to the New World.				
Late 1500s/ Early 1600		Cotton planted in Florida.			
Early 1600s	Cotton planted in Virginia.				
1643	Small group of wool combers and carders emigrate to Massachusetts Bay Colony from England; begin producing finished wool fabric.				
1733			Flying shuttle speeds handweaving.		
1758			Rib attachment patented for stocking frame; beginning rapid developments in patterning of machine knits.		

Year	Fibers	Spinning	Fabric Making	Finishing	Sewing
1764		Spinning jenny, a machine to turn several spinning wheels at the same time, invented in England by Hargreaves.			
1768			Early attempts at knitted openwork net.		
1775			Tricot warp knitting machine produces 16-inch cloth for silk stockings.		
Late 1770s			Experiments and early patents in warp frame knitting.		
1783				Direct roller printing invented.	
1790					First patent issued for sewing machine - does chain stitch.
1793	Cotton gin patented - cotton begins to replace linen in fabrics and thread.				
1801			Jacquard attachment invented - makes patterned weaves economical.		
1812		James and Patrick Clark start thread factory in Paisley, Scotland, selling hanks of cotton thread.			
1815		James Coats starts manufacturing facility for cotton thread in Scotland.	Jacquard weaving becoming widespread.		
1820s				Many experiments going on in machine embroidery.	
1826		J & J Clark (Sons of James) begin winding thread on refillable spools.			

Year	Fibers	Spinning	Fabric Making	Finishing	Sewing
1829				Heilman's handmachine for embroidery patented. Could embroider 20 identical designs simultaneously.	
1830					Thimmonier receives French patent for machine that produces chain stitch imitation of tambour embroidery. Thimmonier begins to adapt mechanism for sewing machine.
1837			Crompton introduces loom for cotton and wool.		
1840		J & P Coats begins selling thread in U.S.			
1839-1841			Jacquard attachment applied to Pusher and Leavers lacemaking machines, making patterned imitations of bobbin laces.		
1841			Bigelow introduces power loom for ingrain carpets.		
1850s					Garment industry begins to use sewing machines.
1850s					Godey's and other ladies' magazines begin running fashion plates with suggestions for how to make the clothes pictured.
1853		Mercerization process invented - increases luster and strength of cotton fibers and woven fabrics.			Sewing machine "combination" formed among sewing machine manufacturers; ends the patent wars over competing machines.

Year	Fibers	Spinning	Fabric Making	Finishing	Sewing
1855	First patent for Rayon issued.				
1856				First synthetic dye, mauve, invented.	Single thread chain stitch introduced.
1860s		Clark's invents a thread even, smooth, and strong enough for sewing machines. Our New Thread (O.N.T.), is a thread cabled of three, 2-ply yarns. Beginning of huge sewing thread industry.		Borers added to embroidery handmachine, could mimic Broderie Anglaise, eyelets, and Ayrshire whitework.	Sewing machines used to outfit Union soldiers: uniforms, tents, blankets, sails, knapsacks.
1861					Singer and other manufacturers selling sewing machines around the whole world.
1863			Knitting machine capable of adding and dropping stitches produces shaped garments.		
1865					Cornely embroidery/sewing machine invented by Bonnas, manufactured by Cornely. Used to embroider outlines on lace and fabrics.
1870s					Major pattern manufacturers starting operation.
1871					First patent for electrified sewing machine.
1870s				Colorfast flosses available; triggers craze for redwork.	

Year	Fibers	Spinning	Fabric Making	Finishing	Sewing
1880s				Schiffli embroidery machines introduced. Could produce openwork embroideries and embroider on net to mimic mesh-based laces.	Zig-zag stitch introduced by John Kaiser.
				Aetz process introduced which dissolves background fabric behind Schiffli-type lockstitch embroideries to produce guipure laces.	Zipper becomes commercially available.
1884	First rayon fibers produced.				
1889					Singer introduces their first electrical machine.
1891	First commercial production of rayon.				
1897				Tension mercerization developed to prevent shrinkage during process.	
1920s					Home electric sewing machines begin to become popular
1930s	Broken ends of rayon filament yarns spun into staple yarn; used mainly for women's lingerie.				
1935	First U.S. production of nylon.				
1939	First commercial production of nylon hosiery.				
1940s					Home zig-zag machine becomes widely available.

Shows and Sales

California

Folk Art to Funk — Textiles, Costumes and Clothing
Annual/ Spring
Wide range of textiles including linens, laces, quilts, coverlets and rugs to vintage fashion.
Santa Monica Civic Auditorium
Santa Monica, CA
For dates and information
310-455-2886
445-772-3272

Textile Costume and Clothing Show
Two shows per year, January and August
Wide range of textiles including linens, laces, quilts, coverlets and rugs to vintage fashion.
Pickwick Banquet and Entertainment Center
Burbank, CA
For dates and information
Caskey Lees: 310-455-2886

Wear and Remembrance Vintage Clothing Show and Sale
Annual sale, Last weekend in April
Yuba City, CA
For information and date: 530-743-1004

Vintage Fashion Expo
Santa Monica, San Francisco, Long Beach CA
For dates and information: 707-793-0773

Connecticut

Vintage Clothing, Estate and Costume Jewelry, and Vintage Textile Show
Two shows per year, usually September and February
Maven Company and Young Management Company
Stratford, CT
For dates and information:
800-344-7469
203-758-3880
www.mavencompany.com

Illinois

The Vintage Show
Two shows per year, winter and fall.
Large show featuring all kinds of textiles including lace and linens, household textiles, costume, haute couture, eighteenth through twentieth century fashion.
Cats Pajamas Productions
Elgin, IL
847-428-8368
thevintageshow.com

Sandwich Antique show
General line antique show that features many textile and fashion dealers.
Sandwich, IL
Lawler, Robert: 773-227-4464
Massachusetts

Antique Textile and Vintage Fashions Extravaganza
Held May through September, the Monday before Brimfield week
Very large show featuring dealers offering all kinds of textiles and vintage fashion
Host Hotel
Sturbridge, MA
Zukas, Linda: 207-439-2334

Auctioneers

Caddigan Auctioneers, Inc.
Joan Caddigan
1130 Washington St.
Hanover, MA (South of Boston) 02339
Phone 781-826-8648
Fax 781-826-2438
Holds two or three auctions per year featuring fine pre-1950s and Victorian vintage fashion, and other textiles.

Robert Eldred
Robert C. Eldred Company
1483 Route 6A
P.O. Box 796
East Dennis, MA 2641
Phone 508-385-3116
Fax 508-385-3116
Oriental Art Auctions, including silks, paintings, kimonos, etc. and Americana, featuring quilts, samplers

New York

Stella Triple Pier and Decorative Arts and Textiles Antique Show
New York, NY
Stella management company has be experimenting with some large, new shows that feature textiles and decorative arts. Dates and formats have been changing, so contact the management company for current information.
Stella Show Management Co.
Phone 212-255-0020
antiqunet.com/stella

Vintage Fashion and Antique Textile Show
Metropolitan Art and Antiques
New York City
Several shows and sales per year. For information and dates contact:
Lily Kesselman
Phone 212-463-0200
212-463-7099

William Doyle Galleries
175 East 87th St.
New York, NY 10128
Linda Donahue, couture and textile specialist
Phone 212-427-2730
Fax 212-369-0892
A couple auctions per year featuring great collections of haute couture and other textiles
Phillips, Christies, and Sotheby's New York branches include textiles in Decorative Arts and other auctions.

Pennsylvania

Alderfer
501 Fairgrounds Road
Hatfield, PA
215-393-3000
www.alderfercompany.com
auction@alderfercompany.com

Texas

Victorian Elegance
Richardson, Texas
February and September
Very large shows featuring all kinds of textiles and vintage fashion.
For information and dates
1000 14th St., Suite 201
Plano, TX 75074
Phone 972-235-5139
rmaster904@aol.com

Virginia

Williamsburg Vintage Fashion and Accessory Show
February
Part of Williamsburg Festival week, which includes four different festivals. The only one that is antique related. 25 vendors of vintage textiles, including quilts, fashions, lace, linens, Mancuso, David and Peter
215-862-5828
www.quiltfest.com

Washington

Best of the Past Vintage Clothing and Textile Sale
Last weekend in March, second weekend in October
Seattle Center Pavilion Building
Seattle, WA
Fifty plus dealers, vendors from six states, includes sewing patterns, sewing fabric, elegant to funk, Victorian to 1960s. Lace, linens, household furnishings, towels, curtains, quilts, coverlets. European and American textiles.
J.R. Promotions
509-375-5273
vintagev@aol.com

Canada

Toronto Vintage Clothing Show
Troy, June C.
Phone 905-666-0523
905-666-3277

England

Antique Textile Fair Manchester, England
Annual show, usually in the Spring. Large show, with wide range of vendors featuring all types of textiles and vintage fashion.
Margaret Bolger
Loch Bay Boathouse
Waternish, Isle of Skye
IV55 8GD, United Kingdom
Phone 01-470-592-361
margaret_bolger@compuserve.com

Mail Order Auction

James J. Reeves
P.O. Box 19
Huntingdon, PA 16652
1-888-574-6229 or 814-643-5497
reeves@vicon.net
Diahann Moiser, textile and vintage fashion specialist
Large direct mail auctions, including large selections of vintage fashion and textiles. Phone or email for catalog.

Resource Directory

The following directory lists those who present themselves as dealers, collectors, and appraisers. This list is for information only. We do not certify the expertise or credentials of any listed here.

Some dealers may be willing to identify and appraise vintage clothing, textiles, and linens. Expect a charge for their services. Do not expect each to be an expert in everything or anything.

California

Jules and Kathe Kliot
Lacis
2982 Adeline
Berkeley, CA 94703
Phone 415-843-7178
Extensive line of vintage fashion, linens, and laces. Supplies and books for lacemaking and crafts. Appraisals, repairs, restoration.

George Waldman
Waldman Appraisal Co.
22311 Ventura Blvd. Suite 117
Calabasas, CA 91364-8073
Phone 818-591-8073
Fax 818-591-2073
Vintage clothing.

Susan Narens
45 Morning Glory
Rancho St. Margarita, CA 92688-1523
Phone 714-830-6868
Fax 714-472-9378
Quilts, textiles.

Leslie Vitanza
Peregrine Galleries
508 Brinkerhoff Ave.
Santa Barbara, CA 93101-3441
Phone 805-963-3134
Vintage clothing.

Brian and Stephanie Morehouse
894 S. Bronson Ave.
Los Angeles, CA 90005
323-939-2240
By appointment. Appraising, and consulting buyers and sellers for rugs and tapestries, ethnic textiles. Couture and fashion, general textiles.

Textile Group of Los Angeles
Phone 323-939-2240
Specializes in all areas of textiles.

Kathleen Mitchell
Old Pump Antiques
P.O. Box 774
San Bruno, CA 94066-0774
Phone 415-588-4894
Textiles.

Jude Allen
Vintage Collection
356 Main St.
Half Moon Bay, CA 94019
Phone 415-712-0366
Shop; linens, lace, old yardage, fabrics.

Janene Fawcett
Vintage Silhouettes
1301 Pomona St.
Crockett, CA 94525
Phone 510-787-7274
Men's and women's vintage clothing and accessories, 1850s to 1950s.

Paul Freeman
Textile Artifacts
12589 Crenshaw
Hawthorne, CA 90250
Phone 310-676-2424
Fax 310-676-2242
textileguy@aol.com
www.textileguy.com
Shop, website, shows
Wide range of textiles, Arts & Crafts linens and textiles, lace, ecclesiastical embroideries.

Holly Hess
Janet Russell
Atelier P.O.lonaise
4610 1/2 Park Blvd.
San Diego, CA 92116
Phone/fax 619-291-8700
Authentic period and bridal apparel

Julianna Greenberg
2695 W. Mesa
Fresno, CA 93711
209-436-8633
High quality fashions, linens and laces. Shows and by appointment. Has display in local antique mall; call for information.

Leigh Leshner
Thanks for the Memories
P.O. Box 55113
Sherman Oaks, CA 91413
Phone 800-981-8433
Website. Shows and by appointment
venture18@aol.com
www.tias.com/stores/memories
Showcases at Sherman Oaks Antique Mall.

Kathryn Mancini
Ages Ahead
Palo Alto, CA
Phone 415-327-4480
Fax 415-326-2573
Vintage clothing and bridal.

Janice Stockwell
The Stage Stop
4330C Clayton Road
Concord, CA 94521
Phone 510-685-4440
Men's and women's vintage and collectible clothing.

Lauriks Imports
3790 El Camino Real, Suite 103
Palo Alto, CA 94360
Phone 415-949-1096
Fax 415-948-5512
Antique laces, lace clothing by appointment, and catalog.

Jim Thomas
1080 Scots Lane
Walnut Creek, CA 94596
Shows and by appointment

Emma's Trunk
1701 Orange Tree Lane
Redlands, CA 92374-2857
Phone 800-448-7865
Fax 909-798-7386
5,000 sq. ft. mall with lots of textiles of all kinds.

Paris 1900
2703 Main Street
Santa Monica, CA 90405
Phone 310-396-0405
Shop; vintage clothing, bridal, textiles, linens and lace.

Urban Mermaids
1807 Divisadero at Bush
San Francisco, CA
Phone 415-775-7774
Vintage clothing, glitz, drag, and unusual pieces from the 1950s to 1970s.

The Paper Bag Princess
8700 Santa Monica Blvd.
W. Hollywood, CA 90069
Phone 310-358-1985
ZZZ.PaperBagP.com
Vintage couture and designer resale.

Herb Wallerstein
Calico Antiques
611 N. Alta Vista Drive
Beverly Hills, CA 90210
Phone 310-273-4192
Fax 310-273-1921
Fine quality pre 1930 quilts.

Museums

The Lace Museum
552 S. Murphy
Sunnyvale, CA 94087
Phone 408-730-4695
Extensive collection of lace and lacy vintage fashions. Some always are on display. Classes in lacemaking.

San Jose Museum of Quilts
and Textiles
110 Paseo de San Antonia
San Jose, CA 408-971-0323
Jane Przybyz, Executive Director

H.M. deYoung Memorial Museum
Golden Gate Park
75 Tea Garden Drive
San Francisco, CA 94118-4501
Phone 415-750-7609
Fax 415-750-7692
Diane Mott, associate curator of textiles
Dmott@farnsf.org
Wide range of vintage textiles. Rarely on exhibit, but available for study.

Colorado

Sharon Daugherty
The Lace Chest
101 South 25th St.
Colorado Springs, CO 80904
Phone 719-632-1771
Shop; antique linen and lace.

Rebecca Nohe
Quartermoon Market
315 E. Pikes Peak Ave.
Colorado Springs, CO 80903
Phone 719-630-8961
Shop and by appointment. Fine textiles, whites; unusual and high end., quilts, samplers, old buttons.

Connecticut

Debra Bonito
Images
32 N. Colony Road
Wallingford, CT 06492-3650
Phone 203-265-7076
Heirloom linens, lace, textiles Early textiles, needlepoint, tapestry, tablecloths, sheets.

Laurie Brady
Stonington Antiques and Fine Linens
123 Water St.
Stonington, CT 06378
Shop; shows; linens and lace.

Stephen & Carol Huber
40 Ferry Road
Old Saybrook, CT 06475
Phone 860-388-6809
17th and 18th century needlework.

Patricia Lea
Orkney & Yost Antique Center
Cutler Street
Stonington, CT 06378
Phone 860-464-0466
Fine linens and lace, and textiles. Tapestries, victorian draperies. 1950s drapes, Velvets, French Silks.

Patricia Menson
The Linen Merchant
494B Heritage Village
Southbury, CT 06488

Lydia Reed
Wyndham Needleworks
Box 65, 2333 Old Colony Road
Eastford, CT 06242
Phone 203-974-1214

Museums

Windham Textile History Museum
Willimantic, CT
Located in 19th century
textile company.
jquilt@aol.com

Florida

Helen Board
5946 Holly Bay Road
Jacksonville, FL 32211
Phone 904-743-4974
Lace and linen collector.

Teresa Dunn
5146 Grandview Court
Tallahassee, FL 32303
Phone 904-562-5681
Victorian white clothing; doll trimmings.

Paivi Roberts
3100 Vincent Road
West Palm Beach, FL 33405
Phone 561-659-3896
Fax 407-835-0079
Fine linens and lace. Shop; antique shows across the country.

Georgia

Rittenmeyer
Reminiscent Rose Antiques
1032 Wildwood Rd.
Atlanta, GA 30306
Phone 404-892-9611
70224.335@compuserve.com
Linens.

Reminiscing Vintage Fashions
1579 Monroe Drive, Box 200
Atlanta, GA 30324
Phone 404-815-1999
dgkg123@aol.com
Quality vintage fashions by mail.

Illinois

Jan Barishman
Findings of Geneva
307 W. State St.
Geneva, IL 60134
Fine vintage linens and lace; shop and shows in Chicago area.

Maury Bynum
Textile Conservators
Chicago, IL
Phone: 312-329-0097
www.textileconservators.com
maurybynum@textileconservators.com
Quilts, coverlets, hooked rugs, extraordinary vintage textiles. Buy and sell, repair, restoration. By appointment.

Sabine Casten
The Lace Collection
558 Monroe
River Forest, IL 60305
Phone 708-366-0756
Vintage linens and clothes. Chicago area shows.

Nancy Cordero
AdVintageous
101 Glenlake Avenue
Park Ridge, IL 60068
Phone 847-823-8451
Wearable Vintage, 1920s to 1950s. Shows and by appointment.

Tari Costan
Silver Moon
3337 N. Halsted
Chicago, IL 60657-2426
Phone 773-883-0222
Antique clothing, wedding gowns, textiles.

Dotty Day
Vintage Days
Nine 4th St.
Carrollton, IL 62016
Phone 217-942-3996

Chris Ebert
Chris' Antiques
5152 Harlem Road
Rockford, IL 61111
Phone 815-654-1610
Quilts, linens, vintage clothing.

Evelyn Forstadt
Swell Stuff
Evanston, IL
Phone 847-475-5716
Wide variety of linens, textiles, Victoriana, laces. Shows and by appointment.

Ellen Germanos
Suburban Chicago, IL
Phone 847-670-4440
Wide range of textiles, linens, vintage clothing. Shows only.

Bill Kohanek
Antiques and Decoration
121 West State Street
Geneva, IL 60134
Phone 630-232-0552
Wide range of vintage textiles for decorating.

Rick Lidinsky
2935 W. Byron #1
Chicago, IL 60618
773-583-7309
Hawaiiana, draperies, odd lots 50s and 60s, Hawaiian rayon yardage. Shows and by appointment.

Christine McConnell
Crystal Lake, IL
Phone 815-338-7265
Wide range of vintage and textiles; shows only. Coverlets.

Nancy Pratt
203 Sunset Drive
Libertyville, IL 60048
Phone 847-367-8456
Shows and by appointment. Also exhibiting at Volo Antique Malls II and III, Volo, IL. Does lectures on hats and clothing, 1890s through 1940s. Vintage furs, apparel, and hats.

Nancy Schofer
Chicago area, IL
Phone 708-251-4840
Creating clothing and household items from vintage fabrics. By appointment only.

Denise Stehman
Gemini Antiques
43B Garden Market
Western Springs, IL 60558
Phone 708-246-6968
Wide range of vintage accessories, fashions.

Lavinia Tackberry
Eye on Design
Hinsdale, IL
Phone 630-986-5228
African, ethnic textiles.

Cindy Warrington
The Blue Parrot
Springfield, IL
Phone 217-793-2986
Vintage clothing for men and women. Hats, early 20s to 50s vintage. Shows and by appointment.

Inge Wolf
Antique Market II
301-303 W. Main Street
St. Charles, IL 60175
Phone 630-377-5818
Fax 847-741-1599
Vintage linens.

Geneva Antique Market
227 S. Third St.
Geneva, IL 60134
Phone 630-208-1150
Several textile dealers, including vintage textiles, quilts, Victoriana, linens and lace.

Ophelia's
125 Marion St.
Oak Park, IL 60301
Phone 708-386-9194
Vintage clothes.

Vintage Adventure
403 11th St.
Rockford, IL 66111
Phone 815-227-1892
Vintage clothing and bridal gowns.

Indiana

Bob & Priscilla Brown
18516 E. Redbud Ct.
Hope, IN 47246
Phone 812-546-1100
Hooked rugs and other textiles. By appointment only.

Dawn Karberg
Blue Mirror
2531 Ticonderoga
Schereville, IN 46394
219-365-3825
Shows; shop in Chicago. Assorted vintage clothing and pre-1950s textiles; Barkcloth fabric, draperies, printed tablecloths.

J. Parker
The Hound in the Hat Antiques
Rossville, IN 46065
Phone 765-589-3884
Vintage fashion, linens, lots of notions, ribbons, hats. One of three shops in mall devoted to textiles; Also shows and by appointment.

Michelle Stewart-Pruit
Back Through Time Antique Mall
Junction of state roads 26 and 39
9 West main St.
Rossville, IN 46065
Phone 765-379-3299
Vintage fashion, linens, lots of notions, ribbons, hats. One of three shops in mall devoted to textiles; Also shows and by appointment.

Swartzentruber Auctions
805 N. VanBuren
P.O. Box 331
Shipshewana, Indiana 46565
219-768-4621
Auctions: quilts, from antiques to the latest made, from all over the U.S. Shipshewana is Amish country in Indiana, and these auctions typically includes many Amish-made.

Museums

Indianapolis Art Museum
Indianapolis, IN
Extraordinary collection of late 19th and early 20th century laces and linens. Appointment is needed.

Connor Prairie
13400 Allisonville Road
Fishers, IN 46038
Historic farm and park in the Indianapolis area, focusing on 1836. Has large coverlet collection and other vintage textiles. Jane Leslie, textile specialist
Phone 317-776-6000

Kentucky

Hollis Jenkins Evans
Past Perfect
1520 So. 2nd St.
Louisville, KY 40208
Vintage and collectible clothing; mail or by appointment only.

Jeanne Rhea
Victorian Lady
P.O. Box 248
Murray, KY 42071
Phone 502-759-3249
victorianlady@ldd.net
Website: Ldd.net/victorianlady/victorian/html
Linens, lace, textiles, clothing.

Cynthia Roeder
Ramblin Rose Antiques
4 Colonel Point Space #82,
Duck Creek Antique Mall
(Cincinnati area)
Wilder, KY 41076
Phone 606-441-6254
Linens and lace; vintage hats.

Robert Walker
Just Faboo
107 East Main St.
P.O. Box 3913
Midway, KY (Lexington area) 40347
Phone 606-846-5606
1780-1920 high quality vintage fashions, paisleys. Large shop, shows, and by appointment.

Shelly Zegart
12 Z River Hill Road
Louisville, KY 40207
Phone 502-897-7566
Fax 502-897-3819
Fine quilts bought and sold.

Garbo's Vintage Clothing
Covington, KY
Phone 606-291-9033
Specializing in Men's Wear.

Museum

Museum of American Quilt Society
215 Jefferson
Paducah, KY 42002
Phone 502-442-8856
Permanent collection of quilts. 60 to 70 quilts from permanent collection always on display. Changing exhibits vary from contemporary to antique quilts. Publish newsletter for members.

Embroiderer's Guild of America
335 West Broadway, Suite 100
Louisville, KY 40202
Phone 502-589-6956
Small exhibit of contemporary and vintage embroidery always on display. Extensive library for research.

Louisiana

Victoria Bloom
89 William and Mary
Kenner, LA 70065
Phone 504-469-1847
Linens and lace.

Sherry Kohleri
Erudite Art
605 N. Alexander St.
New Orleans, LA 70119-4511
Phone 504-486-0257, 504-866-7795
Shop: intage clothing, textiles, linens, and lace.

Maine

Marsha Manchester
Milady's Mercantile
21 South Main
Middleboro, MA 02346
Phone 508-946-2121
Shirley Frater
Arsenic and Old Lace
P. O. Box 367
Damariscotta, ME 04543
Phone 207-563-1414
Fine quality linens and lace.

Maryland

Barbara Spaid
Squirrel Cage
130 Chesapeake Ave.
Prince Frederick, MD 20678-4473
Phone 410-535-1158

Barbara Lessig
Lessig's Pleasant Valley Antiques
21000 Georgia Ave.
Brookeville, MD 20833-1138
Phone 301-924-2293301-570-1625
jlessig@lmi.org
Vintage textiles.

Adrienne Moss
Moss Antiques
11510 Parkedge Dr.
Rockville, MD 20852-3729
Phone 301-770-2383
Quilts.

Joan Hurt
Arundel Appraisers
9715 Philadelphia Rd.
Baltimore, MD 21237-3427
Phone 410-686-9598
Quilts.

Massachusetts

Lucia Hotton
263 Union
South Weymouth, MA 02190
Phone 781-337-1982
Vintage linens, lace, apparel.

Skinner, Inc.
357 Main Street
Bolton, MA 01740
Phone 978-779-6241
Fax 978-779-5144
Auctioneers. Various auctions, especially Discovery and Decorative Arts auctions including early American textiles, such as samplers, quilts, coverlets, hooked and other rugs, and lots of mixed laces, linens, and textile fragments.

Old Sturbridge Village
1 Old Sturbridge Village Road
Sturbridge, MA, 0156
Phone 508-347-3362
Lynne Bassett, Curator of textiles and fine art.
Extensive collection of quilts and other early American textiles.

Michigan

Christine Crockett
The Crockett Collection
506 E. Kingsley
Ann Arbor, MI 48104
Phone 313-761-4751
Fine quality linens and lace. Saline (Ann Arbor) show and by appointment.

Judy Frankel
Judy Frankel Antiques
2900 W. Maple, Suite 111
Troy, MI 48084
Phone 248-649-4399
Textiles, by appointment.

Donna Hicks
Aldon Antiques
Kalamazoo, MI
Phone 616-388-5375
Linen, lace, white apparel for ladies and children. Shows and by appointment only.

Jean Kenny
901 Ridgewood
Bloomfield Hills, MI 48304
Linens and vintage; Royal Oak Flea Market and by appointment only.

Ann Rogers Pfrender
5764 Fox Hollow Ct.
Ann Arbor, MI 48105-9510
Phone 313-665-6058
Quilts.

Leslie Saari
Great Lakes Appraisals
201 Iroquois Place
Cadillac, MI 49601-9221
Phone 616-775-6423
Identify and appraise vintage lace and linens.

Sodou, Kathy
Mason Antiques District
208 Mason St.
Mason, MI 48854-1128
Phone 517-676-9753
Vintage clothing dealer.

Denny Tracey
Denny L. Tracey Antiques
2115 Frieze Avenue
Ann Arbor, MI 48104
Phone 313-662-3145
Hooked rugs.

Barbara VanWeinen
Nobody's Sweetheart
953 East Fulton St.
Grand Rapids, MI 49503
Phone 616-454-1673
Shop: wide range of vintage clothing and textiles

I Remember That
2085 E. Main (M21)
Owosso, MI 48867
Pam Yockey
734-459-4238
Memory Designs
Box 3033
Springfield, MI
Phone 417-887-9844
Early quilts. By appointment only.

Minnesota

Cathy Taylor
Victori
126 South Holmes
Shakopee, MN 55379
Phone 612-928-9061
info@victori.com
Antique and vintage clothing 1800 up to 1940 and fashion collectibles. Special pieces shown by appointment. Shows. Does lectures and demonstrations.

Bench Street Antiques
and Mercantile
364 Bench Street, Box 243
Taylors Falls, MN 55084
Phone 612-465-6100
Assorted vintage clothing and textiles.

Winona's Haddit Antiques
Stillwater, MN
Phone 612-452-4865
19th and early 20th century vintage fashions, frills, and fancy hats.

Missouri

Beverly Donze
Odile's Linen and Lace
34 South Third
Ste. Genevieve, MO 63670
Phone 314-883-9871
Linens and lace; new and antique Victoriana.

Suzanne Dryer
4101 W. 83rd St.
Kansas City, MO 64114
Phone 816-246-5117
Stall in Mission Road Antique Mall. Lace, trims, ribbons, textiles.

Diane Huckshorn
Lily Lark Antiques, Inc.
16614 Kentucky
Belton, MO 64012
Phone 816-331-8148
Victoriana, Victorian frills, frippery and finery.

Nebraska

Willa Felzien
1308 Highland Drive
Hastings, NE 68901
Phone 402-463-3620
Linens and lace; quilts; textiles. Shows and by appointment

Nancy Kirk
The Kirk Collection
1513 Military Avenue
Omaha, NE 68111-3924
800-398-2542
402-551-0386
fax 402-551-0971
Kirk Coll@aol.com
KirkCollection@msn.ccon
http://www.auntie.com/kirk
Extensive collection of vintage quilts, vintage and historic fabrics, and supplies for repair and restoration.

International Quilt Study Center
Carolyn Ducey
Phone 402-472-6301
Cducey@unl.edu
The University of Nebraska
HE 234
Lincoln, NE 68583-0838
Open to the public 9 to noon, Monday, Tuesday, Wednesday.
Comprehensive collection that of American and International quilts, both antique and contemporary. Permanent collection contains about 950 quilts. Some almost always will be displayed on campus. Study center also offers quilt-related classes for non-traditional students.

New Jersey

Joan DeBoer
The Painted Lady
16 Greenwich St.
Belvedere, NJ 07823
Phone 908-475-1985
Shop; linens and lace.

International Old Lacers, Inc.
P.O. Box 554
Flanders, NJ 07836
Largest association of lacemakers in the United States. Sponsors regional chapters which hold workshops, demonstrations of lacemaking techniques, and exchange information and patterns.

Stacy Gley
Marilyn of Monroe
39 Godwin Avenue
Ridgewood, NJ 07450
Phone 201-447-3123
Vintage designer clothing.

Ray Smith
Olympic Memorabilia
P.O. Box 254
Elizabeth, NJ 07207
Phone 908-354-5224
Fax 908-352-1576
Olympic: neckties, scarves, flags, banners, etc.

Janice Stillhard
Jan's Wholesale Vintage Textiles
36 Sky Manor Road
Pittstown, NJ 08867-4032
Phone 908-966-1000
Sky Manor Airport - textiles from 1860s to 1970s; handkerchiefs, collectible scarves, draperies, etc.

Fourscore and More Antiques
Box 611
Boonton, NJ 07005
Phone 201-335-2284
English and American samplers, coverlets. By appointment only.

Remmey Galleries
30 Maple Street
Summit, NJ 07901
Phone 908-273-5055
Remmeygalleries.com
Occasional vintage fashion, haute couture, and textiles auctions

New York

Virginia Di Sciascio
230 E. 80th St.
New York, NY 10021
Phone 212-794-8807

Barbara Boyce
Another Time
3164 State Street
Caledonia, NY 11423
boyceTime@aol.com
Phone 716-538-9730
Shop; All kinds of textiles for kitchen, fashion, and the home.

Nioche Brigitte
Your Image Plus
New York, NY
Phone 212-398-9890
Fax 212-398-6675
info@yip.com
Vintage fabrics from 1800s to 1950s.

Iris Brown
Victorian Doll Shoppe
253 East 57th Street
New York, NY 10022
Phone 212-593-2882
Doll clothes.

Molly Carroll
329 Berryman Dr.
Amherst, NY 14226
Phone 716-837-5243
Specializing in Irish Lace. New York Pier shows and by appointment.

Jean Ellis
Sussex Antiques
P.O. Box 796
Bedford, NY 10506
Phone 914-241-2919
Victorian Christening gowns, linens and lace; vintage fashion. Shows only and by appointment.

Cherie Everett
Box 344
Carthage, NY 13619
Phone 315-493-4535
Fax 315-493-3832
cwocgret@northnet.org
Wide range of vintage textiles, linens, and lace. Shows and by appointment.

Laura Fisher
1050 Second Avenue, Gallery 84
New York, NY 10022
Phone 212-838-2596
Antique quilts, hooked rugs, paisleys, coverlets.

Jennifer Grambs
Jennifer Grambs Collection
New York City, NY
Phone 212-737-0798
jennylan@aol.com
Classic vintage clothing.

Renate Halpern
Renate Halpern Galleries
325 East 79th St.
New York, NY 10021
Phone 212-988-9316
Fax 212-988-2954
Antique textiles bought, sold, appraised.

Douglas Hammond
Schmul Meier
Manhattan, NY
Jean Hoffman
207 East 66th St.
New York, NY 10021
Phone 212-535-6930
Bridal veils, paisleys, lace handkerchiefs. Extensive collection of top quality vintage wedding dresses, petit point bags.

John and Martha Jack
46 Woodbury Way
Fairport, NY 14450
Phone 716-223-7142
Coverlets, Samplers. Also museum of coverlets.

David Kincaide
Kincaide and Bragg
130 Water Street
New York, NY 10005
Phone 212-825-1576
oc.davie@aol.com
Lace, quilts, 40s and 50s printed tablecloths, vintage fabrics.

Mallory and Jeanette Merrill
Red Balloons
10912 Main St.
Clarence, NY
Phone 716-759-8999
Shop with exquisite and rare vintage linens, lace, clothing, lingerie, hats, paisleys, unique Victorian textiles and textile arts.

Florence Merritt
Antiques of Merritt
Rochester, NY
Phone 716-271-0912
Quilts, coverlets.

Kay Mertens
1788 Everette Place
East Meadow, 11554
Phone 516-538-9185
All types of quality textiles, linen, lace.

Maria Niforos
39A Lafayette Ave.
Suffern, NY 10901
Phone 914-369-0830
Shop: high-quality textiles, linens, lace, costume. Also shows.

Audrey Paden
Schoharie, NY
Phone 518-295-7220
Textiles, by appointment.

Melanie Rahiser
Docuswatch
990 Sixth Avenue 6L
New York, NY 10018
Phone 212-695-8877
Fax 212-695-8969
Fragments of vintage textiles for designer's inspiration.

Rosse, Betty
Gallerie Enchantment
Hammondsport, NY
Phone 607-569-2809
Shop: vintage clothing, hats, etc.

Susan Simon
New York, NY
Phone 212-663-5318
Shows and by appointment. Very high quality European textiles, late 19th early 20th century. Pillows, silk shawls, bedspreads, table linens.

Stan Slavin
PM Vintage
New York, NY
Phone 212-752-8451
Shows and by appointment. Late Victoria to 1920. Shawls, heavy draperies and brocades.

Ann Solicito
6 Village Green
Bardonia, NY 10954
Linens, lace. Shows only.

Patricia and Richard Dudley
8 Montcalm St.
Glens Falls, NY 12801
Shows and by appointment. Also appraisals and consulting. 19th century and earlier American and Anglo needlework, hooked rugs, textiles of all kind of kinds, blankets, rugs.
Jwww.dudleyanddudley.com

Jana Starr
Jana Starr Antiques
236 East 80th St.
New York, NY 10021
Phone 212-861-8256
Shop. Vintage white dresses, lots of old lace and textiles.

The Fassnachts
American Samplers
Box 795
Canandaigua, NY 14424
Phone 716-229-4199
American Samplers. Shows and by appointment.

Sid Warshafsky
240 Overlook
Woodstock, NY 12499
Designer clothes; lace, linens. By appointment.

Beehive Antiques
Route 21
North Cohocton, NY
Phone 716-534-5770
Shop. Vintage clothing.

Cora Ginsburg
19 East 74th St. 3rd Floor
New York, NY 10021
Shop. Specializes in 17th and 18th century fabrics, tapestries, lace, linens.

Heritage Antiques
42 W. Main St.
Angelica, NY 14709
Phone 716-466-3712
Vintage clothing.

Marie Auermuller
Fine linens
P.O. Box 07936
East Hanover, NY 07930
By appointment.

Metropolitan Antiques
110 West 19th Street
New York, NY
Phone 212-463-0200
Call for information on shows and auctions of vintage fashion, textiles, textile and lace sample books, and other related materials.

Chris Dreissen
Shop: 3256 State Route 30
Esperance, NY 12066
http:www.hickoryhillquilts.com
518-875-6133
Antique quilts, tops, blocks, vintage fabrics, reproduction fabric sewing notions. Restoration, appraisals.

Rabbit Goody
Thistle Hill Weavers
101 Chestnut Ridge Road
Cherry Valley, NY 13320 (near Cooperstown)
518-284-2729
rabbitg@albany.net
www.albany.net/~rabbitg
www.quilthistory.com/thistlehill
Resource on coverlets, quilts, weaving, and vintage fabrics. Specialist in identification of hand-produced textiles, and textiles from the transition period of from home to factory technology, circa 1750 to 1850. Early block, roller cylinder and copperplate prints. Custom textile mill producing reproductions of antique silk, linsey-woolsey, textiles for museums, reenactors, decorators.

Cheryl Anne VanDenburg
Pieces of the Past Antiques
Cuddebacks Antique Center
Canandaigua, NY
Phone 716-396-3224
Shows, exhibits at antique mall. Quilts, and antique textiles.

Museums
Brooklyn Museum of Art
200 Eastern Parkway
Brooklyn, NY 11238
Phone 718-638-0005
Patricia Mears, textiles specialist, Ext. 251

Metropolitan Museum of Art
New York, NY

North Carolina

Elizabeth Bright
Elizabeth Bright Antiques
26 Williams Circle
Lexington, NC 27292
Phone 910-249-2448
Linens and lace; vintage textiles and Victoriana. Shows and mail order.

Ramona Spain
Of Cabbages and Kings
111 West Main
Aberdeen, NC 28315
Phone 910-944-1110
Shop; linens and lace; vintage clothing; quilts.

Ohio

Cynthia Barta
2568 Kendall Road
Shaker Heights, OH 44120-1141
Phone 216-281-1959
Shows and by appointment. 1940s to 1970s men's and women's clothing and accessories featured at Suite Lorain antique mall, 7105 Lorain Avenue, Cleveland, OH.

Linda Bowman
Legacy
12502 Larchmere Boulevard
Cleveland, OH 44102
Phone 216-229-0578
Shows and by appointment. High style vintage clothing from 1920 through 1960

Libby Gower
618 Superior Ave.
Dayton, OH 45407-2303
Phone 937-223-4615
Shows and by appointment. Art Deco and Vintage clothes and textiles.

Linda Ketterling
Toledo, OH
Phone 419-536-5531
Antique linens and lace. Shows and by appointment.

Tim & Barb Martien
1229 Bell St.
Chagrin Falls, OH 44022
Phone 440-338-3666
Samplers. Shows and by appointment.

Betty Parker
Pieces of the Past
159 Franklin
Doylestown, OH 44230
Phone 330-658-6161
Quilts; linens and lace. Shows and by appointment.

MarionSteinbrunner
14747 Sisson Road
Chardon, OH 44024
Linens, lace, and textiles. Shop and Atlantic City shows.

Shirley and Jim Wolf
Stitches in Time
61 Truax
Plymouth, OH 44865
Phone 419-687-2061
wolf@stitchesintime.com
Shop, shows, and by appointment. Wide range of vintage clothes, bridal, hats, etc. from 19th century on.

Mary R. Yarton
Whitehouse, OH 43571
Phone 419-875-5310
Samplers and other American antiques. By appointment.

Reflections of the Past
P. O. Box 40361
Bay Village, OH 44140
Phone 440-835-6924
Website only. Vintage clothing, textiles, linens, lace.

Museums
Kent State University Museum
Kent, OH
330-672-3450
On the campus of Kent State University. Exhibits of vintage fashion, textiles, and related items always on display.

Cleveland Museum of Art
1150 East Blvd.
Cleveland, OH 44160-1797
Louise Mackie, curator of textiles
Christine Starkman, assistant curator of textiles
Phone 216-421-7340

Oklahoma

The International Linen Registry
4107 S. Yale Avenue #247
Tulsa, OK 74135
Phone 918-622-5223 1-800-581-5223
Lace and linens always on display. Classes in lacemaking. Appraisals and identification.

Oregon

Norma Bernady
Vintage Whites
320 Court St. NE
Salem, OR 97301
Phone 503-587-8998
Shop: vintage linens and antiques.

Museum
Latimer Quilt and Textile Center
www.oregoncoast.com/latimertextile
Regional repository of handmade textile arts.

Pennsylvania

Laura Allmond
Route 272
Adamstown, PA 19501
Phone 717-270-9014
By appointment: textiles and decorative arts.

Barbara Q. Kennedy
125 West Lawn Avenue
West Lawn, PA 19609
Phone 610-678-5187
Fax 610-376-5503
By appointment only, vintage textiles.

Helen Lake Smith
Meadville, PA
Phone 814-333-9267
Shows and by appointment only. High end linens and laces.

Katy Kane, Inc.
34 W. Ferry St.
New Hope, PA 18393
Phone 215-862-5873
Antique clothing and fine linens.

Natasha's
Natasha Green
551 Beaver St.
Sewickley, PA 15143
Phone 412-741-9484
Shop, specializing in old linens, laces, and fine vintage fashions. Also shows and by appointment.

Pat Edleman
1945 Meadow Lane
Wyomissing, PA 19610
Phone 610-796-0320
Shows and by appointment. Vintage lace and linens.

Elizabeth Hine
Hinesight
Phone 717-396-9527
717-393-9132
Fine vintage apparel and textiles.

Horst Auctioneers
50 Durlach Road
Ephrata, PA 17522
Phone 717-738-3080
Fax 717-738-2132
Located in Amish country in Pennsylvania, Horst Auctions frequently include samplers, quilts, coverlets, hooked rugs and other textiles.

Amy Finkel
M. Finkel and Daughter
936 Pine Street
Philadelphia, PA 19107
Phone 215-627-7797
Fax 215-627-8199
Gallery and shows. Samplers, embroideries, needlework. Well researched and documented pieces.

Stan Clark
915 Fairview Avenue
Gettysburg, PA 17325
Phone 717-337-1728
Fax 717-337-0581

Museums
Heritage Center Museum
13 W. King Street
Lancaster, PA 17602
Phone 717-299-6440
Moravian and Amish, needleworks, samplers, hooked rugs, decorative towels, quilts, coverlets. Exhibits are constantly changing. Call for appointment to study textiles in any specific area.

Tennessee

Laura Muller
7200 Stamford Cove
Germantown, TN 38138
Phone 901-754-4222
Linens and lace

Ann Williams
P. O. Box 743
Brentwood, TN 37024
Phone 615-373-4725
Linens and lace, handkerchiefs.

Texas

Winston McKenzie
McKenzie Galleries
7026 Old Katy Road, Suite 161
Houston, TX 77024-2110
Phone 713-863-1213
Fax 713-863-1216
Costumes and textiles.

Samuel Abraham
Abrahams Oriental Rugs
5120 Woodway Dr., Ste.6010
Houston, TX 77056-1724
Phone 713-622-4444
Needlework, tapestries, textiles, silks.

June Adair
Adair Appraisals
1311 Devon Glen Dr.
Houston, TX 77077-3211
Phone 713-861-7711
Fax 713-496-6234
Vintage clothing, by appointment only.

Penny Millican
Towne and Country Estates
5319 Holly St.
Bellaire, TX 77401-4805
Phone 713-666-0970
Fax 713-666-2715
Quilts.

Vintage Quilt and Textile Society
vqts1@airmail.net
2401 Blue Cypress
Richardson, TX 75082
Phone 972-783-4149
Lisa Erlandson, newsletter editor
erland@cooke.net
texas_quilt.co@airmail.net
An organization devoted to the studies of vintage quilts, textiles, and related subjects. Holds quarterly workshops in Dallas area.

Vermont

Karen Augusta
31 Gage
N. Westminster, VT 05101
Phone 802-463-4958;
800-OLD LACE
Designer vintage, fine linens and lace. Shows and by appointment.

Virginia

Sally O'Brien
P.O. Box 29534
Richmond, VA 23242
Phone 804-364-3488
Fine 19th century English linens, lace, and accessories. Lectures and programs on linens and lace.

Heart's Desire
7518-E Fullerton Rd.
Springfield, VA 22153
Website through costumegallery.com

Norma Blanchard
Blanchard Appraisals
1222 Aldebaran Dr.
McLean, VA 22101
Phone 703-734-1406
103325.2577@compuserve.com
Appraises quilts, textiles.

Ann Kovalchick
P.O. Box 608
Front Royal, VA
Antique lace, vintage textiles. By appointment

Gretchen Noyes
P.O. Box 948
Alexandria, VA 22313
Phone 703-920-0348
Appraisals of antique needlework and textiles, including quilts, samplers, embroidery, hooked rugs, linens, and lace.

Washington

Nancy Evans
Legacy of Lace
220 South First
Kent, WA 98032
Phone 206-852-0052
Linens and lace, appraisals, repair and conservation.

Maureen Matich
M.A.M.s Vintage Linens
35 Main St.
Edmonds, WA 98020
Phone 206-771-5310
Shop; shows: linens and lace.

Bette Bell
Guildmark Appraisal
P.O. Box 952
Edmonds, WA 98020
Phone 425-775-5650
Fax 425-670-6597
Appraises quilts.

Ann Bodle Nash
Prof. Appraiser for quilted textiles
annbow@c10.net
840 Halloran Rd.
Bow, WA 98232

Washington, D.C.

Museums
Smithsonian
Corcoran Museum of Art
300 Seventeenth Street, N.W.
Washington, D.C. 20006-4804
Phone 202-639-1711
Fax 202-639-1778
Extensive lace collection as well as other textiles.

West Virginia

Dixie Elmore
Rt. 1, Box 211
Washington, WV 26181
Phone 304-863-5460
Vintage clothing, hats, clothing 1800-1945. Linens, lingerie, assorted trims. Shows, and by appointment.

Wisconsin

Joe Vonnie Anderson and Jenne Aton
Vintage Vamps
489 Broadway St.
Berlin, WI 54923
Phone: 920-295-6959 (Joe) and 920-361-2893 (Jenne).
By appointment. Quilts, bed linens, quality linens and laces, kitchen tablecloths and towels, vintage clothes.

Tracey Jones
Retrofit, Pilgrim Antique Mall
W156 N 11500 Pilgrim Road
Germantown, WI 53022
Phone 414-774-6041(Home) Shop 414-250-0260
Men's and women's vintage clothing, soft goods, textiles. Stalls in Germantown and Grafton malls. Shows and by appointment.

Pat O'Brien
Flapper Alley
1518 N. Farwell
Milwaukee, WI 53202
Phone 414-276-6252
Shop, mail order, and by appointment. 19th century vintage fashion, linens and lace.

Dawn Steckmesser
Timeless Treasures
112 N. 8th
Manitowoc, WI 54202
Phone 920-682-6566
General antique plus vintage clothing. Shows and by appointment.

Idlewild Antiques
5121 Glen Road
McFarland, WI 53558
Phone 608-838-8410
Wide range of high-end vintage and textiles. Shows and by appointment.

The Scarlet Letter
Box 397
Sullivan, WI 53178
Phone 414-593-8470, 414-593-2417
Antique samplers and reproduction kits.

J.J. Murphy
920 Emerald St.
Madison, WI 53715-1614
Phone 608-257-3855
Fax 608-257-3730
Collector, seeking rare 19th century printed children's handkerchiefs and bandannas. Author, Children's Handkerchiefs.

University of Wisconsin
Madison, WI
Helen Allen Collection
Phone 608-262-2651
Vintage fashion and textile collection.

Wyoming

Celia Howarth
P.O. Box 4616
Jackson, WY 83001
Phone 208-787-2181
English and French textiles. Shows and by appointment.

Rescued Treasures
Casper, WY
Phone 307-265-3002
Marty Carpenter, Store Manager
Recycling bales of old clothing. Sell old clothing by the pound.

Europe

Italy

E. Kerer
Palazzo Miari (Behind St. Marks Church)
Calle Canonica 4328 A
Venice, Italy
Phone 52.35.485

Spain

Concha B. Roig
Enmedio, N 103 Atico
12001
Castellon, Spain
Phone 964-21.51.75
Specialists in mantillas, and vintage lace.

Pepita Sanchez
Beatriz Castello
Alfonso XII, 63
Detras Clinica del Pilar
08006, Barcelona, Spain
Phone 201.46.89
Vintage clothing and lace

El Nino Seise
Piazza de la Pescaderia 4
41004, Seville, Spain
Phone 95-4561916
Antique laces and vintage clothing

London

Phillips International Auctioneers
101 New Bond Street
London, W1Y OAS
Phone 44-171-629-6602 (textile department)
New York phone for catalogs and sale information 212-570-4830
Regular sales of textiles, about 6 per year, include European band, spot, and European and American needlework samplers from the seventeenth through the nineteenth centuries.

Reenactors

Reenactors are a good source of vintage clothing and textiles information because of their interest in authentically reenacting specific periods. The following offer a starting point for contacting these various groups.

Smoke and Fire News
P.O. Box 166
Grand Rapids, MI 43552
Phone 419-832-0303
Offers a calendar of events, lectures, workshops, museums, and parks, and ads and articles for Early American, Furtrader and Western, 17th century calendar, French and Indian War, American Revolutionary War, 1812, Civil War, Native American. Send $1.50 for sample copy.

Web pages and discussion sites for reenactors. Include a wide range of materials in addition to textiles and costume.

www.netins.net/sowcase/nwta
Northwest Territory Alliance, Revolutionary War reenactors. Revolutionary War discussion group.

www.meridian.com/revlist
http://users.aol.com/canaltwo/sutlers.htm
://jaxnet.com/~ahrendt.suttler.htm
Lists of dealers of goods concerning Revolutionary War reenactors.

Index

Cover Photos

Front cover:

Background:

Nineteenth century bridal veil of English Honiton bobbin lace. Complete veil is shown in Bridal Veils section, page 73.

Top right:

American hooked rug, dated "Feb. 14, 1922" with a trotting horse. Scalloped border is worked in stripes of black, gray, brown, red, blue, and purple yarns. Minor repair, wear, and fading. 29 inches by 39.5 inches. Sold at auction for $1093. Photo courtesy of Skinner, Inc., Boston.

Bottom right:

Dress by Charles James, sold at auction for a record $49,450. One of the premier designers in the 1940s, James brought a unique sculptural quality to couture. Photo courtesy of William Doyle Galleries, New York.

Bottom center:

Bookmark, worked in a smaller version of a Stevengraph design for a sash produced for the International Order of Foresters in the nineteenth century. Extraordinary detail and vibrant colors make this a highly collectible bookmark. A devoted collector might pay up to $100 for such a bookmark.

Sampler, stitched "Lydia Ritter, aged 11 years" with verses surrounded by flower sprays, and urns with flowers. A flowering vine forms the border. Size is 20.2 inches by 24.8 inches. Sold at auction for $1,265. Photo courtesy of Skinner, Inc., Bolton, Massachusetts.

Quilt in center:

Sampler quilt, with thirty different pieced and appliqued blocks arranged in rows. Size 90 inches by 75 inches. Sold at auction for $575. Photo courtesy of Butterfield and Butterfield, San Francisco.

Back cover:

Top left:

Christening gown, probably mid nineteenth century, decorated with cutwork embroidery technique known as Broderie Anglaise. Skirt is over 36 inches long. Christening gowns of this quality and age are rarely found for under $500. Photo by Elizabeth Poder Michael.

Center left:

Fine hats are imaginative sculptures. Details of this hat appear on page 89. Photo courtesy of Red Balloons, Clarence, New York.

Right:

A close look is essential to identifying and evaluating textiles. In embroidery, the relationship of thread, fabric, and the choice of stitches and colors all contribute to the overall effect and value.

Photo of author by Elizabeth Poder Michael

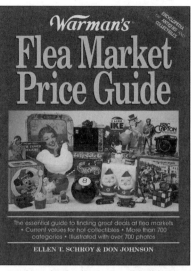
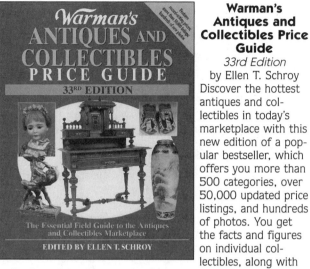

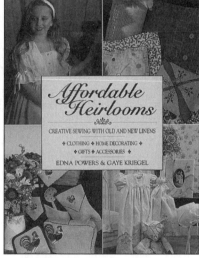

IDENTIFY VINTAGE COLLECTIBLES WITH CONFIDENCE

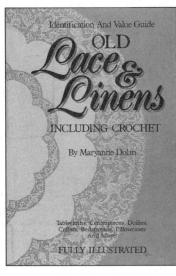

Old Lace & Linens
Identification and Value Guide

by Maryanne Dolan
Tops the collectors' list as the best identification and value guide for hand-stitched artwork of the past century. Tablecloths, doilies, collars, napkins, towels and more are spread out for simple identification, authentication and pricing. Includes crochet.
Softcover • 5-1/2 x 8-1/2
160 pages
227 b&w photos
OLL • $10.95

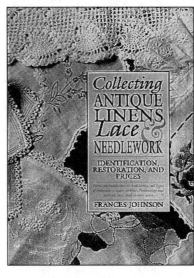

Collecting Antique Linens, Lace & Needlework

by Frances Johnson
Your collecting success is all sewn-up with this comprehensive guide to stitching, needles, pins, thread, embroidery, knitting, crochet, and more. Learn unique uses for old needlework and how to care for old linens and lace.
Softcover • 7-1/4 x 9
208 pages
8-page color section
CALL • $18.95

Vintage Clothing 1880-1980
Identification and Value Guide, 3rd Edition

by Maryanne Dolan
All the fashion raves for men, women, children and infants are dressed with updated descriptions and current values. Maryanne Dolan makes this the perfect resource for costume designers, seamstresses, doll-makers, and historians, too. It's a nostalgic walk down the fashion runway that recalls the outrageous and the conservative clothing of a very stylish century.
Softcover • 8-1/2 x 11 • 304 pages
350 b&w photos 275 Illustrations • 21 color photos
VIN03 • $22.95

Zalkin's Handbook Of Thimbles & Sewing Implements

by Estelle Zalkin
Use this fact-packed, liberally illustrated hand-book to find values for collectible sewing implements, from needlework tools to pin cushions, clamps, work boxes, and more. You'll find a wealth of information on research sources, and learn how to spot variations and reproductions, catalog a collection, and locate other valuable collectible objects.
Softcover • 6 x 9 • 304 pages
16-page color section
THIM • $24.95

WHAT'S NEW IN PRICING YOUR ANTIQUES
Get The Most Up-To-Date Pricing Right Here!

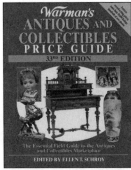

Warman's Antiques and Collectibles Price Guide
33rd Edition
by Ellen T. Schroy
Discover the hottest antiques and collectibles in today's marketplace with this new edition of a popular bestseller, which offers you more than 500 categories, over 50,000 updated price listings, and hundreds of photos. You get the facts and figures on individual collectibles, along with collecting advice, history, tips for spotting reproductions, collectors' clubs, museums, auction houses, and a list of reference books and periodicals relating to each category. Expert advisors also share insider pricing information not available anywhere else.
Softcover • 8-1/4 x 10-7/8 • 640 pages
600+ b&w photos
WAC33 • $16.95

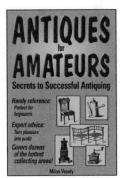

Antiques for Amateurs
Secrets to Successful Antiquing
by Milan Vesely
Satisfy your curiosity about the fascinating-but often difficult to understand-world of antiques with this helpful, informative beginner's guide. Novice antique enthusiasts will appreciate the easy-to-read-and-understand approach to a broad range of categories. Learn what antiques are, how to identify and collect them, and how to successfully buy them so that they grow in value. With so many topics covered in one book, everyone will value this handy reference.
Softcover • 6 x 9 • 192 pages
250 b&w photos • **ANFA • $14.95**

Antique Secrets
How the "Pickers" Find Treasure in Another Man's Trash
by Joe Willard
If you want to make big bucks finding frequently overlooked antiques and collectibles don't miss out on this book! Learn the skills necessary to negotiate profitable deals, how to "get there first", and determine value. Whether you are a novice seeking information on how to get started picking or a professional looking to enhance your skills the down-to-earth concepts and original anecdotes will keep you interested from start to finish.
Softcover • 6 x 9 • 192 pages
28 b&w photos
ANTSE • $14.95

Warman's Americana & Collectibles
8th Edition
by Ellen Schroy, editor
Get the latest prices on today's hottest collectibles in this brand-new edition. From Pez to Hot Wheels to golf collectibles, and from Depression-era to Baby Boomer to Generation X, the 1930s to current day collectibles, this diverse value guide has it all.
Softcover • 8-1/2 x 11 • 400 pages
250 b&w photos
WAMC8 • $17.95

1999 Toys & Prices
6th Edition
Edited by Sharon Korbeck
The newest edition of the toy hobby's bible covers more than 18 categories of toys with detailed information and pricing in several grades of condition. New toy categories have been added bringing this edition to more than 19,000 toys dating from 1843 to 1997. As an added bonus, a toy manufacturers directory and an auction house list are included. Toys featured are Beanie Babies, Stars Wars, tin toys, games, lunch boxes, character toys, restaurant premiums and many more!
Softcover • 6 x 9 • 928 pages
500 b&w photos • 20 color photos
TE06 • $18.95

Today's Hottest Collectibles
by The Publishers of Toy Shop and Warman's Today's Collector
Learn the brief history of many collecting areas, general guidelines, current trends, line listing of prices for items. Includes clubs, newsletters, periodicals and other helpful information to access when looking for more specific information. Collectible areas covered include toys, cookie jars, beer collectibles, books, magazines, Beatles/Elvis collectibles, postcards, records, salt/pepper shakers, trading cards, World's Fair memorabilia, Beanie Babies and much more.
Softcover • 8-1/2 x 11 • 400 pages
1,300 b&w photos
CGA01 • $24.95

Credit Card Customers Call Toll-free
800-258-0929
Dept. ACB1
Monday-Friday, 7 a.m. - 8 p.m.
Saturday, 8 a.m. - 2 p.m., CST

Visit and order from our secure web site: www.krause.com
If you collect it - you'll find it @ www.collectit.net

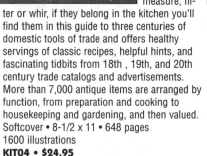